BUILDING DIGITAL LIBRARIES

A How-To-Do-It Manual®

TERRY REESE, JR.
KYLE BANERJEE

HOW-TO-DO-IT MANUALS®

NUMBER 153

NEAL-SCHUMAN PUBLISHERS, INC.
New York   London

Published by Neal-Schuman Publishers, Inc.
100 William St., Suite 2004
New York, NY 10038

Printed and bound in the United States of America.

The paper used in this publication meets the minimum requirements of American National Standard for Information Sciences - Permanence of Paper for Printed Library Materials, ANSI Z39.48-1992.

Library of Congress Cataloging-in-Publication Data

  Reese, Terry.
    Building digital libraries : a how-to-do-it manual / Terry Reese, Jr., Kyle Banerjee.
        p. cm. — (How-to-do-it manuals ; no. 153)
    Includes bibliographical references and index.
ISBN 978-1-55570-617-3 (alk. paper)
1. Digital libraries. I. Banerjee, Kyle. II. Title.
ZA4080.R44 2008
025.00285—dc22

                                                    2008024103

CONTENTS

LIST OF FIGURES

PREFACE

In the digital age, libraries need to preserve and provide access to digital resources, but traditional library procedures and tools from the brick-and-mortar type library are often not suited to this task. Physical libraries and their access mechanisms rely upon a publishing model that has slowly evolved over the past 500 years. In this model, each resource (book, globe, audiotape) consists of an object or objects in a single format, and each object remains static over time. Methods of building and cataloging physical library collections depend on these constants.

A digital library exists within a very different framework. A single resource (e.g., a portal) may consist of objects in many formats (full-text articles, databases, etc.), yet each of these objects is a resource in its own right. These objects may be updated frequently, and their original formats may become obsolete as technological developments lead to new types of information resources. Due to these differences, creating a digital library requires a new set of skills. *Building Digital Libraries: A How-To-Do-It Manual®* is a tool kit for the new world of digital libraries. It demystifies the challenges of designing, constructing, and maintaining a digital repository.

Although there have been many books written on electronic resources management, most have assumed that librarians will be managing subscription databases or collections created by others. *Building Digital Libraries* focuses on locally created digital repositories. A locally created digital repository is designed or maintained by the host institution. Such a collection may contain institutional or archival materials, or it may contain resources created partly or exclusively by parties outside the institution.

The few books that have focused on locally created repositories have been heavily weighted towards the interests of archivists. Archival collections may be the most obvious candidates for digitization, but digital libraries are far from just an archival concern. With the ease of finding general resources on the Web, digital collections have become one of the more unique and valuable parts of many libraries' holdings. In *Building Digital Libraries,* we have tried to speak to the full range of librarians who are, or who will be, involved in digital library projects: Systems librarians, project managers, and students, many of whom will find themselves starting, updating, or maintaining digital collections in years to come.

Building Digital Libraries covers both the fundamentals of digital library theory and the details of how to implement a digital collection. No specific technical knowledge is required. Each chapter discusses the capabilities and limitations of specific technologies and reflects important developments of the last few years, with a focus on tools that are applicable and appropriate to a variety of environments. The most recent and useful third-party technologies are highlighted, including service repositories, Search/Retrieval URL and Search/Retrieval Web Service (SRU/SRW), federated searching, digital object identifiers (DOIs), and widespread adoption of OpenURLs.

After completing the book, readers will have sufficient knowledge to identify and implement the technical components necessary to construct a digital repository from scratch. Our aim is to explain and clarify both the technical and conceptual aspects of digital repositories so that readers can thoroughly understand how to create such a valuable resource for your library.

ORGANIZATION

Each chapter in *Building Digital Libraries* focuses on a step in the process, addressing both how to execute that step and how to combat challenges encountered along the way.

Chapter 1, "Planning a Digital Repository," gives a broad overview of issues surrounding the construction of a digital library. It provides the reader with an understanding of how the integrity of information can be protected over time, how to safeguard a repository against natural and man-made disasters, and how to accommodate the problem of constantly changing formats.

Chapter 2, "Acquiring, Processing, Classifying, and Describing Digital Content," discusses specialized access mechanisms, processing and acquisitions, and maintenance; it also emphasizes the critical importance of good workflow. Chapter 3, "Choosing a Repository Architecture," describes several frameworks for digital libraries and outlines the strengths and limitations of various hardware and software architectures. Choosing an appropriate hardware and software platform is critical to the success of a repository, so it is important to understand how the choice of platform influences how information can be stored and retrieved, which systems the collection can interact with, and how functionality can be enhanced in the future.

Chapter 4, "General Purpose Technologies Useful for Digital Repositories," introduces metadata, particularly the group of technologies associated with eXtensible Markup Language (XML). Chapter 5, "Metadata Formats," explores in greater detail generic technologies and critical standards, such as MARC, Dublin Core, Metadata Object Description Schema

(MODS), and Metadata Encoding and Transmission Standard (METS), providing examples that help the reader understand how these standards can be leveraged to provide services with relatively little effort.

As the number of information providers continues to grow, a repository cannot simply be a silo on the Internet. Chapter 6, "Sharing Data: Metadata Harvesting and Distribution," looks at the role individual repositories play in a shared environment, how they can be normalized and shared for use by diverse systems, and how to make repositories searchable as part of federated collections and make their resources visible to search engines.

Chapter 7, "Federated Searching of Repositories," investigates a wide array of protocols and technologies used for searching materials located in a vendor database or scattered across Web pages. From Z39.50—the original metasearch protocol for libraries—to the latest methods, readers will learn how to layer different search technologies to provide seamless access to diverse resources stored in different systems.

Chapter 8, "Access Management," examines digital rights, protection of intellectual property rights, and monitoring of repository use in long-term repositories. Control mechanisms such as LDAP (Lightweight Directory Access Protocol) Shibboleth, OpenID, and Athens are also discussed.

Maintaining a repository is an ongoing endeavor. Chapter 9, "Planning for the Future," is devoted to managing a living repository and anticipating future needs, as well as issues of updating as technologies and patron needs change.

Chapter 10, "Conclusions," offers a clear outline of the process from start to finish and highlights the global importance of points touched upon in previous chapters.

It is not just the information itself, but the organization, structure, and presentation of that information, that give a repository its value. Digital libraries enhance the value of information resources by allowing users to locate information in contexts that suit their needs. We believe that these benefits of digitization have potential for a wide range of different types of collections and institutions. In *Building Digital Libraries*, we presume nothing except the desire to learn how to help bring libraries into the future.

1 PLANNING A DIGITAL REPOSITORY

The ultimate success or failure of a digital repository is usually determined in the planning stages. A repository must be structured and organized so that users can readily find and use diverse types of resources. It must be easy to maintain and capable of accommodating needs and resources that may not exist at the time the repository is designed.

People charged with implementing digital repositories often focus immediately on the technical aspects of the endeavor. They evaluate software, read about standards, and estimate what type of hardware they will need to make their repository a success. While important, these steps are only a small part of the planning process.

Creating and managing a digital repository is similar to starting a new physical collection. Just as the value of a library is in how it collects, organizes, and presents materials, the quality of a digital repository is measured the same way. It must contain resources that people need and that are easy to find and use. As is the case with any living collection, new materials must be added while those that no longer support the mission of the repository should be removed. Such an endeavor requires a great amount of planning, and managing the resources effectively takes significant ongoing resources and staff time.

WHAT IS A DIGITAL REPOSITORY?

On a basic level, a digital repository is simply a collection of digital resources. These materials may have been converted from an analog format, such as paper, or they may have been born digital. Regardless of the type of resources they contain, one of the primary functions of digital repositories is to preserve electronic resources, though they must also provide a system for cataloging, indexing, and retrieving digital materials. Unlike physical repositories, which exist to preserve specific information artifacts, the purpose of a digital repository is to preserve *access* to information artifacts. In contrast to their paper counterparts, electronic documents do not physically exist—they are a stream of data that must be copied, transmitted across networks, and interpreted by software to be useful. Technology changes rapidly, so the data streams that represent digital resources must constantly evolve in order to remain useful. In other words, even materials that are stored in an "archival" format will most likely need to be converted at some point in the future.

Because digital resources are not stored as physical artifacts, digital repositories must also address issues of provenance and digital security. Organizations, particularly government institutions, will be expected to ensure that resources are not modified after they are stored. This is one of the many challenges currently being addressed by the U.S. Government Printing Office (GPO). Because this is an archival repository of born-digital materials of significant legal, political, cultural, and historical significance, users must be assured that the documents delivered from the GPO digital repository are authentic and have not been modified by an outside source.

THE DECISION TO BUILD A DIGITAL REPOSITORY

Building a digital repository requires a significant and ongoing commitment of staff and financial resources. Although many people treat repositories as short-term projects that can be funded with grants and other nonrecurring monies, the reality is that building a repository is equivalent to adding a major collection of many items that require special handling and ongoing care. The process of identifying, acquiring, processing, storing, and preserving digital resources is very different from that of traditional library materials, and numerous organizational and technical challenges must be overcome for a digital repository to be successful.

Libraries may be traditionally associated with books, but most users expect access to electronic information as well. User expectations and publishing models have evolved with technological improvements, and people now expect to access information using computer networks. Digital technology continues to simplify the publication process, and increasing numbers of items are published in digital form—some *only* in digital form. Likewise, as digital publication methods improve and mature, it becomes more practical to move services to a digital environment. At the same time, the importance of physically possessing resources diminishes, and more value is placed on the ability to locate and download remotely stored resources. In this sense, digital repositories are a logical outgrowth of traditional library services in response to changes brought about by network technology. The overall effect of a digital repository is to allow a library to provide a greater level of access to a more diverse collection than it can with exclusively physical resources.

Now that we live in a world in which physical copies of certain culturally significant information resources are no longer produced, digital repositories become a necessity.

Consider the 2000 United States presidential elections. For the first time, presidential candidates utilized the World Wide Web as a campaigning/advertising platform. As a result, much of the presidential "conversation" took place within this digital space—a space not yet well archived by libraries and other memory institutions. Had this conversation not been archived, this part of history would have been lost quickly. To preserve this record, the United States Library of Congress created the 2000 Election Web Archive. The project captured the content of some 800 unique sites related to the 2000 presidential elections over the course of a year (U.S. Library of Congress, accessed: 2007). Following the 2000 elections, nearly all of this content disappeared from the Web. However, thanks to the Library of Congress's archival effort, these historical documents still exist for research and study. This project illustrates why digital repositories are important and how they meet needs that cannot be accommodated using traditional library methods.

Digital repositories can also provide access to specialized or fragile content that is not generally available. For example, Figure 1-1 shows an image of the city of Corvallis, Oregon, during a 1964 flood. The digital image shows the Willamette River at 12:30 p.m. on Dec. 24, 1964, covering highway 34 and the surrounding farmlands. This image and many others are stored in the Oregon State University Libraries Archives and, until last year, were virtually unknown to the outside community. With just a few keystrokes, this information is now available for a wide range of uses. Ironically, the collection (http://digitalcollections.library.oregonstate.edu/cdm4/client/corflood64/index.html) was launched in January 2005, when the Willamette Valley flooded again. As a result of the public availability of these images, individuals, as well as government officials were able to use this collection to help assess the current flood as well as plan for future ones. For example, in Figure 1-2, one can see that the housing area next to the bridge may be prone to flooding and could be useful in predicting the extent of future floods. This kind of information may be of interest to future homeowners or developers looking to build in and around these areas.

Digital repositories allow organizations to provide information to a much broader audience. In late 2006, the Oregon State University (OSU) Libraries Archives began creating an Oregon Multicultural Archive. This collection was a digital conglomeration of images and text taken from sets found within the OSU Archives collections. Digitizing this collection not only allowed the OSU Archives to provide these materials to the larger OSU community, but these materials were also exposed to users outside of the OSU community. The OSU digital library program makes available all of its collections using OAI (Open Archives Initiative) and other methods discussed later in this book for harvest by Web crawlers and other

Figure 1-1. 1964 Flood in Corvallis, Oregon

Source: John H. Gallagher Photo Collection, 2001: 118. Photos courtesy of the Oregon State University Libraries Archive.

Figure 1-2. Flooded Housing Area

Source: John H. Gallagher Photo Collection, 2001: 118. Photos courtesy of the Oregon State University Libraries Archive.

academic image repositories. Consequently, these images appear in normal Google search results as shown in Figure 1-3, and they can easily be found by users outside of the OSU community.

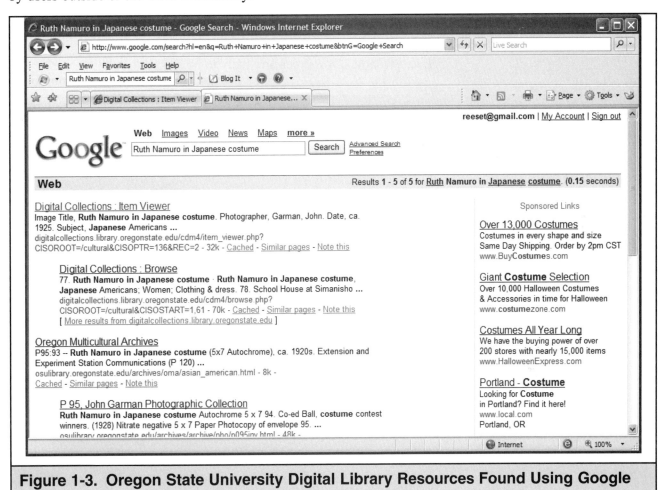

Figure 1-3. Oregon State University Digital Library Resources Found Using Google

Once work on a repository begins, money and staff time must be permanently allocated unless maintenance is transferred to an outside party. Resources in obsolete formats need to be converted. Hardware, operating systems, and software must be maintained and improved with time. Acquisitions, storage, and access mechanisms must evolve to accommodate changing user needs and new types of resources. Electronic resources require considerable maintenance. Paper resources can be very accessible and usable after many years of neglect. However, electronic resources will soon be completely unusable if the hardware, software, and the resources themselves are not maintained.

Designing and building a digital repository is exciting work, but it is a complex endeavor that requires people to work with each other and technology in new ways. For this reason, planners need to answer a number of questions in consultation with staff before starting work. Why should the library build a repository? What needs would it satisfy? What alternatives to building a repository might satisfy these needs? What technical and staff resources are available? How much time do people have to dedicate to the repository and what skills do they have? What staff, financial, and technical resources are likely to be available in the future?

ADVANTAGES OF A DIGITAL REPOSITORY

Building a repository presents many challenges, but it also brings many benefits to the library as well. Aside from improving desktop access to materials, it gives libraries a chance to make unique resources widely available. Electronic resources are usually more convenient to use than paper resources. They don't need to be returned, users cannot damage them, and they do not consume valuable shelf space.

A well-designed repository is very useful for the public image of a library. When libraries demonstrate how effectively they use new technologies and tools, they send a message to their users that they can be trusted to satisfy any information need, even if it requires access to a type of resource that the patron does not even know about. Now that users expect desktop access from anywhere, a well-executed virtual presence is important for maintaining the credibility of the library as well as making it enjoyable. Libraries in beautiful well-conceived buildings with logically organized collections are more likely to be used than those in dingy facilities where finding things is difficult. This same principle applies in the virtual world.

Digital repositories also provide an opportunity for library workers to upgrade their skills. Aside from allowing those who want to learn something new a chance to develop professionally, the possibility of helping improve and maintain a good repository can help attract desirable future job applicants. Digital repositories are still very new, so individuals who work on them are almost by definition on the cutting edge, and they can still have considerable influence over the tools and methods that libraries everywhere use for collecting, preserving, and managing digital resources. As the information that users need is increasingly available only in electronic form, libraries need to adapt their tools and procedures to accommodate those needs. Creating a digital repository is a step in that direction.

There are also significant drawbacks to creating digital repositories. Because they are still on the cutting edge of library services, the tools and methods cannot be regarded as stable. Difficult migrations might be necessary later if a library makes choices that prove to be ineffective in the long term. There is even the possibility that information that a library went to great effort and expense to preserve could be lost.

User expectations for digital repositories are also very high. People may expect that a library can effectively preserve any resource virtually. However, there is simply no effective way to archive certain types of resources that are dependent on specific hardware, software, or other networked resources. Numerous technical and organizational challenges must be overcome for a library to preserve and provide access to resources that are "booklike" in that they can be printed out and used. The issues associated with increasingly common interactive information resources are more complex by orders of magnitude.

Electronic resources are inherently more difficult to work with than their physical counterparts. Staff and users alike are very comfortable working with traditional library materials, such as books and journals. These resources have a very consistent structure that people understand, and the tools and procedures used to work with these materials and make them accessible are very mature. In contrast, electronic resources are available in an enormous variety of different forms—in many cases, it is difficult to identify where one form begins and ends. Processing and access mechanisms are still in their infancy, and it is very difficult to describe and store these diverse materials in a way that makes them easy to find and use.

In addition to the technical and organizational challenges repositories offer, libraries must consider whether the staff who would be responsible for maintenance will embrace their new roles. No particular background is essential, but staff will need to help develop new procedures. They will need to develop new skills and be willing to learn on their own. They will need to be able to help managers evaluate and suggest improvements to tools and methods. They will need to expect that their specific duties will evolve with time and that what they do next year may be very different from what they do this year.

Having said that, a digital repository can be rewarding for patrons and staff alike if appropriate resources can be dedicated to the project. It can help the library improve its ability to deliver the next generation of library services while making new resources available to more patrons than was possible before. And because these resources are still very new, it can make the library more interesting and exciting for both users and staff.

SELLING THE PROJECT

A digital repository needs support from all areas in an organization. While projects to create digital repositories often generate considerable enthusiasm, they should be expected to have a significant impact on the services an organization provides as well as the staff responsible for maintaining these services. For this reason, buy-in from an organization's administration and staff are critical to success. One of the first jobs of those planning a digital repository is to garner this support.

To effectively articulate the value of a specific project to staff and administration, digital repository planners must believe in the goals of the project. The repository planner must convince the organization of the worth of the repository and the viability of the plan. The planner must keep the project on track, motivate others as necessary, and help maintain an expectation among staff and administration that the repository can and will succeed.

In addition to winning the support of staff and administration, a repository also requires organizational support to succeed. While a digital repository administrator/planner must sell and ensure the implementability of the digital repository plan, organizational commitment and ongoing dedication of resources to the endeavor is required for success. Creating a digital repository is a long-term commitment to support a new collection, and the success of this collection will be directly determined by the organization's ability to integrate the repository into the organization's funding and decision-making infrastructure.

As a new collection, a digital repository needs its own funding source to support the ongoing maintenance and development. A successful digital repository will have its own budget to ensure long-term support of the technical infrastructure as well as the ability to bring staff into the project. In addition, the organization needs to find ways to integrate the digital repository into the existing collection development workflow of the institution. For example, providing collection developers with a "digitization" budget for projects relating to the digital repository helps integrate the digital repository into the existing selection process and encourages wider participation within the organization. Having funds explicitly dedicated to digitization also reminds everyone that there are costs to digitizing and adding content to a repository. Staff should be encouraged to interact with the digital repository so that they can come to see it as a dynamic, exciting and integral resource to the organization.

UNDERSTANDING THE PURPOSE OF THE REPOSITORY

Before any work can begin, it is essential to articulate as concisely as possible why the repository is being built—the needs a repository seeks to address must drive the design process. Once the purpose of the repository has been determined, it is then possible to move on to a number of other practical questions that must be answered, such as:

- What type of resources will it contain?
- How big is it expected to grow?
- Who is going to use it and how?
- How can resources be protected against accidental or intentional modification?
- How will access and intellectual property rights be managed?
- What systems does it need to interact with?
- What special capabilities does it need?
- What resources will be available to create and maintain it?

Answering these questions allows designers to specify in broad terms how the repository will work and help identify what functionality is needed as well as the key players and expertise necessary to move the project forward. It is critical for designers to define the purpose of the repository as specifically as possible before attempting to identify an appropriate technical infrastructure, acquire materials, or request funding and staff resources. Even if financial, staffing and technical realities ultimately determine what will be done, it is important to address these constraints only after designers can describe their general vision and articulate what they wish to accomplish.

Understanding the purpose of the repository is important because at some point in time, the almost limitless possibilities that the virtual world has to offer must be reduced to a discrete set of capabilities that will actually be provided. When designing a repository, it is important not to get bogged down in discussions about what *could* be done. Rather, attention must be focused on what *will* be done. Services must be installed and configured before patrons can use them, and they must be maintained using resources that will be available.

Once everyone understands the purpose, repository designers must decide the types of materials the repository will contain. Just as successful physical libraries require a robust collection development process, so do electronic ones. The subject area of the materials, their format, the expertise required to understand them, and the anticipated use inevitably have a profound effect on whom the repository is likely to appeal to; how the repository will be used; and how materials will be processed, stored, accessed, and protected over time.

Establishing a collection development policy is a critical step that tends to be overlooked. Because digital resources ultimately consist of files containing a series of numbers on a hard disk, many people tend to just think of them as mutually compatible "electronic information." However, different types of digital resources present different challenges, so a repository must satisfactorily address the issues presented by the resources it will contain. Otherwise, there is a substantial risk that people will not be able to use the resources as desired, and the information could even be lost forever over time. Chapter 2 explains collection development issues in detail.

It is important to be aware how repository purpose affects initial and ongoing expenses. Except when relatively simple materials are concerned, it is not realistic to expect even the most sophisticated hardware and software to be able to organize all of the data the way people need them. Powerful searches of geospatial or video data may require expensive time-consuming addition of metadata or other processing. Even textual data might require the addition of access points so that it may be accessed by subject area, purpose, associated individuals or corporate entities, or other criteria. Few designers want their repository to function as an information silo on the Internet, and adding the ability to combine search result from different information resources may require data to be translated or standardized. All of these functions require resources to be maintained.

Certain design and functionality choices imply a long-term commitment to specific technologies that may or may not meet future needs. Repository designers should identify what they can work with and focus their collection and preservation activities on those things. If they want the repository to contain a particular type of document, they need to know how they will obtain, process, and provide long-term protection for that type of document with the available resources. As of this writing, there are no reliable methods for archiving certain types of materials, such interactive resources, because these are often dependent on specific software products. Chapter 3 discusses approaches that can be used when there is a need to archive interactive resources or other materials that are especially problematic as well as how to identify appropriate technologies for a digital repository project.

ANTICIPATING USE PATTERNS

Once the purpose of the repository and the type of materials it will contain are understood, attention can shift to imagining how the repository will be used—that is, the actual tasks people will perform when finding information in the repository or adding materials to it. When thinking about anticipated use, designers need to put themselves in the place of the patrons as well as the staff who will interact with the repository. Obviously, needs will be diverse, but it is still necessary to anticipate the broad categories of problems people are trying to solve and to understand which processes make sense and which do not.

Although almost anything is theoretically possible in a virtual environment, hardware and software can only do what they are "told to do."

Search boxes do not appear unless code specifies their size, location, and appearance. Search results do not display unless software determines what information is searchable, how that information is structured and searched, and how results are organized and displayed. Patrons cannot even use text, images, or audio unless they have software that interprets the files presented by the repository.

Some design choices preclude others. Power and flexibility come at the expense of simplicity and speed. For example, if a repository contains a large number of videos and sound recordings or geospatial data, it is highly unlikely that users will be satisfied if the only access mechanism provided is a simple Web-style search box that examines the full text of documents in a handful of formats and a few file attributes. On the other hand, if the purpose of a repository is simply to archive Web pages consisting primarily of text, a simple search box might well be the ideal access tool, while a sophisticated form allowing powerful searches may just confuse people. In practice, storage and retrieval mechanisms that are optimized for a particular type of resource usually prove to be inadequate for other types of resources.

Databases are fast because their indexes physically arrange information so that very little data needs to be scanned before a desired item is located. If electronic items share a similar structure, it is easy to index information within them efficiently. However, if they all are structured differently, it is impossible to create an efficient index without imposing a structure on the information first.

Computers are fast and network bandwidth is plentiful, but it is relatively easy to overwhelm even the most powerful systems. Technology constantly improves, but there are physical limitations to how fast information can be read from disks or memory and then processed. Disks are very fast, but even the drive that can transfer data at 200 MB/second (common at the time of this writing) and takes almost a minute to scan 10 GB of data, and this is assuming that no other process needs access to the drive and that the computer is idle enough to process all the information as fast as it is received. Currently, memory in a mid-range server can be accessed roughly 20 times faster than a hard disk, but even this is not fast enough to search large quantities of unstructured information.

Even the most powerful computers can be slowed to a crawl if forced to scan huge amounts of data sequentially or perform sufficiently complicated operations. Despite the fact that desktop computers today are easily hundreds of times faster than the ones that were available many years ago, most information technology (IT) managers hear constant complaints that the machines are too slow even though people use them primarily to read e-mail, compose documents, and look at a few Web pages. Likewise, today's servers are much more powerful than those of yesteryear, but it is still easy enough to make choices that cause them to run very slowly.

Many content-management systems store information in an "object database"— a specialized type of database that stores information in almost any format. While it is true that any information can be stored in a database, searching and retrieving the information efficiently can be another matter entirely. For example, the Plone content-management system's object database stores all documents, images, and other resources in a sequential file. An index keeps track of the location within the file of each object. In essence, this method is the electronic equivalent of assigning accession numbers to books and placing them on the shelf in the order they are added. Although caching frequently used resources in memory as well as other methods can significantly increase performance, sequential scans of all the objects in the database for desired resources simply are not feasible.

An understanding of how the repository will be used is essential for determining what technologies it will be based on, what access points will be stored, and what the user experience will be like. Though machines can do a great deal with electronic information, even a well-organized collection still requires significant human intervention. For example, it may be possible to encode virtually any relationship using eXtensible Markup Language (XML), but even in a fully automated system, humans must establish the rules that determine which information should be encoded and how it should be stored and searched. Countless lines of code and configuration parameters determine how people store, find, and use items in a repository. To obtain and configure appropriate hardware and software for a repository as well as developing efficient workflows for processing materials, designers need to have a clear picture of how people will interact with the repository.

IMAGE AND TEXT PROCESSING

As digital archives are created, libraries need to understand common processes and best practices associated with image and text processing of digital documents. Many libraries lack expertise in digital data capture, so digitization techniques for repository projects are typically developed by (IT) departments. Starting a digital library program requires planners to understand how to best capture and preserve such digital data so that it can provide maximum benefit to users in the long term.

Fortunately, a number of well-established resources already exist that provide detailed information on digitization topics, such as the capture of digital images. Cornell, for example, has an online tutorial titled *Moving Theory into Practice: Digital Imaging Tutorial* that provides a step-by-step discussion of key concepts and principles of digital-image capture (Cornell University Library, accessed: 2007). Likewise, the U.S. National Archives and Records Administration provides a list of the United States Archives' technical specifications for digital capture and preservation that can be used to determine what level of digital image capture will meet the needs of a particular digital repository program (National Archives and Records Administration, accessed: 2007).

Digital-capture guidelines vary considerably because the best digitization techniques vary depending on the purpose of the organization's digital repository. A digital library program focused on providing archival and public access to materials will utilize a very different set of digitization guidelines that those simply creating digital access copies of materials.

It is useful to be familiar with a few technical concepts relating to digitization. One of the most important is understanding the components of image resolution, since these determine how files can be stored, transmitted, displayed, and converted. Resolution of digital objects is determined by a number of key properties that make up the image.

1. Pixels: Digital images are made up of units known as pixels. Pixels correspond to binary bits that are given a value to represent the tonal (color) of the individual unit of the image. In essence, an image is a large grid on which each pixel makes up one element of that grid. Each pixel has a corresponding value that determines its visible tone. For example, bi-tonal images represent the most basic pixel layout. Bi-tonal images can be either black or white. This means that each pixel is defined as either black or white. For text documents, bi-tonal images often generate the most readable representation of the text—however, the character of the medium that such a text was digitized from will likely be lost (Wikipedia, n.d.).

2. Bit Depth: Most archival images are digitized as color or grayscale images, meaning any individual pixel can take a large number of values (as opposed to bi-tonal pixels; a bi-tonal pixel is represented by a single bit that can only take a value of 1 to represent black or a value of zero to represent white). Shading, depth, and color of an image are captured through the enhancement of bit depth. This allows each pixel to be represented by multiple bits and to represent a larger range of tones. So an image with a bit depth of 8 can represent 256 (2^8) shades, while an image with a bit depth of 24 can represent 16,777,216 (2^{24}) color values.

3. Dots per inch (DPI) or pixels per inch (PPI): The ability to reproduce or modify an image for other purposes is dependent on the DPI of the image at capture. The DPI represents the number of pixels represented per inch of the image. The higher the DPI, the greater the number of pixels that are utilized to represent an image—thus, the larger its size. Images saved primarily for Web browsing

are traditionally saved at 72 DPI archival images are traditionally captured at much higher resolutions. For the sake of comparison, the figures for this book were created at a resolution of 700 DPI.

4. Lossy versus Lossless: This concept relates to what information is retained and lost at the time an image is converted to a storage format. Images saved using a lossy file format suffer a degradation of resolution each time an image is converted or resaved because image bytes are lost during the image-compression process. Lossy image formats traditionally remove data from the image that would be imperceptible to the human eye. However, once lost, this data cannot be restored. This is different from lossless image formats, which save image data without data loss. A digital object saved using a lossless data format always retains the original digitized data from the scanner. For archival purposes, lossless images are generally preferred because they can capture and retain all of a digital objects' digital information. Lossy images tend to be utilized for the rendering of archival images on the Web, since these images will be much smaller in size (reductions of over 90% are common) and easier to render for the user.

Digital repository managers must understand the basic issues surrounding image resolution in order to make informed decisions about how digital resources will be captured. A number of digital archival formats can be utilized but fortunately, a great deal has been written about them over the past few years. A number of the resources discussing formats are listed later in the chapter, and these should be consulted for a fuller understanding of what image formats and techniques are available. A basic description of image formats is provided here.

As is the case with resolution, the best image was storage formats for a repository depend on the purpose of the repository. Are digital images being created primarily for display purposes, or will these images need to be archived for permanent storage? As discussed earlier, lossless image formats are normally preferred to a lossy image format for archival purposes, particularly if users are expected to edit or reuse these resources. On the other hand, lossy formats, such as JPEG, are usually far more practical for casual use. Lossless formats result in such huge files that they become unusable to patrons with slow connections. Moreover, despite the fact that disk space is cheap, lossless image formats can significantly increase processing and maintenance costs.

At present, there are two image formats used primarily for archival purposes and four image formats used primarily for displaying digital data.

ARCHIVAL IMAGE FORMATS

TIF (Tagged Image Format)

The TIF image format represents the current de facto digital file format for archival digital images. A quick survey of file formats supported by digital library programs around the country point to the overwhelming support for the TIF format as the digital archival master-image format of choice. In practice, the TIF file format is used almost universally by digital library projects around the world. A quick sampling of current projects like the Library of Congress (accessed 2007), NARA (accessed 2007) the California Digital Library (accessed 2007), and Stanford University all require the TIF format for all master images. In part, this choice comes from the technical make-up of the file format itself. The TIF file format is a 24-bit, lossless file format commonly used by nearly all image editors. This makes the format ideal for archival image digitization since the saved file always provides an exact digital representation of the digital artifact.

PNG (Portable Network Graphics)

Like the TIF format, the PNG format was developed as a lossless format capable of creating archival images. Few use PNG as an archival image format, in part because the image format was designed primarily as a replacement to the GIF image format. PNG was developed primarily in response to Unisys's decision to enforce a patent related to the compression format within the GIF image format. PNG was developed by the open-source community to provide a standards-based image format, superior to the GIF image format, but meeting the same need. As an archival format, the PNG image format is a lossless image format, but it is not widely supported as the TIF image format. As a result, the PNG image format is used primarily for the creation of display quality images.

DISPLAY IMAGE FORMATS

JPEG

JPEG is the common name for the image-standards format developed by the Joint Photographic Experts Group. The JPEG image format utilizes a lossy compression algorithm, making it ill-suited for archival or preservation purposes. However, as a display image format, the JPEG image format enjoys nearly universal support from image-editing software and Web-browsing software, making it an ideal choice for images such as photographs, which have subtle variations in tone and color. JPEG images perform much worse with text-based images, as the image artifacts created during the compression process become apparent against the sharp lines and harsh contrasts of most digital text representations.

JPEG2000

In 2000, the Joint Photographic Experts Group created JPEG2000 to supersede the JPEG file format. JPEG2000 utilizes a different compression mechanism, allowing the file format to be utilized as both a lossless and lossy image format. One of the important differences between JPEG and JPEG2000 is that the latter can store representations for the master image at multiple sizes and resolutions. This allows images encoded with JPEG2000 to generate display-quality images from a JPEG2000 master while still maintaining the ability to zoom down to the maximum image resolution. On the surface, the JPEG2000 image format seems to be a leading successor to the current TIF image format for archival storage, in part, because JPEG2000 can be saved using a lossless image algorithm and does not require the creation of derivative images (e.g., thumbnails) for display. However, lack of format support by Web browsers and image-editing software has slowed acceptance of the JPEG2000 image format, and patent concerns could ultimately render the format unusable.

GIF (Graphics Interchange Format)

The GIF format has largely started to disappear from Web- and image-editing software packages in large part due to the patent enforcement of the compression algorithm's patent holder, Unisys. As a result of patent concerns, the open-source community created the PNG format, which today has largely replaced the GIF image format. However, prior to the patent action, the GIF format was one of the de facto image formats available on the Web. GIF images were well suited for text-based images, because it is a lossless image format that can represent 256 colors or 8-bit grayscale images. This color restriction, however, made GIF images poorly suited for photographic images, which tend to rely on millions of colors.

PNG

See description above.

SAMPLE ARCHIVAL SETTINGS

Oregon State University Libraries' digital library program focuses on archival digitization of documents using uncompressed TIF and

JPEG2000 images for archival and display purposes. Oregon State University Libraries' current digital guidelines call for the image-capture guidelines in Figure 1-4.

Text processing	Photography
Black-and-white documents	*Black-and-white documents*
1. *Archival object:*	1. *Archival object*
❏ 8 bit	❏ 8 bit
❏ Grayscale	❏ Grayscale
❏ TIF, uncompressed	❏ TIF, uncompressed
❏ 300 DPI	❏ 600, 800, 1200*, 2400*, 3200* DPI
2. *Public object*	2. *Public object*
❏ 8 bit	❏ 8 bit
❏ Grayscale	❏ Grayscale
❏ JPEG2000, lossless	❏ JPEG2000, lossless
❏ 300 DPI	❏ 600, 800, 1200*, 2400*, 3200* DPI
Color documents	*Color documents*
3. *Archival object:*	3. *Archival object*
❏ 24 bit	❏ 24 bit
❏ Color	❏ Color
❏ TIF, uncompressed	❏ TIF, uncompressed
❏ 600 DPI	❏ 600, 800, 1200*, 2400*, 3200* DPI
4. *Public object*	4. *Public object*
❏ 24 bit	❏ 24 bit
❏ Color	❏ Color
❏ JPEG2000, lossless	❏ JPEG2000, lossless
❏ 600 DPI	❏ 600, 800, 1200*, 2400*, 3200* DPI

Figure 1-4. Oregon State University Libraries' Image Capture Guidelines

* slide, film positives, film negatives, glass negatives.

RIGHTS MANAGEMENT

Traditionally, the role of the library has been to acquire and manage resources created by others. By their nature, digital archives allow libraries to distribute locally produced information, as well as to repackage and distribute information produced by others. In this sense, the library adopts the role of a publisher when it starts archiving and distributing electronic information (Jones, Andrew and MacColl, 2006). It is therefore clear that the task of maintaining digital repositories is more than a matter of fulfilling the library's traditional role using new technologies.

Providing electronic archives is not the same thing as publishing, but it does imply a number of responsibilities that are traditionally associated with publishers. For example, digital repository managers need to secure the rights to manage and provide perpetual access to materials as well as the right to migrate these materials to other formats when appropriate. Especially in university settings, where the author may have already signed away some or all of the rights to another publisher (e.g., to allow it to be published in a peer-reviewed journal), obtaining permission to distribute locally produced information may be more complicated than one might think (Jones et al., 2006). Likewise, it may be necessary to place access restrictions on works that are politically, commercially, or industrially sensitive (Jones et al., 2006). It is important to be aware that securing rights to distribute materials does not require authors to grant copyright to the repository. Rather, the repository simply needs a nonexclusive right to distribute the resource.

Copyright issues are a bigger concern for digital repositories than for physical libraries. When paper materials are concerned, if a library owns a book that contains information that infringes on the copyright of someone else or that contains inaccurate information that causes harm to others, the publisher and author of the book are liable. However, when the library acts as a publisher, it will absorb some responsibility, though as of this time, the courts have not addressed to what extent this is the case. Electronic information is particularly troublesome in that it can so easily be copied that there is a substantial risk of accidental plagiarism or copyright infringement. For these reasons, even if a repository contains only freely available items, designers still have to take reasonable steps to prevent copyright infringement and ensure quality control.

Often, managers of a digital repository wish to include high-value resources that are owned by outside copyright holders. When this is the case, the repository must contain suitable access-control mechanisms that can perform basic functions such as limiting the ability to access certain resources to specific types of users. Rights management needs to be built into the design from the very beginning so that appropriate technologies and workflows can be adapted to protect materials and to prevent premature disclosure of information. While most people do not think of library materials as being sensitive, embargo periods for electronic versions of titles have been common for years (Jones et al., 2006). Likewise, theses and dissertations often include detailed information about inventions that are in the process of being patented or findings that must be released elsewhere, or they have some other characteristic that prevents them from being released immediately.

Rights management is a serious issue and the legal issues of copyright are beyond the scope of this book. However, any well-conceived digital repository will want to prominently and clearly state all policies regarding the materials it contains. Such policies must explain what people may and may not do with materials they download, as well as appropriate legal disclaimers. Although these policy statements will help reduce confusion and protect the library, it is important to be aware that not all users on the Internet are human. Unless appropriate barriers are constructed, content providers should be informed that digital archives will undoubtedly be mined by Web spiders and other types of robots (Jones et al., 2006).

Although it is important to take copyright issues seriously, it is also important not to let them derail a digital repository project. The rules of the virtual realm are not as clear as the rules of the physical world (to the extent that those are clear). When a repository is accessed over the Internet, the materials it contains will be accessed from areas governed by different and contradictory laws. It is impossible to anticipate and solve all copyright problems. Rather, repository designers need to identify and manage risks.

ACCOMMODATING CHANGING FORMATS AND DATA STRUCTURES

Historically, libraries have been responsible for preserving the materials that they acquire. Just as most libraries have policies that allow them to reject single issues of serials, low-value books that are falling apart or filled with mold, or resources that cannot be used without special equipment that the library does not have, digital repositories must establish criteria that ensure that the repository only contains materials that can be used and maintained—it is ultimately counterproductive to add enormous files without regard for format to a repository with no long-term plans for dealing with technological change.

It is risky to presume that software produced in the future will address issues of accessing and preserving formats that are currently in use. Although it is theoretically possible to emulate any hardware or software environment, it is unrealistic to expect that this will be done for most resources. Enormous quantities of data encoded in the 1960s, 1970s, 1980s, 1990s, and even in the past few years are unreadable because the required software is no longer available.

For example, well into the 1980s, WordStar was the most popular word-processing program and was considered *the* standard. Nowadays, few people remember WordStar, and it is difficult to find converters that can interpret documents created by the program. Likewise, even documents created by early versions of Microsoft Word cannot necessarily be read easily anymore—even Microsoft cannot guarantee that its programs will read documents created by earlier versions of its own software. The fact is that when a company discontinues support for a program or goes out of business, there is rarely much incentive for someone else to step in since the demise of products and companies is often caused by insufficient demand in the marketplace.

Although paper seems fragile, it is easy to work with and can be stored under a variety of conditions where it can survive many years without attention or maintenance. No special equipment is necessary to view information that is stored on paper. As such, acid-free paper is an excellent archival format.

Electronic information, on the other hand, can easily be copied to new media, but it is unstable enough that it cannot be stored on disks and then ignored for many years. To complicate matters, electronic information can only be used when the right hardware and software are available to interpret it.

To preserve access to books and other physical resources, archivists protect the materials themselves. However, when people use resources in a digital repository, they do not use the actual information that was stored by the library. Technically, they access a reproduction of the resource that was copied into the memory of a computer and they view it with the aid of software. This is what makes it possible for more than one person to use the same resource at the same time. Because the original resource is not actually used and no one interacts with it directly, it is unimportant as an artifact. Consequently, the goal is not to preserve specific bytes as if they were pages of a book but rather to recreate the temporary experience people have had when using the resource (Helshop, Davis and Wilson, 2002).

Figure 1-5 demonstrates this dynamic. Note that the original material is almost irrelevant and that the goal is to reproduce the substance of a particular experience involving an information object.

The model shown in Figure 1-5 is not new to libraries. For many years, libraries have collected sound and video recordings that were originally stored on decaying nitrate films, various disks, obsolete tape formats, cylinders, and other media that are inherently unstable and that require special equipment to use them. Just as it is not reasonable to expect to watch an early silent movie on nitrate film stock using a projector from that era, it is also not realistic to expect to view a WordStar 1.0 document on the CP/M (Control Program/Monitor) operating system. While such a capability may sound obscure, as mentioned, WordStar was by far the most popular word-processing program in 1980, and CP/M was so dominant that few imagined that any other operating system would be used on Intel-based computers (Online Software Museum, accessed: 2006).

Library practice has long been to migrate sound and video recordings to new media that are more stable and usable. While the experience of using a migrated resource is not *exactly* the same, the substance of the information object is preserved. Likewise, digital files must be converted from time to time. Although there is a widespread tendency for librarians to want to preserve the original manifestation of digital works, doing so does not necessarily improve long-term access. The source files can be saved easily enough, but technology cycles are so short that it is impossible to preserve the process of rendering the resources (Helshop et al., 2002).

It is assumed that all formats will eventually become obsolete. As a practical matter, there are only two basic strategies for working with information resources stored in obsolete formats. The first strategy requires emulation of the original hardware and software environment. Even if all technical and financial implications of emulating countless hardware and software combinations is ignored, this strategy still requires knowledge of the reader's environment at a particular point in time (Rosenthal et al., 2005). Many programs (including document viewers) run only on particular versions of Windows, MacOS, or other operating systems. Emulating them all is simply not feasible.

Figure 1-5 demonstrates the second preservation strategy—migration. Many repositories collect documents and materials that originated in a

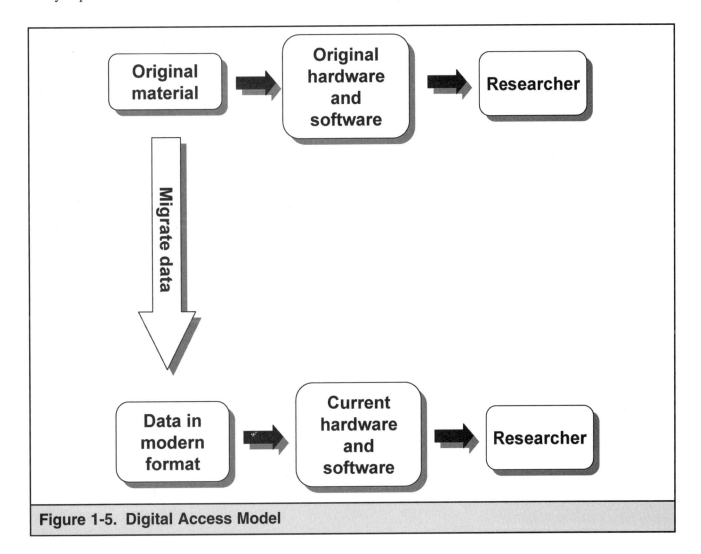

Figure 1-5. Digital Access Model

wide variety of propriety formats. If these are migrated to a standard format at the time they are added to the collection, the long-term prospects for these resources will be significantly improved, even if the only initial effect is to postpone the need for the next migration.

No system lasts forever, so digital repositories must be designed with the presumption that original formats, hardware, and software will become obsolete over time. If migrations are built into the digital repository plan, the likelihood of future data or service loss can be greatly reduced.

Format migrations often result in the loss of some information. While the loss of any information is undesirable, it is simply a reality of working with digital objects. Attempting to preserve all characteristics of an information object can result in an enormous investment of time and money for protecting inconsequential details while more substantive matters are neglected (Rosenthal et al., 2005). Many characteristics (e.g., toolbars, buttons, color schemes, etc.) are simply not essential for most information objects. For a number of reasons, it is generally much more effective to identify which elements of an information resource are essential and focus on preserving them. While the definition of an "important" element can be a matter of debate, resolving conflicts should not be difficult if the archival purpose has been articulated clearly.

Migration is an ongoing commitment, and the magnitude and complexity of this task increases as the collection size increases. For this reason, repository administration can be simplified and resource integrity can be preserved more effectively if data are normalized at the time they are incorporated into the repository. Figure 1-5 diagrams this process.

Normalizing data at the time of ingestion presents a number of advantages. If the normalized data are stored in a format that is specifically chosen for its stability and "friendliness" to the migration process, future migrations are drastically simplified and the need for them is minimized. Limiting the number of formats also simplifies workflow and access because there is less need for different treatment for various information resources. Obviously, normalizing data simplifies management of the repository as a whole and makes it easier to extend the original functionality.

There is no way to predict the future, but the best way to protect data against obsolescence is to limit the number of formats within the repository and ensure that tools for processing those formats are available. Thus, when it becomes necessary to migrate to a different format at a later date, it can be accomplished. Because converting or reformatting digital resources inevitably results in some loss of functionality or information, it is almost inevitable that resources viewed in 50 years will not be the same as the original. However, it is reasonable to believe that they will be functionally equivalent.

Ideally, preservation should be considered at the time of creation so that information loss is minimized. Unfortunately, that is often not feasible because the repository managers do not necessarily have influence over those who create the materials that are kept there. However, if repositories ensure that resources are initially stored in formats that lend themselves well towards archiving, the chances of providing good quality long-term access will be increased.

PROTECTING INTEGRITY OF RESOURCES

Protecting the integrity of digital resources is much more difficult than protecting books, journals, microfiche, and other physical resources. Aside from the inherent problems of managing virtual resources that can be modified easily and quickly, the task of ensuring integrity is complicated by the fact that a document in a digital repository is defined by the content itself rather than the string of bytes used to encode that content. In other words, a slight change to that string of bytes may represent a very serious and undesirable modification to the content, while a very radical change to that same string of bytes might be perfectly acceptable because it was simply the result of a migration that did not change the content of the document at all.

As already noted, electronic information frequently needs to be reformatted or converted to be usable. Any Web page that communicates with a database reformats the information from the database before presenting it. Most organizations try to present electronic information so that it has a uniform look and feel. By definition, any software used to view a document must format the information it is given.

Facilitating legitimate reformatting and modification of resources while preventing illegitimate modification is a difficult task. Once electronic resources are created, they can easily be modified intentionally or inadvertently in seconds by anyone (or any process) with appropriate system permissions. On the other hand, no repository can function unless appropriate individuals have permission to add and modify the data in it.

Cryptography is an effective way to ensure the integrity of data because an encrypted file cannot be modified without rendering it unusable. However, encryption is not a good solution for most digital repositories. If the key used to encrypt the information is lost, so are all resources that were locked with that key. Widely distributing the key used to encrypt the information defeats the purpose of encrypting it in first place. Likewise, if the encrypted file is corrupted at all, the information will also be lost. An alternative to encryption is to generate a checksum by running a known algorithm against the file. However, if a person accessing the file can also access the checksum, he or she can simply generate a new one, which compromises security.

One simple approach for protecting documents is to archive them on media that cannot be modified. For smaller numbers of documents, this method can be quite effective. However, as the number of documents grows, physically managing the disks becomes its own problem, as does verifying that the resource supplied to patrons is the same version that is archived. Another major disadvantage of this method is that it forces documents to be stored as individual entities on a file system that imposes a number of restraints on system design and repository function.

Digital repository designers should take reasonable measures to ensure that the integrity of resources is protected. However, it is also important to keep the problem in perspective and not allow highly unlikely but theoretically feasible scenarios to derail the repository project. In the physical world, as long as repositories have existed, theft, destruction, and mutilation of resources have been problems. Advances in technology have made it relatively easy to forge or alter virtually any document. Thieves and library staff have stolen library resources for as long as libraries have existed. As this chapter was being written, a student assistant at a major university library managed to steal $75,000 worth of books, which he sold through an online retailer before he was caught (*Austin American Statesman*, 2006).

Nonetheless, libraries have been very successful following pragmatic policies regarding security despite constant threats and the occasional loss, theft, or mutilation of materials. Likewise, digital repositories are probably better served by practical measures to ensure the integrity of resources than they are of overzealous measures designed to eliminate problems entirely. Perfect security is impossible, and excessive measures can lead to poor service and high costs.

Fortunately, a reasonably high level of protection can be achieved by following a few simple practices. One of the most obvious is simply to keep multiple copies of resources.

LOCKSS (LOTS OF COPIES KEEP STUFF SAFE)

One of the simplest ways to protect resources is to retain multiple copies. If copies of digital resources are stored in separate locations managed by different people, resources and collections of resources can be protected reasonably effectively against accidental modification or deletion of data as well as intentional efforts to suppress or modify them.

The idea behind LOCKSS is simple—multiple copies of documents are stored at different libraries. Documents that have been modified can easily be detected and repaired because copies at the different libraries are constantly compared. If a discrepancy is found, the different LOCKSS servers "vote" to figure out which copy is correct and the damage is automatically repaired. Because LOCKSS retains multiple copies of documents, backups are not necessary. Figure 1-6 illustrates how LOCKSS works.

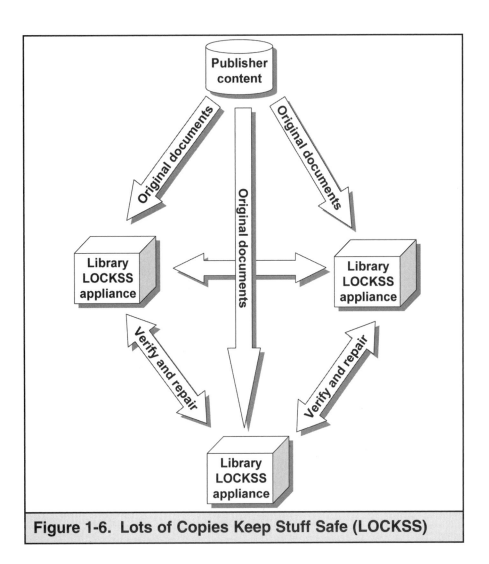

Figure 1-6. Lots of Copies Keep Stuff Safe (LOCKSS)

LOCKSS has the support from major publishers and many libraries. However, LOCKSS is designed to ensure access to content that a library has purchased, and then it can only be used if the publisher has granted explicit permission. As of this writing, several thousand titles can be stored in LOCKSS appliances, but they are only a small part of the information a library is likely to want to include in a repository. In addition, LOCKSS presumes that multiple libraries will want to store local copies of resources maintained by others. For purchased journals, this is a safe assumption, but for local digital repositories, this is not necessarily the case. Universities that store theses, dissertations, and faculty preprints might find that other institutions are not interested in archiving and maintaining this information. Nonetheless, LOCKSS offers a practical, simple, and relatively cheap model for providing access to digital resources.

DISASTER PLANNING AND SECURITY

Just as the buildings that house physical libraries need adequate security to protect library resources, the computer systems that make up a digital repository must also be adequately secured. Generally speaking, the same precautions that would normally be taken with any important computer system are also appropriate for protecting digital repositories. The list below is not comprehensive, but the following are examples of good policies:

- Good physical security is needed for repository hardware. Unauthorized users should not be able to access machines.
- Everything should be backed up regularly and stored in a different location.
- Staff should monitor system logs and use or write software that alerts them to unusual systems activity.
- The operating system and software should be kept up-to-date.
- Staff should join announcement lists that share news about any developments that concern the software.
- Administrators should take measures to ensure users have appropriate systems permission, and they should be careful when creating group accounts.
- Staff should not use powerful administrative accounts except when necessary to perform specific tasks.
- Encrypted connections should be used to connect to servers, particularly those working off-site.
- Unnecessary software should be disabled.

MANAGING WITH AVAILABLE RESOURCES AND CHANGE

Just as any library would plan carefully before agreeing to take on the responsibility of absorbing and nurturing a new physical collection indefinitely, it must also do the same for electronic collections. Although there is a widespread tendency to think that digital materials take few resources to work with or maintain, implementing a digital repository is a major commitment that requires significant staff and funding resources.

When digital resources are involved, it is natural for people to want to build all the good features they have seen in other systems into their own. While it is perfectly reasonable to want the greatest level of functionality possible, it is important to be aware that every feature complicates configuration and increases long-term maintenance commitments.

Launching a digital repository is an exciting process, but long-term success depends on a viable long-term plan. Such a plan requires a realistic view of how much time and money it will take to achieve each goal. The library must have access to adequate technological resources as well as sufficient expertise to set up, configure, and maintain systems properly. The library also needs adequate staff to perform acquisitions and processing tasks. If the resources are not sufficient to implement the plan, it may be necessary to adjust the goals to achievable levels. A high-quality repository with a modest scope is more valuable as a resource than an overly ambitious project for the simple reason that with the former, people can reasonably know what they can expect to find.

Acquiring and processing new electronic resources takes time and significant staff resources. An acquisitions model that presumes that authors and others will consistently identify valuable materials and submit them using an online submission form is not realistic—few people are nearly as interested in archiving or in open access as the library (Jones et al., 2006). Depending on non-experts to create helpful metadata is equally unrealistic. History has yet to provide an example of a good library with a collection development policy based primarily on letting authors and users determine all acquisitions. Nor has any library succeeded in organizing a major collection by having ordinary information providers and patrons catalog and shelve materials in the way they believe will be most useful.

It may be easier to understand the basic acquisitions and processing challenges by examining a case study. The Oregon Documents Repository (ODR) provides electronic access to government documents produced by the State of Oregon. These documents can be created by any agency and may be in any format. When the ODR was being designed, planners enjoyed two advantages that, they hoped, would drastically reduce the amount of work required to identify and process materials. The first is that the State of Oregon had participated in the Government Information Locator Service (GILS) for more than five years, and extensive training had been provided to agency staff on the importance of providing metadata for documents, as well as guidance on how this should be done. The second advantage is that a significant percentage of Oregon documents are created within a content management system (CMS) that requires people to submit metadata about each document at the time of submission. Some metadata, such as the date, are automatically provided by the system, but authors provide subject and keyword data.

Despite the extensive metadata training provided to agency users, ODR designers quickly discovered that the author-supplied metadata was virtually useless. Many authors submitted a few hopelessly vague terms that had at best tangential connection to the document. Others provided long lists of keywords that appeared to be designed to make the document appear as often as possible, whether or not it was needed for the search. Even metadata elements as simple as the title were often useless. Generic titles such as "Report" were common.

State agencies are legally required to deposit documents with the Oregon State Library, but what constitutes a "document" in the eyes of people who do not work for the library is very different from the librarians' definition. Some people believe that all meeting minutes should be archived, while some who create significant publications that are heavily used, such as high-level budget reports, do not regard the documents as important. The most common problem is that people tend not to think of the library or repository at all. The ODR was designed so that people could suggest inclusion of particular documents, but library staff use other means to identify most documents that are actually added to the collection at this time.

In the end, the Oregon State Library developed a number of automatic and manual processes to identify documents to be cataloged using procedures that are very similar to those for physical materials. Even though the ODR is searchable through the State of Oregon's search mechanism as well as with popular search engines such as Google, usage statistics indicate that the library catalog (and library catalogs that have downloaded MARC records from the State Library) are the primary routes used to locate documents in the ODR.

As the ODR case suggests, a significant part of a repository's value is based on the judgment and efforts of library staff. The ODR planners' decision that it was best to ignore metadata provided by non-experts (many of whom had received training) implies that repository designs predicated on the assumption that users will do work traditionally performed by library staff may lead to poorly organized collections of highly variable quality.

Selection and organization are the qualities that give libraries their value. People will not use materials that they have no need or desire for, and it does little good to have excellent materials if people cannot find them. For this reason, a critical part of formulating a good digital repository plan is determining how the desired materials will be identified and processed using available resources.

Digital repositories are completely dependent on technology, and it is easy to underestimate the costs of long-term system support, especially when a system is developed in-house. When a digital repository is new, people remember the planning process, they are familiar with the components used to build the repository, and it is easy to find people with detailed knowledge of how things work. As a result, most things function as designed, and while the repository is still new problems are solved rapidly.

After some years have passed, supporting and improving the system becomes more difficult. The software for any digital repository will have many dependencies, and it may turn out years later that individual components are dependent on specific versions of software that are no longer maintained. This problem can occur with proprietary as well as open-source software. Key players may no longer be available, and critical details will have been forgotten. Consequently, maintenance and troubleshooting that was previously simple can become very difficult, and complex operations such as systems migrations can become overwhelming. Once a system reaches the point where it cannot be supported properly, all of the resources in the repository are at risk of being lost.

Maintaining a digital repository in the long term is more complicated than maintaining an integrated library system (ILS). Over the past few decades, the ILS market has become relatively mature. Bibliographic, patron, and vendor data have become more standardized. Future migrations may be costly and complicated, but they are certainly feasible.

Conversely, digital repositories are still in an embryonic stage that is currently in a period of rapid development. Divergent and incompatible methods are used to store complex information. It is still unclear which architectures will survive even in the medium term. It is important to design the repository so that it is easy to maintain using resources that will be available after some time has passed. In many cases, this means setting relatively modest goals. Sophistication and complexity go hand in hand while simple, elegant, designs tend to be more robust.

FURTHER INFORMATION

While we hope that this book provides readers with the information needed to start and maintain their own digital repositories, the diversity of projects and rapid technology cycles makes it impractical to address all needs comprehensively. Information related to the digitization of images as well as the economics of digital libraries are well-established topics, and a great deal of literature is currently available for readers wanting to additional information about these topics.

The Cornell Libraries and the NARA both provide extensive tutorials detailing the technical and procedural methods for digitizing of images. Cornell Library's online tutorial, *Moving Theory into Practice: Digital Imaging Tutorial* provides a straightforward, yet accessible, approach to digital image capture geared primarily towards information technology with little appearance in libraries. The tutorial offers many examples, linking to other projects and technical specifications and covering a wide range of topics without boring the reader with technical jargon. Anne Kenney's work, "Digital Benchmarking for Preservation and Access," should also be consulted as a companion to the preservation and access elements of Cornell's tutorial. Together, these two documents provide a great deal of information that will be useful to both the novice and experienced digital repository manager.

NARA's *Technical Specifications* cover the technical specifications currently in use by NARA's digitization programs. However, in addition to procedural specifications, there are also technical specifications, including information on the digitization station setup with a list of hardware specifications that will guide readers planning to start a digital library program. In addition, many large digital library projects currently make their best practices available for download. For example, the Collaborative Digitization Program in Colorado (www.cdpheritage.org/digital/ index.cfm), the California Digital Library (www.cdlib.org/inside/ projects/), the University of Michigan (www.umdl.umich.edu/docs/ index.html), and the University of Virginia (www.lib.virginia.edu/digital/) all provide Web sites that document best practices, image digitization guides, and hardware specifications currently used by each project. This information can be invaluable for novice digital library developers.

Likewise, a number of books have recently been written on creating a successful digital program. Recently, two amazing texts targeting electronic theses and dissertations (ETD) development and the acquisitions of digital materials have been made available to the library community. The first, *Electronic Theses and Dissertations: A Sourcebook for Educators, Students and Librarians* is a compilation of articles on the development of an ETD program (Fox et al., 2004). The book covers topics ranging from the motivation for starting such a program to the technologies used for the development of such a program. The text provides a wide breadth of information dedicated to this one specific digital library program, though many of the concepts can be applied more universally within one's digital repository program. The later text, *Handbook of Electronic and Digital Acquisitions* (Leonhardt, 2006) offers in-depth insights into collection, selection, and evaluation of digital materials.

SUMMARY

To be successful, digital repositories must be planned carefully. Designers need to understand the goals of the repository, the target audience, and the resources that will be available to create and maintain the repository. The real costs of a repository are in the long-term upkeep, so it is important to address practical issues such as who will identify and process materials and how these will be maintained. Although a digital repository is a highly automated environment, a great deal of human judgment and manual work is necessary to develop a high-quality collection. All systems and software eventually become obsolete, and future data loss and service disruptions can be minimized by normalizing data at the time resources are ingested into the repository and by thinking about migrations from the outset. Generally speaking, it is best for a library to start with a simple but extendable design and add functionality and complexity as staff become experienced in facing a wider variety of challenges and systems mature.

REFERENCES

California Digital Library. *Digital Image Format Standards*. Available: http://chnm.gmu.edu/digitalhistory/links/pdf/chapter3/3.29b.pdf (accessed April 10, 2007).

Cornell University Library. *Moving Theory into Practice: Digital Imaging Tutorial*. Available: www.library.cornell.edu/ preservation/tutorial/contents.html (accessed April 1, 2007).

Fox, Edward A., Shahrooz Feizabadi, Joseph M. Moxley, and Christian R. Weisser. 2004. *Electronic Theses and Dissertations*. New York: Marcel Dekker.

Helshop, H., S. Davis, and A. Wilson. 2002. "National Archives Green Paper: An Approach to the Preservation of Digital Records." Available: www.naa.gov.au/recordkeeping/er/digital_preservation/ Green_Paper.pdf (accessed September 30, 2006).

Jones, Richard, Theo Andrew, and John MacColl. 2006. *The Institutional Repository*. Oxford: Chandos.

Kenney, Anne R. 2000. "Digital Benchmarking for Preservation and Access." In *Moving Theory into Practice: Digital Imaging for Libraries and Archives* (pp. 24-60). Mountain View, CA : Research Libraries Group. Available: www.rlg.org/preserv/mtip2000.html

Leonhardt, Thomas W. 2006. *Handbook of Electronic and Digital Acquisitions*. New York: Haworth Press.

National Archives and Records Administration. "Digital-Imaging and Optical Digital Data Disk Storage Systems: Long-Term Access Strategies for Federal Agencies." Available: www.archives.gov/preservation/technical/imaging-storage-report.html (accessed April 10, 2007).

National Archives and Records Administration. "Technical Information." Available: www.archives.gov/preservation/technical/ (accessed April 1, 2007).

The Online Software Museum. "CP/M." Available: http://museum. sysun.com/museum/cpmhist.html (accessed October 1, 2006).

Rosenthal, David S. H., et al. 2005. "Transparent Format Migration of Preserved Web Content." *D-Lib Magazine* 11, no. 1. Available: www.dlib.org/dlib/january05/rosenthal/01rosenthal.html (accessed September 30, 2006).

"Texas Tech Book Theft Spurs Changes." 2006. *Austin-American Statesman* (September 19). Available: www.statesman.com/news/content/news/stories/local/09/19/19Library Theft.html (accessed September 30, 2006).

United States Library of Congress. "Election 2000 Web Archive." Available: http://lcweb2.loc.gov/cocoon/minerva/html/elec2000/elec2000-about.html (accessed April 11, 2007).

United States Library of Congress. "Technical Standards for Digital Conversion of Text and Graphic Materials." Available: http://memory.loc.gov/ammem/about/techStandards122106.pdf (accessed April 10, 2007).

2 ACQUIRING, PROCESSING, CLASSIFYING, AND DESCRIBING DIGITAL CONTENT

The value of a repository is measured by how it selects, organizes, and presents information. While a great number of powerful tools such as approval plans, OCLC cataloging, and the MARC format have been widely and successfully used to perform these tasks for physical resources, analogous standard procedures for identifying, processing, and organizing digital resources have yet to be widely implemented. The highly distributed nature of the virtual world presents some unique challenges that must be addressed if a library is to develop a coherent, high-quality digital collection.

PLANNING WORKFLOW

Libraries depend on a variety of procedures to incorporate materials such as books, journals, and government documents into their collections. A collection development process determines what materials will be added to or removed from the collection. An ordering and acquisitions process determines how libraries locate and obtain desired items. Physical processing and cataloging procedures preserve and organize resources so they can be readily found and used by future generations.

Workflows define the physical and conceptual processes that occur when libraries acquire new materials, organize or manage the collection, and provide access. They determine who does what: what level of staff are needed, what specific skills these staff need, and what actual tasks are performed. Different workflows are necessary because managing a library collection is a relatively complex operation. Most people have difficulty finding things that they bought for themselves fairly recently even though they choose where those things are kept. These same people, however, would not expect to have trouble finding a resource in a library even though it may have been acquired decades ago and stored on the shelves based on the decision of one of hundreds of staff members working at the library over the years. Reliable workflows and procedures make this possible.

Collection development specialists must know the collection and what resources patrons need. Acquisitions staff need to know how to obtain whatever resources the collection development specialists may identify, no matter where they may be. Technical services staff need to be able to preserve and organize materials that may be in foreign languages about unfamiliar subjects and that may be published on media with poor archival qualities.

Performing these functions so that patrons will be able to find what they need requires specialized knowledge. Different staff and procedures are needed for different functions or even to perform the same functions with different types of resources. The procedures and skills required to add the latest issue of a popular magazine to the collection are very different from those needed to add a specialized monograph written in foreign language that can only be acquired from an overseas publisher.

Physical libraries develop a variety of workflows that are optimized to address the practical challenges presented by different types of resources. It is common for libraries to select and acquire materials meeting certain criteria with an approval plan, but to select and order other resources individually. Many, if not most, libraries use batch processes to handle the most common types of resources but invoke a completely different mechanism to incorporate specialized or valuable resources into the collection.

Most challenges in incorporating physical materials into the collection also occur when digital resources are involved. A mechanism to systematically identify materials to add to the collection must exist. Technology constantly changes, so electronic resources must be reformatted or converted so they can be preserved and made accessible. The items must also be described using metadata or a catalog record. As with physical resources, some digital resources must be handled individually while others may be processed in batches.

The value of a digital collection is measured by how well it helps users locate what they need rather than by the number of items it contains. This means that to be useful, digital files must be selected and processed before they are stored. However, the process for selecting, acquiring, processing, and organizing digital materials varies with the type of resource as well as how they will most likely be used.

Digital repositories vary significantly in terms of purpose, what they contain, and the technical and personnel resources available to support them. For this reason, solutions developed in one environment may or may not work in other settings. Libraries should take advantage of lessons learned at other institutions, but they must evaluate their own needs and create their own workflows rather than simply adopting those developed elsewhere. If a repository will be maintained by existing library staff, planners must remember that maintaining a digital repository requires a number of skills that many (if not most) staff will not have. The workflows must take into account what staff can realistically be expected to achieve after a reasonable training period.

Although there are many ways to develop workflows, the most effective approach is often to identify what major tasks need to be accomplished and then to determine how those tasks can be broken down into discrete procedures. Figure 2-1 illustrates the basic steps common to the workflow

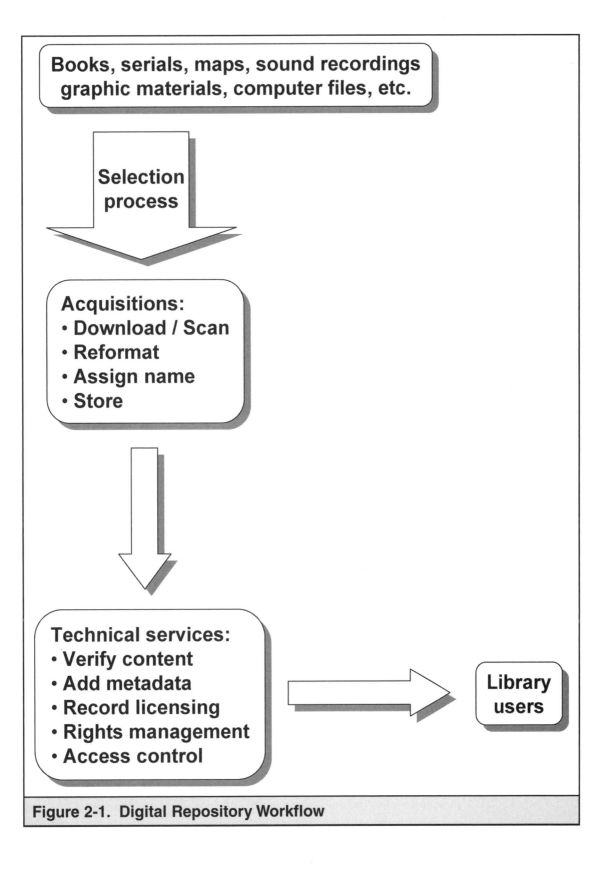

Figure 2-1. Digital Repository Workflow

for most digital repositories. Note that the major functions in digital repositories are for the most part analogous to those in traditional libraries.

DEVELOPING THE COLLECTION

Once the purpose of a repository has been established, the first question digital repository planners must ask is that how content will be selected and acquired. The selection process is critical, but it is frequently neglected because many planners fail to appreciate how different the process for selecting digital content can be from the familiar process for selecting physical content.

For paper resources, selection and acquisitions are heavily influenced by a publishing model that has been slowly evolving for over 500 years. Publishing and distributing paper resources is a complex and expensive process. Because publishers and distributors lose money if no one is interested in a book or journal, mechanisms are built into the publication process to ensure that an item in question is valuable to enough customers to be marketable. By its nature, the publication process imposes a minimal level of quality and directly contributes to the traditional association of good libraries with large collections. It also has led to a variety of mechanisms such as catalogs, approval plans, and other ways to help librarians learn about and obtain materials that might be of interest to users.

The Internet has lowered the barriers to distributing works to the point that anyone can completely bypass the publication process and distribute virtually anything to a worldwide audience at negligible cost. Aside from dramatically increasing the number of authors, materials need not be edited, marketed, or be of any interest to any particular audience. Distribution has become so decentralized that it is not reasonable to believe that librarians can rely heavily upon marketing literature, catalogs, approval plans, or other mechanisms used with print resources to identify materials for the collection. Consequently, they must find other means of learning about and acquiring digital resources.

Adding materials to the collection simply because they are available, requiring content providers to submit resources, or expecting librarians to discover resources through serendipity are three common methods that usually prove unsatisfactory unless used in combination with other techniques. Acquiring resources because they are available electronically makes no more sense than acquiring resources simply because they are available in paper. Content providers cannot be expected to consistently provide information because many of them will either not be aware of the library's need to archive materials or simply will not care. It is not realistic to depend primarily on individuals encountering useful resources primarily by means of serendipity. For these reasons, the workflow itself needs to include a reliable means for systematically identifying high-value resources that users expect while avoiding low-value materials that clutter search results.

Just as it is common in physical libraries to use different selection methods for different types of resources, it is appropriate to use a combination of methods to identify materials for a digital collection. Selection requires understanding what resources are available and what practical challenges they present given the goals of the repository and the technology it is based on.

For a selection process to be successful, the following questions must be addressed.

- **What resources are desired and where are they?** The success of a repository depends on effectively identifying resources that can be used to build a coherent collection. For this reason, the single most critical aspect of the selection process is to define as clearly as possible what should be included and where it can be found. The selection process must address a number of questions: How can a selector identify a desirable resource? Who is the target audience? Are the resources a physical collection waiting to be digitized? Are they oriented towards a particular topic or purpose? Are they in a content management system (CMS) or database? Who currently creates and maintains them? Are they part of a collection now, and, if not, are they scattered across multiple Web sites? If they are stored in multiple systems, how can the selector know where to find them? What formats are they in?

  The answers to these questions will vary greatly from one digital repository to the next, so there is no "best" way to identify resources. If the purpose of the repository is to provide specialized information on a given topic, the first task is to identify where the desired information is and who maintains it. If it turns out that the resources in question are created or maintained by a small number of content providers, it may prove feasible to ask content providers to manually or automatically help identify useful resources. On the other hand, if the resources are created or maintained by a large number of individuals with diverse interests, it is unrealistic to expect consistent assistance with identifying relevant items, so alternative methods need to be explored.

- **How will different versions of documents be handled?** Depending on what type of resources a repository will include, version control can be a serious issue. Although many resources do not change after they have been created, digital resources are inherently different from their physical counterparts in that they can be easily modified. If the collection development policy includes resources that might change, which version(s) will be kept? The decision to retain or not retain different versions of resources has implications for workflow, staffing, systems resources, and access.

If every version of a resource is retained, procedures need to be developed so that repository staff knows when a new version is available. Time will be needed to process the document, and systems resources will need to be allocated accordingly. Even if changed resources can be easily identified, and staff and systems resources are plentiful, how will users search for and use these materials? If seven versions of a resource are available, how does the user know which one to choose?

Retaining only a single version of a resource has its own problems. If only the most recent version is retained, staffing needs will be roughly equivalent to those needed for retaining every issue because a single resource may need to be replaced many times. Similarly, a mechanism for informing staff of updates will be needed. Although confusion with duplication in the repository is reduced when only one version is kept, problems could emerge when a version that a user cited as an authoritative source is replaced. A similar problem will occur if the library only retains the first version that it encounters, but a user cites a later version.

- **Who should participate in the selection process?** Will specialists locate and identify works to include, and if so, how will they accomplish this? Will an automated or semi-automated process identify resources of interest? Will content providers be expected to submit resources via a Web page? The process of determining which resources are desired, where they are, and what tools exist to detect them should help identify who should be involved in the selection process.

Just as it is extremely useful in the physical world to have people with subject expertise help select materials in those topics, it is also very useful to have people who can be considered experts help select digital resources. The Web is only a delivery mechanism, so it makes no more sense to have systems personnel or low-level staff choose electronic resources than it does to have them select paper journals and books in subjects they lack expertise on.

- **What tools exist to help automatically detect resources?** Can Web spiders, data extractions from a CMS or other system, scripts, or other tools be used to identify desirable materials? Even the serials module for a library's integrated library system (ILS) could prove useful for tasks such as alerting staff to new issues of publications on the Web since it is already designed to help staff know when new issues of paper journals are expected.

Identifying digital resources is often complex, so multiple methods should be employed simultaneously. Automated tools can be very useful for identifying desirable resources, but, in most cases, the identification process will still involve a significant amount of manual labor. For example, if a spider or data extraction is used, how will the desired resources be separated out from the vast bulk of resources that are not desirable?

ACQUIRING DIGITAL CONTENT

Once a selection process exists, it is necessary to determine how materials will be acquired. Intuitively, one would expect that the basic options would be to have content providers submit materials, have staff or an automated process collect materials, use software to "slurp" desired content, or load large numbers of resources into a system using a batch process.

However, acquiring resources for a digital repository is an inherently complex endeavor because it is often unclear what needs to be archived in the first place. Electronic resources frequently lack obvious boundaries. Web resources typically include a variety of images, links to other pages or documents, and other objects. Some of these linked objects are an integral part of the resource while others are not. Some of the linked objects themselves contain links or relationships that are also important. Many electronic resources are generated dynamically every time they are viewed, so archiving them in a repository that does not use the same software to display information is inherently problematic. Except for document-like objects—resources that can easily be printed and bound because they are discrete items with a linear structure like physical materials—acquiring electronic resources is a problematic task that requires substantial compromises.

Although there are many potential methods for addressing the challenges presented by complex resources, most fall into one of four general approaches: (1) not including troublesome resources in the repository;

(2) reformatting materials so that they are easier to process and preserve; (3) presuming that future technological advances will solve the problem; or (4) contracting the responsibility for preserving the resource to an outside party.

All approaches have substantial advantages and disadvantages. Limiting the types of resources that can be added to the repository greatly simplifies workflow, storage, access, and long-term preservation. However, by effectively defining the problem away, valuable items might be excluded simply because of their format. On the other hand, it is common practice for libraries to require certain physical characteristics as a condition of materials being added to the collection. Most libraries do not accept materials that are falling apart or have some other problem that means they can only be preserved at a very high cost (if at all). Nor are most libraries willing to accept unreadable and obsolete tape, cylinder, punch card, or disk media. It is common for libraries to accept only materials that can be made available over the long term, and there is no compelling reason to abandon this long-standing practice simply because a resource is accessed by computer.

Reformatting materials has most of the advantages of limiting the types of resources that can be added to a repository. Reformatting inevitably results in loss of information and functionality, and converting some resources can be difficult. Nonetheless, as Chapter 1 explains, migrating resources to an archival format as they are incorporated into the collection is usually the most practical approach. By supporting only a small number of formats chosen for their archival qualities, libraries can significantly reduce the likelihood of information loss while drastically simplifying future migrations.

Ignoring the problem by assuming that technological advances will later resolve the problem is possibly the riskiest strategy of all. Historically, this approach has been very unsuccessful, so it is highly recommended that repository planners address access, processing, or preservation issues as early as possible. Few libraries manage to upgrade brief bibliographic records that are more than a few years old. It therefore seems highly unlikely that they will suddenly acquire the considerable additional staff and money needed to identify all the materials in the collection in problematic formats and take whatever action is necessary to make them usable—especially since this is far more complex and time consuming than upgrading substandard records. Although it is conceivable that future library workers will find software that addresses the challenges of presenting resources in a wide variety of formats, most libraries already struggle to meet current demands. For this reason, hoping that some unspecified future development will solve problems is not a realistic preservation and access strategy.

The option of contracting the responsibility for preserving some resources to outside parties may appear to contradict the very idea of a digital repository. However, just as the principle of access has been displacing that of ownership for purposes of evaluating library collections, there is nothing inherently wrong with digital repositories relying on third parties to provide access to certain resources. In many ways, purchasing database access is effectively outsourcing a portion of the collection. Besides, it is now common for libraries to outsource operations that were considered core library operations a few decades ago. It is also common for libraries to use vendors and approval plans to select new materials. OCLC and contract cataloging have replaced large, slow, and expensive cataloging departments with smaller, faster ones. Collaborative virtual reference services such as L-Net allow patrons of a library to have their questions answered any time of the day or night, even when the local library is closed. It is common for interlibrary loan processes and data to be hosted by service providers such as ILLiad.

Contracting the responsibility for providing perpetual access to materials can be appropriate in certain cases, particularly for interactive resources that are data or software driven. As Chapter 1 describes, two basic strategies can be used to ensure that resources will be available when technology changes: emulation and migration. For a variety of reasons, it is not feasible to emulate complex software environments. On the other hand, there is no way to archive or migrate interactive resources based on databases or services distributed across multiple machines.

Relying on third parties does not necessarily require the library to even pay to have access to important resources maintained. In its simplest form, the library need only create a formal agreement with the agency that currently maintains the data, stating in effect that the data are important and must be maintained indefinitely. In certain cases, relying on organizations with an inherent interest in the resource to be responsible for preserving that access is appropriate as well as cost effective. Just as it is perfectly reasonable to trust that the Patent Office will provide perpetual access to patents and that the appropriate departments will maintain court proceedings, organizations vested in providing certain information services are in a better position than the library to provide perpetual access to that service.

For resources that will be stored physically in the repository, some degree of reformatting is necessary. For example, a Web page consists of many components (text, images, javascript, stylesheets, links, etc.) that are stored in different physical files and that may be on different machines. When a page is copied, the dependent files must also be stored, and the links in the original page must be changed to reflect the new location of the component. This process may sound straightforward, but it can be difficult to implement in practice. Although major archiving software such as CONTENTdm and DSpace provide the ability to ingest Web documents, some materials do not archive well.

Consider the rather common scenario in which the main document is a table of contents with links to component subdivisions. These subdivisions also contain dependencies (images, stylesheets, etc.) as well links to supporting documents that may or may not be in HTML. Especially if the document is within a page containing global navigation links, instructing the software to make copies of everything down to a depth of three links could result in the retrieval of many hundreds of files. Some of these may be in proprietary formats that will be unreadable in a few years. Other pages may "talk" to live services that cannot be archived or even intentionally designed so they cannot be copied easily. Likewise, if the original site uses Flash or other proprietary technologies to create navigational elements or other critical aspects, some features in the stored version of the resource may not work as desired.

Just as libraries have established procedures to preserve paper resources that they acquire, digital materials also need to undergo preservation so they can still be used by future generations after the technologies used to create the original resources become obsolete. Format standardization, as illustrated in Figure 1-6, is an important part of the workflow and can be quite difficult depending on what types of resources the repository contains. For example, if a Web page that contains links to a Microsoft Word document, an Excel spreadsheet, and a Visio diagram are all considered part of one resource, all of these materials must be reformatted. The Word document may contain live links to certain areas of the spreadsheet, and modification of the Word document might be necessary to prevent the reference from becoming completely useless after the conversion process (presuming that the link structure was not incompatible with the copying process to begin with). All references in the Web page to the documents in their native formats also need to be changed.

Acquisitions is a much simpler process if the desired resource in question is a single document. However, even if all that is needed is an individual document stored in a single file, the first task is to determine how it will be transferred to the repository and stored in a normalized format. Especially for resources consisting of many files, written detailed procedures will be needed so that staff know how to normalize and ingest materials into the collection. This normalization and ingestion process may be automated, but some materials may need to be downloaded, reformatted, or have other procedures performed on them manually.

It is important to be aware that if the repository does not assign names or identifiers to resources as they are ingested, staff will need to perform this function later. Although the name of a resource in a system can be considered arbitrary, it is generally advisable to establish predictable conventions to prevent staff from employing widely divergent schemes that may lead to future confusion. Examples of naming conventions might include a simple accession number, a numeric date stamp modified to make it unique, or a string based on the responsible agency, subject, or other significant attribute. Observing consistent practices within the repository will simplify maintenance, so staff need to know where to store files, as well as what to name them.

PROCESSING AND ORGANIZING DIGITAL CONTENT

After digital content has been acquired and normalized, searchable representations of items (i.e., metadata or catalog records) need to be created so they can be searched by author, title, and other access points. The first step to developing a workflow for processing resources and adding appropriate access points is to consider what types of materials will be added, how they will be searched, and what the expected size of the repository will be. If the repository consists of portable document format (PDF) documents or simple image files that are uploaded to a server, the processing required will be substantially different from processing Web pages or an eclectic collection of multimedia resources. Likewise, completeness and consistency of metadata are far more important for repositories that contain millions of items than for collections containing only a few thousand resources.

A repository's usefulness is heavily dependent on how it is organized, that is, how well it associates similar items and allows users to find what they need. There are many ways to organize electronic resources, but one of the time-tested ways to provide access is by creating metadata that is either embedded in the resource or stored in a separate record. Major repository software, such as DSpace and CONTENTdm, use metadata. In fact, the traditional library catalog card is just metadata written on paper.

The quality and completeness of metadata are critical to its usefulness. Although it is administratively convenient to store information in its original form and rely on automated means to provide all access, this approach rarely leads to adequate long-term access. Resources—especially those consisting of images, video, or sound—lend themselves poorly to keyword searching. File formats become obsolete or require users to install software (which may be expensive or difficult to find, if it is available at all). Even if resources already contain metadata, one cannot assume that it is useful. For example, when the State of Oregon was developing the system to archive electronic documents (see Chapter 1), it hoped to use metadata from the state CMS to provide access. Even though staff were required to receive training and supply metadata for every document as a condition of adding documents to the CMS, the metadata supplied varied so in quality and completeness that it was virtually useless.

The general problem with patron- or author-submitted metadata is that the patron/author is usually not concerned with how his or her work fits in the collection as a whole or how it will be used by the repository's many users. Rather, metadata terms supplied by individuals who do not manage the collection will very likely reflect the interests of the individual rather than those of the digital repository and its broad user community. In the Oregon example, some content providers listed literally hundreds of metadata terms that had little bearing on the resource—clearly they wanted the resource to be found as often as possible. Others provided only a term or two that were too vague to be useful. Many simply re-entered terms from the title. Some content providers did suggest excellent metadata terms, but they were a small minority. In short, the metadata were inconsistent. Web search-engine companies such as Google have known this for a long time and ignore user-supplied metadata for that reason.

Providing full-blown cataloging of electronic resources is often impractical, but it is important to develop procedures that produce metadata consistent enough in terms of quality and completeness to reliably identify resources. Methods used by major search engines usually prove ineffective for digital repositories because the algorithms these search engines depend on only work effectively with very large numbers of resources. Search engines base results on factors such as the number of linked resources, clickthrough activity, document formatting, and a number of statistical criteria. These methods are highly effective when used on huge numbers of heavily used documents. However, when these same methods are used on relatively small collections containing predominantly low-use resources, they provide much less satisfactory results.

It is important to develop workflows that staff find intuitive. Consider how most libraries process paper resources—staff know what to do with a particular book or journal by which cart it is on, where the cart is located, and whatever notes are attached. Although electronic resources can be placed in folders and notes can be applied to them, it is easier for them to get lost or placed somewhere in a system or on a hard drive where they are ignored because they lack a physical embodiment—this is particularly true of "problem materials." To ensure that staff understand and follow procedures, it is normally best to have the people who will actually perform the work help develop the procedures.

Besides describing and organizing digital resources, the processing workflow must also address how materials will be preserved. Preserving digital content typically requires storing resources in one of a small number of standard formats. Although it is also desirable to store documents in their native formats, it is generally advisable to store them in an archival format to ensure that as much information and functionality are retained as possible over time.

Although one would expect repositories to provide access to items in their archival format, often this is not a practical option. For example, if an old book is scanned and stored in tagged image file format (TIF), the archival copy could easily consume hundreds of megabytes. This is too large to be usable even with high-speed connections. It is much more practical to convert the TIF file to searchable text and let users view either the text representation or highly compressed joint photographic experts group (JPEG) images. For this reason, it may be necessary to store resources in a presentation format that lacks the fidelity of the archival format, but which is more practical for most users. Since it is generally desirable for the archival and presentation copy to be one and the same, the conversion to a preservation format is only done when it is impractical to provide the archival format. Figure 2-2 extends the model described by Figure 1-6 to illustrate this process.

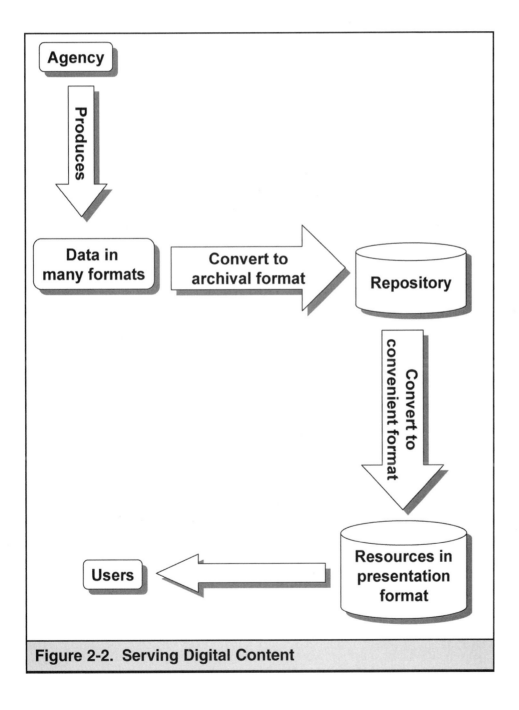

Figure 2-2. Serving Digital Content

ORGANIZING RELATED WORKS AND SUBCOLLECTIONS

Metadata/cataloging can be used to organize works into virtual subcollections, but one should be aware that it is sometimes desirable to use other methods to impose a structure on a resource that was not present in the original source materials. For example, many organizations issue newsletters, bulletins, regular reports, and other materials in a pattern that follows a serial publication pattern. The Web sites frequently include a link to the current issue, and links to older issues may or may not be provided. If these issues are simply treated as electronic documents, the effect would be similar to creating a new bibliographic record in a traditional catalog for every issue. Aside from filling the catalog with enormous amounts of duplicate data, navigating and locating specific issues would become very awkward since it would not take long for a frequently produced publication to be represented by hundreds of entries in the repository. A rather obvious solution is to create an index page listing the issues in reverse chronological order, even if the original publisher provides no similar navigational tool.

Although electronic serials could be made navigable with the appropriate metadata, such a solution requires the system to properly interpret and sort a wide variety of enumeration schemes. These various enumeration patterns would invariably need to be entered as plain text because there are too many different patterns for a system to list them all. Also, the serial title would need to be entered exactly the same way in each record. Otherwise, even minor discrepancies would cause different issues to appear under different titles—which would make it effectively impossible to browse issues.

Likewise, digital resources are even more likely than physical resources to be multipart monographs—works that consist of many individual components. With paper materials, the indexes, appendices, and other supplementary materials are usually bound with the main work. However, large digital documents frequently store each chapter or major division in a separate file, and appendices as well as other supplementary material are often stored as separate files, particularly when the supplementary material is in a different format from that of the main document. Although it is possible to express the relationships between the various components with metadata, it is very difficult to do this in a way that will allow the work to be used as an integrated whole. As is the case with serials, the slightest typographical error can separate the components from each other. Again, to make the resource usable, a simple index page listing the components in an appropriate order might be far more helpful than complex metadata.

Despite the challenges it presents, good quality metadata is usually the core of any good organizational scheme. Metadata can store information about format, purpose, associated people and organizations, time, place, relationships with other resources or collections, and any other appropriate information. It is important to be aware that the system has to be able to interpret the metadata for it to be useful—there is little, if any, value in storing information that systems do not use. With few exceptions, storing metadata that current systems cannot use is unproductive.

For example, over the years, catalogers have spent enormous amounts of time meticulously encoding cryptic fixed fields that store information about various types of illustrations and tape formats, as well as whether the item contains conference proceedings, is a Festschrift (a memorial, or tribute, publication), or contains bibliographical references. No widely used ILS uses any of these fields or a number of others not mentioned. Most of these fields are ignored outright, and there is little or no patron demand to see or search them. Consequently, it is unlikely that this information will ever be usable. It is not difficult to imagine scenarios in which some obscure bit of information would be useful. However, the fact that someone might conceivably find a use for the information does not justify storing it. Creating metadata is an expensive, time-consuming process, and storing information "just in case" someone may need it at a later date takes resources that would probably be better spent providing information and services that people already need.

As metadata becomes more detailed and complete, the possibilities for searching and organizing a collection increase. However, creating elaborate metadata is expensive and time consuming, as well as prone to errors and omissions. Metadata must be applied consistently to be useful, or systems will either ignore it or normalize it to a simpler form. For example, in addition to the cryptic fixed-length fields described above, the MARC standard for bibliographic records defines dozens of variable-length note fields. Despite the fact that notes in the catalog record are stored as free text, different MARC fields are used for notes depending on whether they concern bibliographical resources, summaries, translations, reproductions, access restrictions, file type, dissertations, or a number of other things notes may be written about. Each MARC field is associated with a separate numeric tag and may contain a myriad of subfields. Guidelines for inputting notes exist, but the notes themselves vary considerably in terms of structure and completeness. This should not be surprising given that cataloging rules change over time, practices vary from one library to the next, and notes consist of free text. To compensate for the variability of how notes are input, the vast majority of systems treat almost all note fields identically. In other words, catalogers at many institutions spend countless hours encoding information that will never be used. The notes may be useful, but the specific fields, indicators, and tags are not. The lesson to be learned is that repositories should only require metadata that can be entered consistently.

Consistent metadata structures are essential, but it is also important to ensure that the contents of various metadata fields are normalized as much as possible. This means that when subjects, names, organizations, places, or other entities are associated with a resource, staff should be selecting from an authorized list of preferred terms rather than typing in free-text entries. To help users, metadata must categorize resources, and categorizing requires entering these resources consistently. If the documents created by an author named James Smith appear in the repository under "Jim Smith;" "Smith, James;" "J. T. Smith;" "Smith, James T.;" "Smith, J."; and a number of other variations, finding documents that he authored and distinguishing him from other authors with similar names will be difficult. Likewise, if subjects are not entered consistently, documents about the same topic will be assigned different subject headings—this makes it significantly harder to find materials about a resource or topic. Authority control can seem slow and expensive, but it is worth the trouble. Without it, a database may be filled with inconsistent and unreliable entries.

When determining how to use metadata to organize resources, repository planners should take reasonable steps to ensure that the metadata is compatible with that used in other collections that users will likely want to search. There are so many sources of information that it is unreasonable to expect people to search each one individually; the repository should be designed so that it can be included in federated searches.

The best way to give users the capability of searching the repository and other collections simultaneously is to employ a robust metadata scheme that is applicable to as many different types of resources as possible. Simple but versatile metadata schemes, such as Dublin Core, are most likely to prove robust enough to meet the evolving needs of the repository and its users. Alternatively, the repository should use metadata that can be accurately translated into Dublin Core or other widely used formats. Key metadata schemes are covered in Chapter 4 in detail. In particularly, complex and nonstandard metadata should be avoided, generating them is expensive and they can create compatibility problems when used with other systems or when the time comes to migrate to another platform.

RIGHTS MANAGEMENT

Rights management must be built directly into the standard workflow unless the same access will be granted for all resources. Librarians are accustomed to embargo periods for journals, but they often must be negotiated for other resources as well—even those produced by the same institution. For example, when the Oregon Documents Repository (ODR) first started, one of the early issues that had to be resolved was how to process documents that were produced using money generated from their sale. The legislature had passed a law requiring agencies to make documents available to the State Library so that they could be archived in the ODR, but if the library provided free access to materials that had to be sold in order to create the next edition, the repository could have the effect of eliminating publication of valuable resources. In the end, it was decided that the repository would provide access to these resources only after sufficient time had passed for the current edition to recover its costs, but the workflow for these documents had to be adjusted so that they did not simply appear right away, as the other materials did.

Workflow modifications might also be necessary to limit access to authorized users, and it certainly needs to include steps to record licensing information as well as any processing necessary to make the restrictions effective. Depending on the repository architecture, these workflow modifications may be as simple as setting attributes in the system and entering a few notes. On other systems, files may need to be placed in different areas and special procedures might be necessary.

BATCH PROCESSES

Considerable staff resources can be saved when processes can be automated. However, automation works best for repetitive tasks. There is so much variability in how digital resources are obtained and processed that many tasks in a digital repository do not lend themselves well to automation.

Nevertheless, a number of tasks can benefit from at least partial automation. Automation can easily be used to identify new files, but it is important to be aware that hundreds (if not thousands) of documents might be created or modified on a single system on a given day. For example, if a significant number of resources that will be included in the repository are located in a small number of systems, the administrators of those systems may be willing to send daily or weekly alerts containing lists of new and recently changed files. Any systems administrator should be able to generate such lists easily using standard utilities included with the operating system.

Even when system reports are not an option, programming Web spiders to look for new materials is an option unless prohibited by policy or technical barriers. Web spiders can be configured to follow all links on particular sites or within certain domains. They can be programmed to follow a certain number of links, and they can be given criteria for including or excluding files according to name, format, or location. If spiders are used to identify documents, they should be configured to determine the properties of existing files only and not actually retrieve them. Spider activity can look like a denial-of-service attack to systems personnel, so it is good practice to notify administrators of sites that will be crawled systematically and to harvest data at night or other times when system load is low.

Spiders can only find documents that have been linked to. Many important documents will not be linked to from a public Web page because people are expected either to access them directly or with the aid of a special search engine. Depending on the software used, it may be necessary to load spider reports into a database to identify new and changed documents. This task should not be difficult for most systems personnel.

The Oregon Documents Repository (ODR) uses a system report provided by the CMS and a primitive spider to identify new documents. Every day, the CMS posts a list of new and changed documents. A script at the ODR retrieves each file in the list and then stores essential information about each item (e.g., title, the agency that produced it, and location) in a database. The database contains rules that automatically discard or assign particular statuses to incoming documents based on their file properties. For example, meeting minutes and agendas, job announcements, news releases, forms, and calendar items are systematically discarded. When staff process an item, the system remembers what decision was made for that file. Consequently, if that file is modified, it will automatically be assigned the correct status.

Figure 2-3 shows the screen that ODR staff see. Note that despite the fact that filters prevent most documents from ever being seen, 406 potential documents of interest were located in a single day. Even with the ability to automatically identify and process documents, staff must work hard to keep up with the flow of new documents. Without this automated tool, staff would

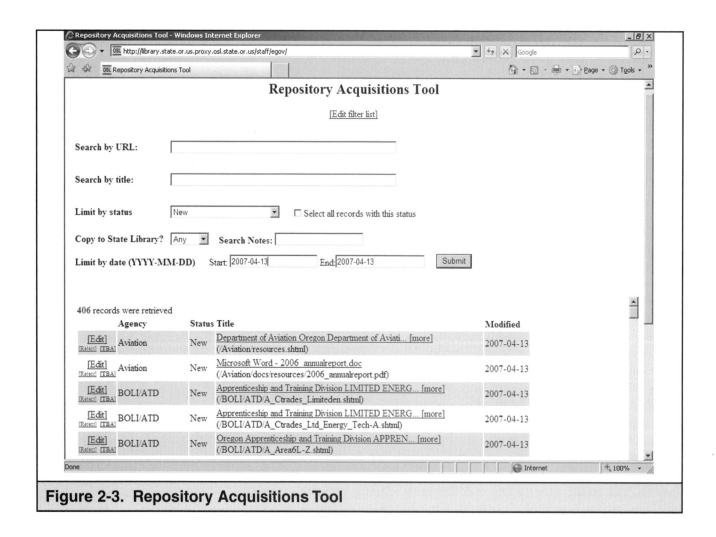

Figure 2-3. Repository Acquisitions Tool

only be aware of a miniscule percentage of the documents they need to include in the repository.

Resource identification is one of the most difficult tasks to automate. Because it is highly unlikely that everything of interest to a library would be located on the same system, multiple systems need to be monitored. Even if only a small number of systems need to be monitored and accurate information can readily be obtained, many of the new items detected might be components of other documents rather than independent documents. For example, it is common for reports to include individual chapters as well as supplementary materials (appendices, tables, maps, spreadsheets, etc.) stored as separate files. When these files are detected, they often appear to be independent documents as there is no reference to the parent document in their content, nor will any relationship be obvious from the file name or location. In fact, the only way to know about their relationship would be to have seen the parent document that links to them.

Nonetheless, automated system monitoring can be effective. Rather than simply looking for any new document, programs can look for materials containing text that indicates that they are especially likely to be relevant. For example, a resource might contain words such as "table of contents," "author," "abstract," "handbook," "technical report," or a number of other terms indicating that it is a target document. Likewise, words indicating periodicity such as "annual report" or "quarterly report" indicate a serial publication that may be of interest. Experience teaches that certain directory paths are likely to include items that are consistently of interest or that should systematically be ignored. Similarly, programs can be told to ignore resources that contain terms such as "meeting minutes," "press release," or other terminology indicating that the file does not fit within the scope of the repository. In short, automation can be very useful as an aid in identifying files, but additional manual identification is almost always necessary.

Reformatting and renaming documents lends itself particularly well to batch processing. Since reformatting normally requires the same process to be performed on all files of a certain type, there is no reason to do it one resource at a time. It is important to be aware that the reformatting process for materials consisting of multiple resources in different formats is inherently more complex because different conversion processes must be run and the links between the various components of the resource also need to be changed so they point to the reformatted documents.

Some reformatting processes are inherently problematic. For example, if an HTML document is saved, staff must ensure that core information and functionality are retained by the conversion process before storing it—even if the document will be stored in HTML. Unlike other formats, HTML cannot simply be copied and be expected to work. An HTML document rarely consists of a single file. Normally, HTML resources are composed of files stored in multiple locations or even on multiple servers. In addition, HTML documents often contain dynamic content. It makes little sense to store documents that cannot be used without the assistance of files stored on other servers. Nor is it feasible to presume that file structures required by the HTML documents can be duplicated in the repository. As a result, the files that an HTML document relies on must be downloaded and stored, and the links between the files need to be modified to reflect their new locations in the repository. Likewise, documents that were created using special features of particular software programs may be difficult to convert in a manner that preserves essential functionality. For example, if a spreadsheet references cells in other documents or contains formulas, these need to be converted to static values unless users will be expected to view the information using particular versions of the spread sheet software. If the data are converted to static values, staff must ensure that document can still fulfill its original purpose.

Adding of metadata is another task that can benefit from partial automation. For personal and corporate names, subject headings, keywords, dates, and other fields to be useful, they must be consistent. Resources on the same subject should have the same subject headings. Similar documents should have similar keywords. Dates should be automatically recorded or formatted consistently with the aid of simple programs if manual input is required. If someone creates multiple resources, his or her name should be entered exactly the same way each time. Otherwise, search results will be unpredictable.

If the contents of metadata fields are automatically compared with authority files, staff can identify and rectify inconsistencies much faster than they can if they simply have to guess or manually look up the appropriate forms of entries. Assignment of subject headings and keywords can also be partially automated by having programs recommend terms based on statistical analysis similar documents.

ERGONOMICS

Acquiring, processing, and managing documents requires considerable human judgment and manual labor, so time, money, and staff effectiveness can be maximized if tools are optimized to accommodate workflows. For example, in the ODR case discussed earlier, a single staff member may be required to evaluate hundreds of documents for inclusion in the repository in a single day. As described in the previous section, an automated process identifies most potentially useful documents for a database while discarding most undesirable resources. The same process assumes that if a resource is updated, the new version should be processed the same way so that staff do not need to keep making the same decisions about the same resources.

However, many new documents arrive every day. When the staff member decides that a resource will be added, she often wants to know what was done with similar types of resources in the past. Besides providing a list of documents likely to be of interest, the ODR search interface allows staff to search by any field, and it updates results with every keystroke so staff can very quickly see what materials can be found with a particular status, with certain text in notes, the title, URL, or materials that were created within a certain date range. Search results containing thousands of items can be generated in a fraction of a second and can be quickly sorted and reviewed to reduce the amount of time spent on the search process itself. Certain statuses can be assigned directly from the search-results page so it is unnecessary to click into full-record view or even go into an edit mode to perform some of the most common tasks. By designing the interface to minimize the number of operations, keystrokes, and mouse clicks necessary to perform a task, substantial amounts of time are saved to free staff to perform other work.

In contrast, Figure 2-4 shows a page that acquisitions staff at Oregon State University use to add a resource to a CONTENTdm installation.

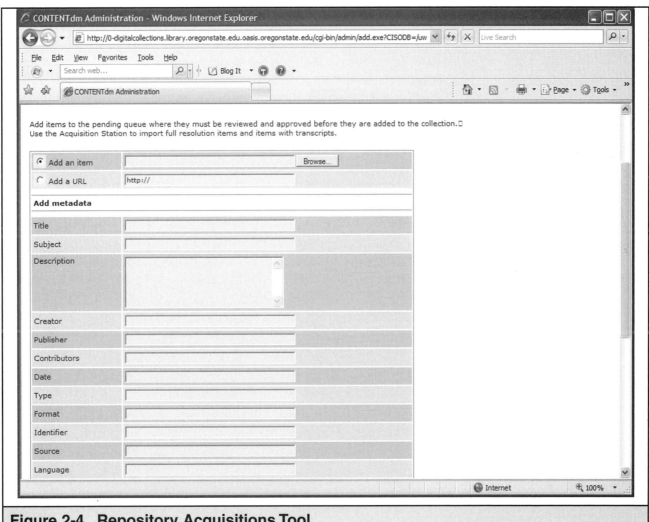

Figure 2-4. Repository Acquisitions Tool

Staff must already know what will be added from some outside source. No information is automatically provided. Many forms must be filled out. Because CONTENTdm has its own database and does not automatically share information with other systems, such as the online catalog, the information must be added manually to other systems if that is desired.

SUMMARY

The workflow for acquiring and processing digital resources is often more complicated and laborious than that for processing paper materials. Granted, there is no need to open boxes or apply property stamps, tattle tape, or labels. Nor is there any need to shelve the items. However, production and distribution of electronic resources is so decentralized that it is difficult to know which ones should be acquired. Once they are identified, they may consist of multiple interdependent files that require reformatting. Moreover, navigating a digital resource is inherently more more difficult than browsing a physical volume that has an obvious structure and extent.

Identifying, obtaining, reformatting, cataloging (i.e., creating metadata), and properly protecting digital resources can be very time consuming. However, the value of a repository is more in how it organizes, presents, and preserves resources than in how many resources it contains. Therefore, to reach its full potential, a repository must have both well-conceived workflows that support its goals and tools optimized to facilitate those workflows.

3 CHOOSING A REPOSITORY ARCHITECTURE

Because it is an integral part of all interactions with the repository and the resources it contains, the platform is inseparable from the repository. By determining how information is added, processed, stored, searched, and used, the platform has an enormous impact on the user experience as well as on all staff functions relating to the repository. Because physical distance is not an issue in the management, organization, or use of electronic resources, repository planners can decide between a number of divergent conceptual and technical approaches. Choosing the right architecture requires understanding the opportunities and challenges different approaches present.

QUESTIONS TO ASK BEFORE CHOOSING AN ARCHITECTURE

The best architecture for a repository depends on the purpose of the repository and its anticipated use. For this reason, it is worthwhile to construct a list of required and desirable functions before making any technical decisions. As of this writing, digital repository software is still maturing, so the architecture that best meets an individual repository's needs may be lacking some desirable features.

The following lists outline a number of general required features and desirable features that a library should consider. Digital resources are fragile and no system lasts forever, so the most important functions allow for proper maintenance of all repository materials and the ability to migrate resources and metadata to a different platform in the future. Once those requirements are met, the information in the repository is safe. However, depending on the needs of an individual project, many items listed here as desirable may actually be required to meet repository goals.

When a library is at the stage of actively evaluating different platforms, requirements need to be enumerated in far more detail than is presented here. For example, the specific formats repository planners wish to support must be spelled out, search capabilities need to outline the specific types of searches that can be used, browse capabilities need to be defined, and metadata requirements will need to specify which fields are supported from the outset.

REQUIRED FEATURES

General

- Accepts content in many formats.
- Ingestion/addition mechanism is not limited to existing formats.
- Scalable. Performs well, even under constant growth and heavy usage.
- Secure.
- Ensures appropriate privacy.
- Monitors system and resource health.
- Provides reports about metadata, resource, and system activity.

Interface

- Accessible to staff and patrons with disabilities.
- Browse and keyword search are appropriate to materials.
- Displays content on the Web.
- Must be able to search materials within the repository, as well as other desired collections, simultaneously.
- Reference tools allow creating lists and performing other functions that help users find resources.
- Cataloging tools allow the creation of standard metadata.

Metadata

- Descriptive—identifies items.
- Technical—details requirements for using a resource.
- Administrative—describes usage restrictions, rights, original source, etc.
- Structural—defines relationships with other resources.
- Must be able to add new metadata fields or schema to accommodate future needs.

- Automatically records and stores time and date of creation and modification of resources.
- Automatically assigns unique identifiers that are independent of location and protocol.

Maintenance and data preservation

- Content preservation is not dependent on hardware or software.
- Exports resources.
- Exports descriptive, administrative, structural, and technical metadata.
- Ensures data integrity.
- Has robust backup and restore capability.

DESIRABLE FEATURES

General

- Modular: It supports open interfaces that can interact with local applications and external systems.
- Able to incorporate existing identifiers into system identifier.
- Patrons can easily verify integrity of the retrieved resource.
- Supports user-selected output methods (print, view on Web or PDA, etc.).

Data management

- Converts data to archival and presentation formats.
- Controls various versions.
- Handles different lifetimes for different materials.
- Detects duplicates.
- Maintains authority control.

Access control

- Precise control limits can be placed on staff and user functions.
- Controls automated deposit of resources and metadata.

- LDAP (Lightweight-Directory Access Protocol).
- Shibboleth (security program).
- Manages licenses.

Workflow

- Flexible: Procedures can be adjusted to support different needs.
- Sophisticated job control specified for tasks involving multiple individuals and groups of individuals.
- Manages rights.
- Supports embargos.
- Serial support (easy to add individual issues, browse an entire run, etc.).
- Automatically extracts metadata from resources that contain it (e.g., Word, PDF).
- Has a convenient mechanism for ingesting individual resources as well as collections of resources.

Share information with other systems

- SRU/SRW (Search and Retrieve via URL/via Web).
- OAI-PMH (Open Archives Initiative Protocol for Metadata Harvesting).
- Accepts harvested resources and metadata.
- Transforms metadata to different formats as required.

FRAMEWORKS FOR DIGITAL REPOSITORIES

The ubiquity of network computing has fundamentally altered the way users expect to interact with resources. Just a few decades ago, people's expectations could be satisfied reasonably effectively by services delivered according to the traditional library model. This service model presumes that the library is a centralized location to store and access content. When someone needs information, he or she goes to the library and searches the catalog or indexes to find what is available. The desired materials are found nearby on the shelves.

The Internet and cheap storage space have changed those expectations. Patrons want to copy digital information so they can manipulate it and use it for other purposes. They no longer view libraries as the place where all the information they need can be found. Patrons know that content is everywhere, so digital repositories must be part of an "information fabric" rather than silos that must be used alone (Walters, 2006). This means that patrons expect to search and use repository materials while simultaneously working with other resources—interoperability is one of the key attributes of a good digital repository.

Expectations have changed for content providers as well as for patrons. One of the major differences between traditional libraries and most digital repositories in the United States is that authors can choose whether their material is added to the repository. In many cases the material is not included unless the author chooses to do so (Lynch and Lippincott, 2005). This fundamentally changes the collection development process and puts the library in the position of needing to convince information providers of the value of submitting materials. It also means that the platform should be set up in such a way that contributing material is as convenient as possible.

In short, digital repositories are very different from their physical counterparts, so before selecting a platform, planners must define what basic and specific functionality is needed. That functionality is largely determined by the purpose of the repository, which needs to be defined as covered in Chapter 1. Once the purpose of the repository is understood and broad functional goals have been outlined, it is then possible to move on to understanding what basic technological components are available, what their relative strengths and weaknesses are, and how they can be used together to provide service.

Digital repositories are still so new that the tools and methods have not yet matured to the point that planners can simply implement solutions developed at other institutions. Few vendor and open-source solutions exist, and many of those that do require significant local expertise and customization. Technology cycles are short and, as of this writing, it is still too soon to be sure which systems, tools, and methods are best in the long run. It is therefore crucial that repository designers choose a platform and procedures that can evolve, or even be abandoned, as librarians learn to manage the digital realm and technological change. At this point in the process, the most important thing to keep in mind is that digital repositories require a high level of interoperability between independent technologies.

It is not necessary to develop a framework from scratch. A number of digital repository frameworks have already been developed, but describing each of these frameworks or providing a detailed analysis of the similarities and differences between different applications for managing digital content is beyond the scope of this book. Having said that, it is useful to have a basic familiarity with a few options that have attracted a significant user base.

The flexible extensible digital object and repository architecture (Fedora) open-source software project deserves special mention because it is probably the best known and most widely implemented at the time of this writing. Also, Fedora is a rich enough framework that basic knowledge of how it works can be useful for many applications related to digital repositories. Fedora is different from systems designed to manage all resources through a single user interface such as DSpace, Plone, CONTENTdm, Greenstone, and others in that it is implemented as a set of Web-based services rather than as an application (Lagoze et al., accessed: 2006). In other words, although Fedora is a content management system (CMS) that allows users to manage and distribute digital resources, it has a generalized architecture that makes it unnecessary to use particular applications or user interfaces. Figure 3-1 illustrates the basic Fedora model.

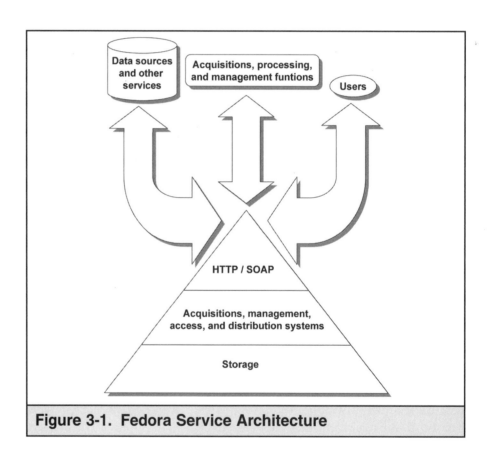

Figure 3-1. Fedora Service Architecture

The storage mechanism for the CMS is at the base of the Fedora model. The acquisitions, management, access, and distribution systems use the storage mechanism to perform their respective functions. Most digital library software consists of these two levels, where the staff and user interfaces are applications that communicate with a storage mechanism. With Fedora, an additional layer is present. Rather than communicating directly with the storage mechanism, the applications staff and patrons communicate with Fedora by sending simple object access protocol (SOAP) messages over hypertext transport protocol (HTTP). Fedora translates these SOAP messages to various staff and user functions that interact with the storage mechanism.

Fedora's structure has two major advantages: (1) the various components that make up the repository could theoretically be located anywhere because all functions are performed by passing XML over the Web; and (2) by adding an abstract layer that allows other systems and applications to communicate with it, Fedora can interoperate with any application that can interact with it using SOAP messages. That is, the staff and patron interfaces as well as collections within the repository could be located on a wide variety of hardware and software platforms. Fedora is open archives initiative (OAI) compliant, so it can act as a metarepository that provides access to content maintained by others. Fedora defines some broad service categories, but there is nothing to keep the repository from developing other services necessary to make resources usable. For example, a resource consisting of many high-resolution images might be associated with a service that converts the images into an easily browseable collection in which the images are delivered in a more Web-friendly compressed format (Fedora, accessed: 2006).

Because file systems and Web services can be used to store and deliver any kind of electronic information, virtually any repository software can be used for a given project (Dahl, Banerjee and Spalti, 2006). When selecting the ideal technology for a specific project, planners should keep in mind that different tools and methods meet different needs and require different levels of technical expertise. Despite its flexibility, Fedora is not an appropriate choice for all environments. As is often the case with open-source projects, substantial technical skills are required to implement and maintain Fedora. So if the needs of the repository are modest, a simpler mechanism would be more appropriate. For example, Fedora is not appropriate if a repository is expected to consist primarily of static pages. The same procedures used to manage a Web site might be perfectly adequate and would be far simpler to implement.

PLATFORMS OPTIMIZED FOR SPECIFIC PURPOSES

Different products are optimized for different purposes for the simple reason that they were initially created to attain different goals. For example, some libraries use DSpace to provide access to all types of resources, but the application was initially conceived as a way to disseminate research throughout user communities and it is still best suited to that task. According to this community-based model, it is assumed that resources can be understood, described, and organized best by experts who are not necessarily part of the library. The assumption is that the digital repository is essentially a collaborative endeavor, and authors are largely responsible for providing and organizing materials.

In contrast, CONTENTdm is based on a very centralized model with tools to support the type of content management and workflows often found in libraries. Rather than relying on authors to choose and organize what belongs in the collection, library staff fulfill these functions. However, like other centralized approaches, CONTENTdm implies a significant staff commitment to metadata management and other workflow issues, such as rights management. Different technical models are best suited for different types of collections. Centralized solutions imply collection development policies geared towards providing access to specific types of resources, while community-based models grow organically as the interests of the participants evolve.

The difference between these platforms extends beyond philosophical and staffing matters into very practical concerns. In contrast to DSpace, which began as a way for faculty to share research, CONTENTdm was designed to provide access to still images. As a result, CONTENTdm makes it relatively easy to browse images, and the features of the program facilitate image presentation. Libraries seeking to establish an image repository are likely to find that it meets their needs better than DSpace, the platform that is normally preferred for disseminating faculty research. In addition to determining what functionality is available, platform choice has an enormous impact on the staff as well as the user experience. Each platform provides different interfaces because it is based on a different assumption of who is responsible for doing what and how tasks are performed. Consider Figure 3-2 and Figure 3-3.

Both figures depict interfaces designed to add resources to a digital repository, but they do this in very different ways. The CONTENTdm page addition form shown in Figure 3-2 assumes that library staff will add resources to the repository. Instructions at the top of the page make it clear that the form is a part of a larger workflow that includes other processes. Staff are expected to know how to fill in the Dublin Core fields without additional instruction. For example, the *Creator* field does not specify that it should be used for the primary author with the surname given first, followed by a comma, followed by the first name and other names, initials, or titles, as prescribed by AACR.

DSpace's resource addition form in Figure 3-3 assumes that non-librarians submit materials for inclusion in the repository. Much less information is requested (for example, they are not expected to fill an *Identifier* or *Type* field), and it is not assumed that submitters are familiar with library procedures or terminology. While on the surface it might appear that DSpace is superior because it utilizes a simpler form that anyone can fill out, this is accomplished at a cost. Because it presumes much less

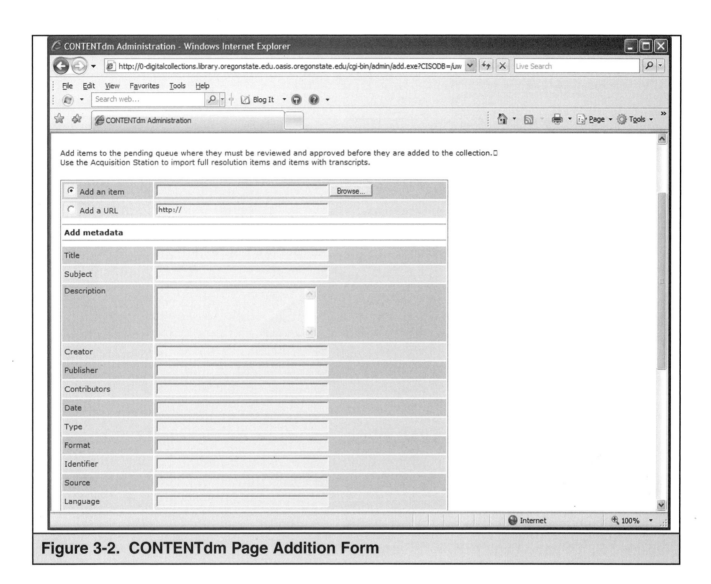

Figure 3-2. CONTENTdm Page Addition Form

structure, DSpace also provides less control over what information is included in the repository and how it is searched. CONTENTdm allows controlled vocabulary to be defined using the form shown in Figure 3-4. Repository managers can specify which fields employ authority control using forms such as Figure 3-5. Even when two platforms perform a similar task such as defining which fields display to users and how, functionality can still differ considerably depending on the platform. A quick glance at Figure 3-6 shows that CONTENTdm offers considerably more granular control over fields than DSpace. This is not to say that one is superior to the other. Rather, it reflects the philosophical differences

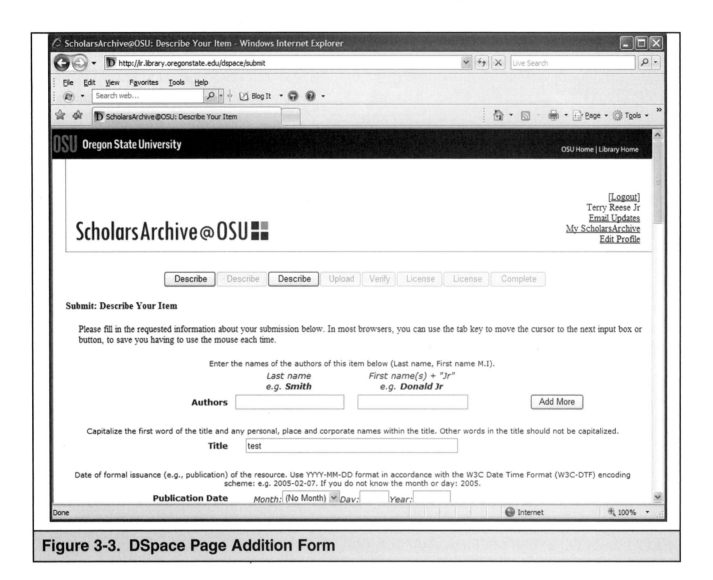

Figure 3-3. DSpace Page Addition Form

between them. The important lesson is to choose a platform that best reflects the goals and processes envisioned by repository designers.

Although DSpace and CONTENTdm are currently the most widely used repository platforms, there are other platforms optimized for special purposes that may better meet a library's needs. For example, bepress was specifically designed to disseminate scholarly information primarily in textual format, so it offers excellent full-text searching. Bepress must be licensed, but EPrints is an open-source alternative that also is optimized to work primarily with sharing research that is mostly textual in nature. However, these two platforms that do so well with text lack capabilities for processing and browsing

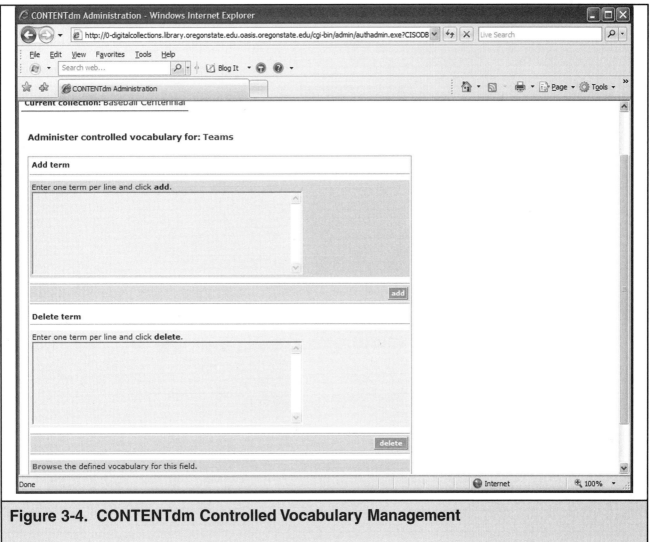

Figure 3-4. CONTENTdm Controlled Vocabulary Management

images and video, even if they do include support for media types other than text.

While almost any of the applications discussed here can be used for managing a digital repository, they are very different in terms of what types of materials they work best with; what workflows and organizational models they are compatible with; and the fiscal, staffing, and technical resources necessary to maintain them. Some digital repository software is open source, so it can be obtained free of charge, but such solutions normally require substantial systems expertise to maintain. Other products may be purchased, or even licensed as a hosted solution.

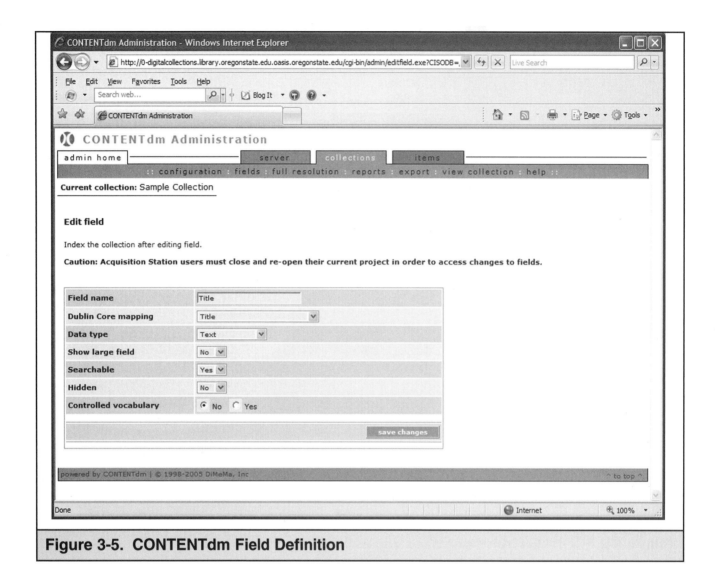

Figure 3-5. CONTENTdm Field Definition

As time passes, software capabilities change. For example, the developers of DSpace and CONTENTdm have extended the functionality of the repository software to include other types of media and to accommodate purposes that may not originally have been envisioned. CONTENTdm has added optical character recognition (OCR) and full-text indexing, which makes it relatively well suited for creating collections of scanned books that can be searched and browsed (Dahl et al., 2006). However, both DSpace and CONTENTdm are still heavily influenced by their original respective purposes and neither may be

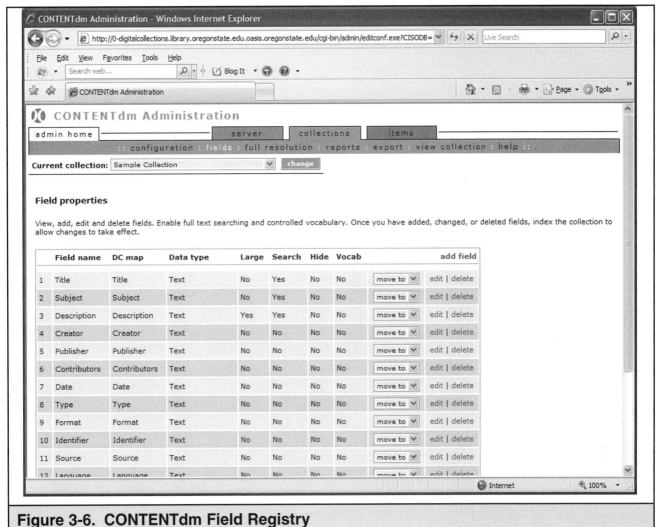

Figure 3-6. CONTENTdm Field Registry

good for certain tasks, such as managing resources based on publication patterns.

It is important to be aware that even relatively well-established digital repository solutions often do not contain basic functionality that has been taken for granted in the traditional ILS (integrated library system) for many years. For instance, neither DSpace nor CONTENTdm provides a specialized mechanism for acquiring, processing, or accessing serials despite the fact that this is a common need and serials have traditionally played an important role in most library collections. There is nothing

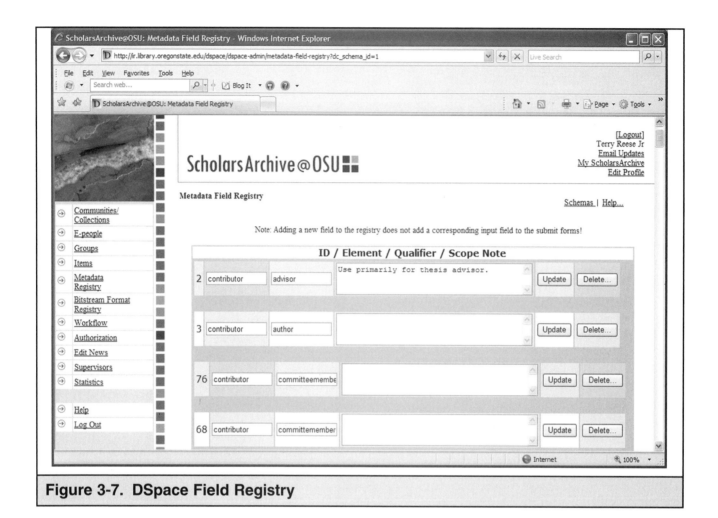

Figure 3-7. DSpace Field Registry

unusual about a library spending 80 percent of its acquisitions budget on serials. Considering the priority that these resources receive in their physical form, it would be a mistake to presume that their role in a repository will not be significant enough to justify tools and workflows optimized to address the challenges they present unless the collection development policy excludes them. Librarians have long been able to assume that any major vendor's serials module will alert staff when new issues are expected. They have come to expect that staff can control how their system displays and sorts issues, and that this will be done consistently across all titles. However, at the time of this writing, digital repository software has not yet matured to the point that these features are supported. One hopes that, as awareness of the importance of workflows increases within the computer science community, this problem will gradually go away.

EVALUATING REPOSITORY FUNCTIONALITY

Virtually all digital repositories must support a certain set of basic functions, such as adding, processing, managing, storing, and displaying resources. Because the way in which these functions are implemented makes an enormous impact on how much time and effort it takes to do things, it is important to ensure that they are executed in a way that is compatible with local needs. Once planning has reached the stage at which these operations and specific tasks are discussed, staff members who will actually be performing the work will need to participate (as will some representative users if they will be contributing resources directly). The repository designers need to articulate a clear vision for how day-to-day tasks will be performed, and developing this vision requires the input of people with sufficient operational knowledge to recognize system characteristics that will aid or hinder the work.

RESOURCE IDENTIFICATION AND INGESTION

The most basic function for any repository is adding resources. The first step in determining how resources will be added to the repository is to understand where they originate. Unless content providers will be expected to contribute resources directly, procedures for identifying materials must be established and documented. In the physical world, collection development librarians learn of new resources using a variety of manual and automated mechanisms: approval plans, catalogs, reviews, patron or faculty requests, recommendations from trusted entities, and other means. With digital resources, many of these methods are not available or appropriate. Depending on whether materials are stored on disks, found on the Internet, part of a CMS, or in a physical format that must be digitized, the digital repository software should provide automated assistance in the resource-identification process.

If the resources are located in a CMS, it is best to use system reports or data extractions to assist with identification of new and changed files. More likely than not, the vast majority of files created on a given day will not be of interest, so program logic needs to be developed so that those responsible for adding resources to the repository are not deluged by a never-ending torrent of meeting minutes, agendas, memos, notes, temporary lists, policies, directories, and other ephemeral documents. As Chapter 2 describes, even if the CMS requires authors to supply metadata, anecdotal evidence suggests that it is likely to be so varied in quality as to be useless. Presuming that users with diverse interests, backgrounds, and responsibilities will consistently expend the time and effort necessary to provide useful metadata is unrealistic. Remember that most authors do not care as much about preservation issues as librarians, and that to many people supplying metadata is just an extraneous step that makes submitting work take more time than it should.

When a CMS cannot be used for resource identification, then server, Web spider, or even search engine logs can be very useful if they can be obtained. Server logs show what files are actually accessed as well as entry points. On a typical system, too many files are accessed for it to be practical for staff to scan for new or changed files. However, if rules that identify resources likely to be of interest, that ignore files that staff have already processed, and that ignore irrelevant materials are applied to the list of files accessed, then Web spider, access, or even search engine logs can be valuable resources for locating materials that should be archived in the repository.

If many of the target resources are on a small number of systems, it is worth contacting the administrators of those systems to discuss the repository's needs. Many systems administrators may be willing to provide a list of new or changed files that appear within the publicly available directories because doing so will not create any security, privacy, or technical problems. By definition, no information would be given beyond what is already publicly available, and it takes much less time and fewer resources to generate a list than it does to obtain this information using spiders or other resource-intensive means. Besides, actually generating such a list is trivial from a programming perspective—in both the Windows and UNIX operating systems, this can be accomplished with a single command.

Even when a CMS can be used to identify new and changed documents, what is discovered will frequently be components of the resources the library is interested in rather than the target materials themselves. For example, a report may be divided into many parts or contain references to spreadsheets and other supplementary material. When these components are created or modified, they will appear as new or changed documents. In many, if not most, cases, it will not be apparent which document they are associated with unless an explicit reference is made inside the file, the filename or document location makes the relationship obvious, or metadata is supplied that shows what is happening.

If all that is in hand is a supplementary file, identifying a parent document is usually more of an art than a science since the only clues available may be the content, name, and location of the file. However, if the library has access to the server access logs where the file is stored, discovering the parent documents is sometimes easy. Standard Web server configuration records certain information when a file is accessed, such as the address of the machine making the request, the date, time, command, browser, and also the referring URL. If anyone has looked at the document and clicked on the link that led to the supplementary file, the parent document will be found. In many cases, it is not even necessary for a user to click on a link for this relationship to be apparent. Some browsers, such as Firefox, "prefetch" pages, that is, they download pages that they expect the user to follow without the user taking any action. Although this practice is somewhat questionable from a systems and privacy perspective (prefetching causes users' computer addresses to be recorded as visiting services that they may not wish to be associated with, allows them to accept cookies, etc.), it also can reveal relationships between linked documents. The entry below illustrates what an access in a server log file might look like:

209.237.92.45—[27/Nov/2006:00:37:35   +0000]   "GET   /reports/ waterqual.xls HTTP/1.1" 200 19893 **"http://myserver.university.edu/ reports/soilcons.html"** "Mozilla/5.0 (Windows; U; Windows NT 5.1; en-US; rv:1.8.1) Gecko/20061010 Firefox/2.0"

If a content management system report or other mechanism has informed staff that a file named *waterqual.xls* was created or modified within the *reports* directory of a server, they may determine from inspection that it is supplementary material for something else. However, it may be unclear that it is a supplement to a file named *soilcons.html* if it is in a directory that contains hundreds of reports, the filename is not similar to the parent document's name, or the supplement contains no reference to the parent. However, the Web server log entry above shows that the referring URL is *http://myserver.university.edu/reports/soilcons.html*. While there is no guarantee that *soilcons.html* is the parent document, because theoretically any file could link to the *waterqual.xls* spreadsheet, this potential relationship can be quickly verified.

Whenever automated means are used to identify documents, whether they are in a CMS or just on the Web, a number of relatively simple techniques can be used to identify resources likely to be of interest while eliminating those that are not. Documents have a greater likelihood of being of interest than executable files and small images. The location of a resource can be a good indicator of whether or not it is likely to be of interest. File sizes can also provide some hints; unless the collection development policy includes very short resources, small files in self-contained document formats such as Word and PDF can be ignored. The specific file characteristics likely to indicate desirable or undesirable resources will vary with the purpose of the repository, but programs that prioritize materials based on these characteristics can significantly reduce the amount of staff time needed to identify and acquire new or updated resources.

The contents of the files themselves can be automatically scanned for clues to their purpose. For example, key phrases such as "table of contents," "abstract," "summary," "author," or "final report" indicate a document or an index page that points to the various components of the resource. There are many text strings that indicate desirable resources, and trial and error can be used to identify those that support the goals of a particular repository. Likewise, filenames containing terms such as "final," "rpt," "report," or "assessment" may indicate a resource that is very likely to be of interest.

Conversely, documents can be systematically rejected based on their filenames, location, or content. For example, filenames that contain strings such as "mtg," "meeting," "agenda," "notes," "calendar," "draft," "announcement," or a few dozen variations of how dates might be expressed (e.g., "20061009," "Oct9," "Thurs," "10-2006," etc.) frequently indicate mundane administrative information that may not be desirable. Experience may indicate that certain directories consistently contain important or unimportant resources.

Even programmers with modest skills can quickly look at many variations of certain patterns using what are known as "regular expressions." A regular expression is a sequence of characters used to match multiple variations with a single line of code. Regular expressions are extremely useful because they make it unnecessary to enumerate every pattern that must be matched. For example, the regular expression "[0-9] [0-9]?[\-_]? [0-9] [0-9]? [\-_]? [0-9] [0-9]" will detect "10-9-2006minutes.doc," "20061009_agenda.doc," "notes_9-10-2006.pdf," "job_listings_2006_10_09.html" and countless other variations. Although regular expressions can become quite complicated, matching many date formats using full or abbreviated months or days of the week in combination with different date syntaxes can be done very easily. A detailed explanation of the construction of regular expressions is beyond the scope of this book, but it is important to be aware that they are extremely powerful and useful for identifying desirable/undesirable materials. All programmers should be expected to know how to use them.

Adding single files is intuitively simple, but a mechanism to add collections of resources in a variety of complex formats must also exist. For some repositories, satisfying the need to add resources may require only a Web page that allows staff, content providers, or others to upload files. However, different types of resources present different challenges. For example, the library needs to determine the steps necessary to add a resource consisting of multiple components. This task becomes more complicated if one or more components also consists of multiple parts (e.g., Web pages) rather than simple files. Even presuming that all the files can be attached as desired, the submitter needs a way to express the relationship among the component parts. Since many components may have been created using proprietary formats, the problem becomes even more complex if the various files must be converted to an archival format.

If authors and users may submit resources directly to the repository, more likely than not, when staff add resources, they will use a different mechanism that has greater functionality and is more complex. If digitization work must be performed, the capture mechanism must be efficient and easy to use. If one of the goals of the repository is to house a large collection—a reasonable desire considering that many libraries have millions of books—there must be some way to add materials in bulk rather than requiring staff to upload resources one by one.

Fortunately, adding multiple resources to a repository is usually not as complicated as it appears on the surface. This is true because in most settings, the resource to be added has the properties of a document. Its boundaries can be easily identified; it has a title and other properties that librarians and users are familiar with; and the structure is obvious. Consequently, the need addressed by adding multiple files typically falls into at least one of two relatively simple scenarios, both of which require only the ability to express very basic relationships between objects. As a result, software can be used to define most of the relationships automatically.

In the first of these scenarios, the library may need to add an entire electronic collection that has already been cataloged or described using metadata. In this case, all that is needed is the ability to import Dublin Core or metadata in some other appropriate format along with a mechanism that can retrieve the actual files. For practical purposes, Dublin Core is a "lowest common denominator" XML standard that can be used to describe virtually any information resource. Dublin Core can be regarded as a *lingua franca* for describing resources, and it is supported by most major repository software. Chapter 5 discusses Dublin Core and other metadata standards in detail.

In the second of these scenarios, a resource may consist of multiple files, but humans still think of it as a single resource—this is generally the case with Web pages, documents containing supplementary materials, and other types of resources commonly found in digital repositories. In these situations, the resource only needs to be described once, and the related resources only need to be stored and linked. Having said that, it is important to be aware that if the related resources are automatically converted to an archival format as they are imported, it is possible for some undesirable data loss or modification to occur. However, for most common document formats, automatic retrieval and conversion works relatively well.

Although it is easy to conceive of situations that do not fall into one of the two scenarios described above, many repository projects never will have to address these possibilities, and most that do will only have to do so rarely. When a library is working with resources that are especially difficult to archive (e.g., dynamic Web resources), it is worth considering working with content providers or other third parties as described in Chapter 2, under "Acquiring Digital Content." By definition, the best tools and methods for working with new types of resources appear only after the resources have been available for a certain amount of time. Document-like electronic files have been around for decades, so tools for working with them are sophisticated and constantly improving. On the other hand, many dynamic objects have only recently appeared on the information landscape, and not enough time has passed for robust archiving tools to be widely available. When there is a need to store such resources, the best policy is to work closely with those who have direct knowledge of their structure and a vested interest in their preservation. For example, an information provider that relies on GIS (Geographic Information Systems) data for its existence is probably going to be better equipped to address changes in GIS technology than librarians who are not GIS specialists.

Finding tools that ingest Web materials as desired can be surprisingly difficult, particularly when the resource to be archived is not structured like a document. It is easy to purchase archiving software that can be configured to follow a certain number of links and exclude external links if desired. Occasionally it is necessary to follow multiple levels of links from pages containing large numbers of links to external resources. In such cases, following to a depth sufficient to capture all desired components of the resource could significantly slow down the acquisitions process, drastically increase storage requirements, and maybe even cause problems with system administrators who mistake archiving activities for a denial-of-service attack. It is very easy for a single item to consume hundreds of megabytes—a size that requires significant bandwidth on almost any network. It is good practice to inform systems and network administrators when planned activity will result in abnormal systems or network usage. The realities of modern network computing require administrators to be vigilant, and some will be more responsive than others about restoring user or staff functions that have been crippled because of a security mechanism that was triggered by unanticipated activity.

Pages that link to resources in proprietary formats or pages containing dynamic content or streaming media present special archiving challenges. If proprietary formats are stored without modification, they will be unusable as soon as the format becomes obsolete. However, if they are automatically converted as materials are ingested, the process could have unpredictable results if it is not monitored and controlled on a case-by-case basis.

Ingestion is the process by which digital resources are copied from their original location into the repository. Ingesting materials cannot be fully automated, and it is difficult to design tools that allow operators to provide input when it is needed. Consider the following rather common scenario in which an online journal keeps a few years' worth of archives online. Any Web archiving software can download all the existing issues. However, what happens when new issues come out, particularly if older issues are removed? Re-ingesting the entire site every time a new issue comes out is time consuming and wastes system resources. Besides, such a solution systematically introduces massive duplication to the repository. Even if one had the excessive system resources necessary to reingest the entire serial run every time a new issue is available, it still would be impossible to easily browse all issues of a title. If the decision is made to ingest each issue individually, repository planners still would have to address the problem of how to associate each item with the other issues that have already been acquired.

Web resources present a broad range of challenges. Even performing a task as simple as archiving an online journal for which all issues are listed on a single page can be problematic. For example, what happens when an organization lists all issues from a number of journals on a single page or buries this information at the bottom of a page containing information that may not seem related? Aside from possible technical difficulties, users might not realize where to find the issue they are seeking even when they have the archived resource loaded in their browser. Clearly, a mechanism that allows partial archiving of a single page—the portion that contains the item of interest—must be available.

As of this writing, the ability to selectively archive content from a single page is not yet widely available. Digital repository software is still very new, but perhaps this functionality will soon be common. In the meantime, a number of simple methods have proven effective in a practical setting.

The Oregon Documents Repository (ODR), a collection of government documents produced by the State of Oregon, developed a few simple tools to address the problems presented by online journals and pages that must be selectively archived. When an online journal is archived, the ODR creates a special index page. This index page looks like an ordinary Web page, but the structure is designed so that functions such as adding new issues or reordering existing ones can be performed automatically. When a new issue must be added to a serial, staff need only know the document number for the serial and the location of the new issue. The ODR software is specifically designed to work with serials, so it automatically retrieves the issue and modifies the index page so that the issue is displayed properly. When only part of a page must be archived, the process is more primitive. Until more sophisticated tools are available, copying and pasting desired sections or even manually editing HTML has proven the most effective ways to selectively archive a page. Although these methods may sound cumbersome, they are reasonably effective and require only modest technical skills. No new staff were hired to maintain the ODR. The software was developed by existing systems personnel, and the repository itself is maintained entirely by technical services staff.

As the case of archiving an online journal illustrates, it is important for tools to accommodate workflows that are peculiar to certain types of common resources as well as the ability to override default automated behavior. When ingesting resources, it is important for staff to be able to select what is needed and eliminate information that will make resources harder to use.

Depending on the repository's collection development policy, version control can be problematic. On a basic level, there needs to be a simple way to add supplements or updates to resources that are already in the repository. Although it is feasible to simply download another copy of a resource, repeatedly doing so is likely to lead to inconsistency in the repository if key metadata points are not populated consistently. Even if users and/or staff who add materials are very consistent in their use of metadata (unlikely, given that studies show that even trained catalogers do not apply access points consistently), duplication will inevitably result. For example, if six updates to a resource are stored, they can all appear in search results. Patrons may be confused by seeing the same title appear multiple times, and they may not notice other useful resources that might satisfy their information needs; most retrieval mechanisms only display a limited number of matches on each screen. Duplication will make the repository more difficult to use over time. Usually, the best way to address the multiple versions issue is to either maintain a policy of retaining the latest version or configuring the display to make it clear that multiple versions of the same resource are available. It is important to be aware that the latter path absolutely requires metadata to be used consistently.

AUTOMATING MANAGEMENT AND ORGANIZATION

Automation can simplify management and organization of the collection, but a significant level of staff intervention is almost inevitable. It is no more realistic to presume that disparate content providers or patrons will effectively organize a digital repository than it is to think that they can catalog and organize materials in a physical library.

Nonetheless, a number of tasks can be performed much more efficiently with the aid of automation. For example, if a repository has any serials, a good platform must have some method for managing and displaying the online serials. Otherwise, the process of adding issues will be time consuming and error prone. In other words, repositories that collect serials without the aid of an effective serials management module will incur higher costs while delivering a lower level of service. At the time of this writing, major repository software such as DSpace and CONTENTdm treat issues of serials like any other electronic resource. Issues must be uploaded one at a time, and metadata must be added to each issue. Obviously, this mechanism is very wasteful of staff resources and needlessly difficult for patrons who are browsing issues.

A good serials module must allow staff to perform common, repetitive tasks efficiently. Staff need to have a way of knowing when new issues are available—it is unrealistic to expect people to alert those who maintain the repository of new issues or require staff to manually scan spider reports or Web pages. Many serials are issued regularly, so software should predict or detect the appearance of new issues. Once a serial run or even a single issue can be identified, a number of other specialized tools are necessary. A mechanism for adding individual or multiple issues must exist. Staff must have a way to describe how issues are related so that patrons can browse them. The repository will be easier to use if issues for various publications are organized and presented consistently (e.g., reverse chronological or chronological order). For this reason, staff need a mechanism that allows them to quickly reorder lists containing issues. In addition, pages containing links to issues of publications may also include a significant amount of extraneous information, so there needs to be a way to selectively archive portions of the page. This task is easy when only a single link is desired, but it is much more difficult when the desired section occupies a quarter of a page of complex HTML.

Organizing the collection is one of the most important and difficult tasks a repository faces. The construction of access points and linkages between related resources determines how users can navigate the collection, but it also has an enormous impact on the quality of their experiences. For this reason, it is crucial to have robust tools and effective procedures for organizing the collection.

It is impractical to fully automate organization of a repository because many people do not worry about establishing meaningful titles, assigning useful filenames, or being consistent with past practice. However, it is feasible to provide automated means to make it easier for humans to organize materials. For example, at Oregon State University, a program that suggests subject headings and call numbers based on statistical similarity of title keywords makes it easy for staff to classify Internet resources quickly. Human operators can ignore headings that obviously are not applicable, and they can add headings that are missing. By allowing staff to quickly browse headings that are statistically associated with similar works, they can quickly find good terms to organize the collection without having to remember headings that were previously assigned or run multiple searches on the collection.

INDEXING FOR EASY RETRIEVAL

There are two basic methods for locating items in a digital collection: searching the resources directly and searching representations of the materials. In a physical library, it is usually impractical to satisfy information needs by examining books, journals, and other items one by one. Instead, representations of the items are searched: the catalog and indexes. Works by authors known to be experts on subjects of interest are retrieved.

Although digital information can be scanned much more quickly than information stored on paper, searching representations of items is often more desirable than searching the resources themselves. Most resources are known by a title or are associated with individual or corporate authors. Subjects capturing the "aboutness" of a resource provide functionality that cannot be achieved with full-text searches alone. Specialized access points such as document numbers, format and language information, or even date of publication can be useful for helping people find what they need.

It is especially important to have good representations of items when the resources are not textual in nature, for example, images, maps, sound recordings, video, and the like. Most digital repositories contain nontextual materials, so it is worth spending some time establishing procedures for applying metadata to organize these resources and make them easier to browse and find. Simple search boxes are popular, but, as Chapter 2 explains, Web search-engine techniques are problematic when used in a digital repository context. Technical challenges aside, it is important to be aware that Web search engines are designed to satisfy a type of information need that is not always applicable in a library setting.

Ranking algorithms work best for satisfying information needs that do not require retrieval of particular resources. However, a library is an archive, and it should be possible to reliably locate any resource. Ranking algorithms are especially effective for retrieving textual resources containing specialized vocabulary. If a resource contains only common words or is not textual in nature (e.g., diagrams, images, sound recordings, multimedia, etc.), it may be difficult or even impossible to construct a query that will retrieve the item. These algorithms are complex, and there is no way to predict exactly how an individual resource will be treated.

One can presume that ranking algorithms will sometimes make even textual materials unfindable. This is not acceptable in a library setting. It is a good idea to provide convenient mechanisms that allow people to quickly find at least some resources when they are not certain what they need, so it may be desirable to provide a simple search box that allows user to search the repository. However, library staff and knowledgeable users should be able to locate any resource in the archive. Given technologies and methods currently available, this need can only be satisfied effectively with the aid of at least some metadata.

Although there is a significant amount of confusion in the library community over what metadata refers to, it is conceptually identical to cataloging. The only difference between how metadata is applied in practice and traditional library cataloging is that the former might be used to record virtually any information about a resource, while the latter only records information prescribed by cataloging standards such as AACR (Anglo-American Cataloging Rules). In fact, some metadata standards such as Dublin Core generally involve recording less information about a resource than appears in a typical catalog record. Chapter 4 describes metadata standards in detail.

Good digital repositories must be able to take advantage of the enormous amount of past work invested in organizing the collection. They also must be flexible enough to accommodate needs that have not yet been imagined. If a digital repository stores information in such a way that it cannot be searched along with other library holdings, it is likely to be quickly marginalized because it will represent only a tiny fraction of available holdings. On the other hand, if it fulfills a new need and can extend the functionality of existing systems, it could easily become a popular service.

While many people view the catalog as outmoded, it is still very important to leverage the enormous wealth of information that it contains. Many large libraries have millions of volumes, and they can quickly search other libraries' collections on systems such as OCLC's WorldCat because of widely followed cataloging standards. In practical terms, this means that if the digital repository is intended to be used as part of the larger library collection, it will be necessary to store author names, titles, and subjects using practices that are compatible with those that describe other resources.

There is nothing to stop a library from creating its own metadata schemes to organize repositories. However, even if it is considered desirable for the repository to function as an information silo, it will eventually be necessary to migrate to another system. If the repository relies on a custom-designed system that relies on a custom-designed metadata scheme, it will be difficult, if not impossible, to migrate to an off-the-shelf system in the future.

This is not to say that digital repositories must be designed so that all resources receive full MARC cataloging. Rather, it means that the infrastructure must exist to share metadata with MARC-based systems. For example, author fields in MARC records follow a very precise syntax that specifies how the surname, additional names, titles, birth/death dates, and other relevant information is structured. If the repository uses only one field to contain all the elements of authors' names, it must structure them the same way as is found in the catalog. If the names are formatted differently, users will have to execute more than one search to find all works by an author if they wish to search both the repository and the catalog. However, it would still be perfectly acceptable to store the various name elements in separate fields so long as the system can assemble them into a compatible format.

Syntax is only one form of compatibility. Library catalogs employ authority control because it is extremely useful for identifying works created by authors with common names, corporate entities that might be known by many different names, or distinguishing the many publications that do not have unique titles (e.g., *Bulletin, Annual Report, Proceedings*, etc.) from each other. Even if entries are formatted properly, repositories that do not use authority control may well encounter problems because of similarities between unrelated entries. Although Web resources that rely on social tagging—i.e., metadata provided by authors and consumers of information—initially did not use authority control, larger projects soon found how essential it was. For example, Wikipedia's *disambiguation* process works very much like standard library control procedures down to qualifying topics in parentheses, naming conventions, and establishing rules for constructing entries for particular types of entries, such as ships (Wikipedia, accessed: 2006).

Although content-related issues, such as authority control, may seem to be related more to the workflow than to the platform, the repository can function much better if it is designed to provide automatic support for slow, repetitive tasks. For example, if someone enters a heading, the software should automatically consult an authority file and suggest alternative spellings if no exact match is found. It should be possible to ingest, convert, and provide metadata for multipart resources that have individual components in different formats without executing multiple manual processes.

OTHER STORAGE CHALLENGES

The most difficult aspect of developing robust storage procedures involves the conversion of materials to an archival format. As Chapter 1 explained, storing resources in their native format is likely to cause serious problems in the future unless the native format is one of the archival formats supported by the repository. Converting regular documents composed on standard word-processing software is a simple process, but conversion becomes much more problematic when the original format contains functionality that is not present in the archival format or if the resource consists of multiple files in different formats.

In a digital repository, the platform, policies, and procedures are closely related. For example, repository designers need to decide how regularly issued documents (e.g., serials) are stored. These can be treated like stand-alone documents, but it may be desirable to create a separate index page for them or even to locate the files together. Similarly, the components of a multipart monograph can be stored together or separately, and planners may decide whether creating a navigational page is desirable. If the resource is currently in a CMS, those developing the storage procedures need to determine whether common graphical and navigational elements should be removed. If not, the library needs to decide whether it considers the resource to be updated when the CMS templates are changed. If the wrapper is removed, a procedure needs to be developed for doing this. Off-the-shelf software can be used for many storage and reformatting tasks. However, it is virtually guaranteed that repository designers may need to develop special procedures or even special tools for storing some materials.

Once the resource is in its archival format, it must be named and placed in an appropriate area on a file system or in a database. Generally speaking, it is preferable to use automatically generated names that are guaranteed to be unique rather than having staff or other submitters make them up as they go along. Aside from promoting consistency and reducing confusion, automatically generated names save time and could prevent the accidental creation of names containing characters that may cause technical problems. If a resource is subject to an embargo period or other access restrictions, the storage procedure may be different from that for other resources.

A frequently overlooked aspect of managing digital repositories involves ensuring the integrity of files. By definition, electronic files can be modified by anyone with adequate systems permissions, even if good security practices are observed. One of the easiest ways to ensure the integrity of files is to generate a checksum for each file as it is added to the repository. A checksum is simply a value that results when a mathematical algorithm is applied to the file. If the same algorithm is applied to the file at a later date and a different checksum results, then the file has been modified and it may be necessary to restore it from a backup. It is important to be aware that the checksum cannot be used to determine what changes were made to a file—it only can indicate whether a file has been modified.

A number of algorithms can be used, but the MD5 algorithm is present on most operating systems. In Windows with the correct utility installed and many flavors of UNIX, simply typing:

md5sum file_to_be_examined

at a command line generates a value that will change if the file is modified, even if the total length is identical. It is important that the checksums be maintained in a different area from the files they describe. Otherwise, anyone who modifies the files can simply generate new checksums. Automating the process of generating and securely storing checksums can save enormous amounts of staff time. Likewise, if the files are migrated to a new format at a later date, new checksums will need to be generated, so that process also must be automated. Other methods can be used to ensure integrity of files. For example, encryption is very effective. However, if the encryption key is ever lost, the files become unreadable.

REPOSITORY ADMINISTRATION

The administrative capabilities of a platform are essential to the long-term success of a repository. Many resources require access controls, so it is essential that the repository software ensure that people can only view or modify resources when appropriate. In addition, routine administration of the repository hardware and software needs to consume as little staff time as possible. If too much time and money are expended on day-to-day upkeep, staff resources may be insufficient to expand the capabilities and collections of the repository later.

Although libraries were early adopters of technology and many had their own systems departments, a growing trend in recent years has been for the hardware and software that libraries rely on to be hosted outside the library. Campus or municipal IT departments often manage the systems that libraries use, and a growing number of functions have gradually been migrating outside the library. More often than not, the tools that large libraries use for providing cataloging, interlibrary loan, federated search, or even reference are hosted by external entities. Given the technical complexity of managing a repository, it is reasonable to presume that many libraries will want to have librarians with relatively little systems training administering the functionality of systems that are maintained elsewhere. With this in mind, the library needs repository software that allows administrators to define which tasks various users can perform.

If systems will be hosted locally, it is essential to have tools that make it easy to perform routine maintenance tasks and monitor the health and operation of the system. For example, backing up data may seem mundane, but it is a critical task that can demand excessive staff time if not adequately planned. Computers are fast and disk arrays store enormous amounts of data, but network capacity has not advanced nearly as quickly. It is not practical to transmit more than a few gigabytes over the Internet, and even that takes hours with a fast connection. As a practical matter, this means that network-based backup procedures must be based on incremental processes, such as LOCKSS (lots of copies keep stuff safe) or rsync, a protocol that allows files to be copied efficiently to multiple servers. If backups must be made to tape and the repository is large, it is important to use equipment that is fast enough to back up the data without taking the system offline for long periods of time. At the time of this writing, even high-end equipment takes many hours to back up a terabyte (1,000 gigabytes) of data, and it is impractical to perform this task with the modest drives and tapes found in many departments. When one considers that active files cannot be backed up (though some CMSs contain backup utilities that can be used on a live system) and that multiple tapes will most likely be necessary, it is important to ensure that the repository is set up so that backing up the system will require minimal downtime and minimal staff intervention for tasks such as swapping tapes.

Many repositories contain resources that cannot be made freely available. For example, many scholarly journals will not accept research that has been published elsewhere. If a university stores theses and dissertations in a repository, it may need to limit access or enforce embargo periods so that this research can be published. Certain resources may require access restrictions because they contain sensitive information or the copyright holder has limited distribution rights. Tools must be built directly into the repository software to prevent the need for awkward adjustments to the workflow for items with access restrictions.

Virtually all medium and large libraries use standard authentication mechanisms to control access to the desktop computers, the local network, e-mail, databases, and other functions. In most cases, these authentication mechanisms can be used to define rights for groups as well as individuals. Although it may be useful for repository software to contain a built-in authentication mechanism, long-term administration will be greatly simplified if the repository can take advantage of authentication mechanisms that are already in use. Most organizations already have a Lightweight Directory Access Protocol (LDAP) server that can be used for authentication purposes. However, LDAP is most useful within the context of a single organization. If the library needs the authentication mechanism to be connected to the local CMS or to share authentication credentials securely with other organizations, the repository needs to support a compatible distributed authentication mechanism such as Shibboleth or Athens. Chapter 8 discusses access control in greater detail.

SUMMARY

Repository functionality is closely tied to the platform. Because digital repository needs vary from one environment to another, it is important to choose software that is compatible with the goals of the project at hand. Some platforms are better suited to centrally managed repositories while others are based on a community model. Likewise, various platforms are usually optimized for working with specific needs and types of resources. Acquiring and processing digital resources can result in a great deal of work, so the platform should facilitate identification, acquisition, manipulation, organization, and presentation of materials. The platform must also be designed to make administrative functions such as access control and routine maintenance as easy as possible.

REFERENCES

Dahl, Mark, Kyle Banerjee, and Michael Spalti. 2006. *Digital Libraries: Integrating Content and Systems*. Oxford: Chandos.

Fedora. "Getting Started: Creating Fedora Objects and Using Disseminators." Available: www.fedora.info/download/2.1/userdocs/tutorials/tutorial2.pdf (accessed November 9, 2006).

Lagoze, Carl, et al. "Fedora: An Architecture for Complex Objects and Their Relationships." arXiv e-print. Available: http://arxiv.org/ftp/cs/papers/0501/0501012.pdf (accessed November 9, 2006).

Lynch, Clifford A., and Joan Lippincott. 2005. "Institutional Repository Development in the United States as of Early 2005." *D-Lib Magazine* 11, no. 9. Available: www.dlib.org/dlib/september05/lynch/09lynch.html (accessed November 1, 2006).

Walters, Tyler O. 2006. "Strategies and Frameworks for Institutional Repositories and the New Support Infrastructure for Scholarly Communications." *D-Lib Magazine* 12, no. 10. Available: www.dlib.org/dlib/october06/walters/10walters.html (accessed November 1, 2006).

Wikipedia. "Disambiguation." Available: http://en.wikipedia.org/wiki/Wikipedia:Disambiguation (accessed December 5, 2006).

GENERAL PURPOSE TECHNOLOGIES USEFUL FOR DIGITAL REPOSITORIES

As noted in previous chapters, planning for and implementing a successful digital repository requires careful consideration at many levels. For many, concepts such as workflow and acquisitions planning are easy to understand because they directly relate to the information object. However, what is often overlooked or not fully considered is the role that metadata plays in creating a successful digital repository. If the value of a digital repository is measured by the content found within it, then the success of that repository will be defined by its ability to surface that information to its users.

A digital object is of little value to a potential user if that information cannot be found in the system that stores it. For print materials, this is easy to understand. If a book or physical object isn't indexed and then placed into storage, there's a high probability that it will be lost. Within the digital world, this concern is exacerbated by the fact that the "storage" location for a digital object is the entire World Wide Web. The availability, the flexibility, and the quality of one's metadata will ultimately determine the relevancy of one's digital repository within this expanded information ecosystem. This chapter will focus on the technologies that make up today's current digital repository systems, XML (eXtensible Markup Language) and SOAP (Simple Object Access Protocol). Chapters 5 and 6 will focus on specific metadata schemas and the tools needed to use those schemas both inside and outside the context of the digital repository.

THE CHANGING FACE OF METADATA

The foundation of any digital repository is the underlying metadata structures that provide meaning to the information objects that it stores. However, this isn't new for libraries. Libraries have traditionally treated the creation and maintenance of bibliographic metadata as one of the core values of the profession. Findability—the ability to create access points between an organization's indexing system and the physical location of the piece—has long been a hallmark of library science. How that metadata was created, captured and stored has changed throughout the years as printed catalog cards gave way to the Integrated Library Systems (ILS) and the MARC (MAchine Readable Catalog) metadata schema. As metadata became digital, organizations like OCLC and the Research Libraries Group (RLG) were formed to promote shared metadata and a common set of bibliographic descriptive standards. From within the library community, standards like AACR and AACR2 recognized the changing face of metadata and helped create a homogeneous metadata ecosystem around the MARC schema, allowing metadata from one institution to be used by another. In these efforts, libraries and their partners have been so successful that many have difficulty seeing a need to move away from the status quo, and even more struggle to embrace new metadata models as more and more information is born digital. This makes the decision to build a digital repository a difficult one because it represents a dramatic change in an organization's information ecosystem, as one finds a way to reconcile metadata for the digital repository with the organization's legacy systems and data-capture procedures.

Unfortunately, in many cases, organizations simply are not equipped to evaluate the metadata requirements for a digital repository. Bibliographic metadata has become so homogenous and print-centric that many organizations lack the metadata expertise in house to evaluate new and emerging metadata frameworks, or there is no one on staff with enough familiarity to utilize the new metadata schemas. Moreover, many organizations have difficulty integrating new metadata schemas and bibliographic descriptive guidelines into existing workflows designed primarily for print materials. As noted in previous chapters, building a successful digital repository requires new workflows and new acquisitions processes to accommodate the dynamic nature of the materials. Individuals like Roy Tennant of the California Digital Library have long argued that for libraries to truly integrate their digital content, their bibliographic infrastructure must change dramatically. This change must include both the metadata creation and delivery methods of bibliographic content. The days of a homogenous bibliographic standard for all content are coming to an end as more specialized descriptive formats are needed to describe the various types of materials being produced today and into the future. This means that organizations will need to look beyond MARC and instead focus on bibliographic schemas that offer the highest granularity of bibliographic content.

XML IN LIBRARIES

Given the nature of the current bibliographic landscape, it might surprise some that the library community has traditionally been one of the early implementers of XML-based descriptive schemas. As lines between the library and publishing communities have blurred, more libraries have found themselves producing digital publications or digitizing existing works. Issues of document delivery, indexing, and display have pushed the library community to consider XML-based markup languages as a method of preserving digital and bibliographical information. Organizations like OCLC, the U.S. Library of Congress, and the Lane Medical Library at Stanford have been at the forefront of XML research and development in the library community. Each represents an organization that has explored ways to make better use of their bibliographic and digital content by looking at how markup formats limit or enhance metadata usability. In many ways, it's from their research and successes that the current generation of digital repositories have been constructed. However, before looking at how XML is used in libraries today, it is best to first take a step back and look at XML in general.

For many, the definition of XML has become understandably muddled. It has been extended to include not just XML, but the many technologies that have come out of the XML specification. This is very much like the definition of MARC today. Like XML, the term MARC is often used to represent the bibliographic descriptive rules and interpretations used to create a MARC record. MARC21 users equate MARC field 245 with a title—even though the MARC specification itself makes no such determination. In part, it is this fusion of rules and specifications that often makes MARC difficult to work with outside of the library community. In reality, the MARC format at its most basic is just a container for the data. The Library of Congress developed MARC as a distribution format that could be used to capture information from a card catalog in digital form for transfer to other systems. In the same way, many tend to fold technologies like XSLT, XLink, or XQuery—all technologies that have been developed out of the XML schema—into the definition of XML. While simplistic, Figure 4-1 shows an abbreviated version of the XML family tree. From the tree, one can see the many different technologies that have been derived from the XML specification.

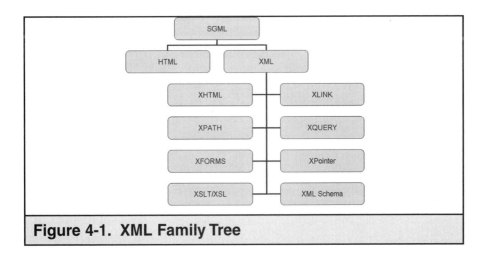

Figure 4-1. XML Family Tree

XHTML

XHTML marks what many hope will be the next evolution of the HTML markup language. It is an extension of the current HTML document type (HTML version 4), which is XML conforming, meaning that XHTML documents can be viewed, edited, validated, and acted upon by XML tools (W3C XHTML Working Group, 2002). The current interest behind XHTML is its adherence to a strict set of validation rules. Since XHTML is XML conforming, it must respect the same strict set of document validation and well-formedness rules for tags and character data. This is very different from the current implementation of HTML, which is, in many respects, a sloppy markup language that has been loosely interpreted by today's Web-browsing technology. It is this promise of markup standardization and strict validation that continues to excite those developing for the Web.

Additionally, the fact that XHTML documents can be validated and acted upon by XML tools and technologies like XPATH and XQUERY should not be underestimated. XHTML documents allow Web developers to build documents for display while still allowing the documents to be parsed and acted on by other groups and users. For institutions that want to make their content available for users to build services, or "mashups," on top of their collections but lack staff with the expertise to provide a fully functional Web-based application programming interface (API), offering content in XHTML can help expose the collections or services.

Likewise, there are many examples of services moving in this direction. Probably the best known example is OCLC's WorldCat.org service. WorldCat.org provides a publicly searchable portal to the OCLC digital properties. However, what's more interesting is OCLC's decision to have World-Cat.org generate content in XHTML. By providing content in XHTML, OCLC has provided a minimal tool set necessary to parse and extract data from the WorldCat.org project and to embed it into other services. For example, using an XPATH statement (which will be defined and explained below), one can easily extract the holding libraries from a document.

So how does one identify XHTML records? XHTML records can be identified by the document type defined at the top of the source code. Look at the source for the following record: www.worldcat.org/oclc/ 26557254&referer=brief_results. The following statement is found at the top of the XHTML file: *<!DOCTYPE html PUBLIC "-//W3C//DTD XHTML 1.0 Transitional//EN"*

"http://www.w3.org/TR/xhtml1/DTD/xhtml1-transitional.dtd"><html xmlns="http://www.w3.org/1999/xhtml" xml:lang="en" lang="en">

The source code identifies itself as XHTML to the Web browser in the first line of the source, that is in the DOCTYPE statement, which defines the (Document Type Definition) DTD that defines the parsing rules and elements that can legally be used in the document. Because this is an XHTML document, each element or tag can be parsed using an XPATH expression, in which the HTML tag is represented as the root tag in the XML tree.

XPATH

XPath is a methodology for addressing parts of an XML document. XPath is a technology designed to be used with XSLT and XPointer (W3C XML Working Group, 1999). It defines a syntax by which XML data can be extracted and acted upon. In a conceptual sense, an XML document is really like a tree, with each element a different node, or branch, on the tree. XPath defines a method for accessing the individual nodes on the tree. For example, consider the following XML snippet:

```
<?xml version="1.0" encoding="utf-8" ?>
<cars>
        <item>
                <model>Toyota</model>
                <make>Rav4</make>
                <year>2007</year>
                <hybrid>no</hybrid>
        </item>
        <item>
                <model>Toyota</model>
                <make>Highlander</make>
                <year>2006</year>
                <hybrid>no</hybrid>
        </item>
        <item>
                <model>Ford</model>
                <make>Escape</make>
                <year>2007</year>
                <hybrid>yes</hybrid>
        </item>
</cars>
```

XPath statements allow a process to access an individual node within an XML file by naming its location in relation to the root element. In this case, a process looking to extract the *make* and *year* from the *second item* tag group would create an XPath statement that navigated the document nodes. In this example however, the node *item* is not unique; it appears multiple times at the same level within the XML document. XPath accommodates this by allowing access to the *item* group as elements of an array. XPath arrays, however, differ from traditional array structures in that XPath arrays start at one, while an array in PERL, C, or C# would start at zero. Accessing the second node from the example above would use the following statement: */item[2]/make,* which illustrates how the data in the second *item* node would be addressed. When coupled with XSLT, XPath allows an individual or process to loop or extract items from the XML document to transform the data to something new.

When dealing with XML-based metadata formats, XPath and XQuery represent the two primary methods for working with the metadata. Currently, most of the transformation of data between metadata formats, or metadata crosswalking, is done with XSLT style sheets. These style sheets make liberal use of XPath statements to process elements within the XML document to extract or transform the XML document into some other useful format. Library of Congress, for example, is producing a number of XSLT style sheets that make liberal use of XPath statements to provide crosswalking functionality between MARC21XML (an XML representation of MARC21) and other metadata formats, like MODS and Dublin Core. These crosswalks can be found at the Library of Congress's MARC Web site at: www.loc.gov/marc/

XFORMS

XForms was designed by the World Wide Web Consortium (W3C) as a technology to replace the current form methodology found in HTML 4.0. It was designed to work as a companion technology to XHTML (W3C XForms Working Group, 2006). Unfortunately, there are very few real-world implementations that use XForms, in part because many current generation browsers provide only slight support for the protocol, and current development tools do not take advantage of the XForms syntax. With that said, XForms, like XHTML, represents the future of HTML and Web development, so the technology should be monitored as it continues to mature and become more universally supported.

XSLT

Standing for eXtensible Stylesheet Language Transformations, XSLT represents one of the technologies that can be used to generate display elements from XML. XSLT's primary function is to translate XML metadata to other document types—be that HTML or another XML format. Essentially, an XSLT document is made up of XPath statements constructed in the form of "templates" that are used to process specific elements within an XML or XHTML document. Chapter 6 takes a closer look at the mechanics of XSLT and how it can be used in the crosswalking of XML metadata (W3C XSLT Working Group, 1999).

XLINK

The XLink specification defines the methodology for the creation and description of links between XML documents (W3C XLink Working Group, 2001). In essence, the XLink syntax provides simple HTML linking between XML documents. However, unlike traditional HTML links, XLinks treat links as objects that can have properties and actions associated with the link itself.

XQUERY

XQuery represents an attempt to build a general purpose query language for XML documents. In some ways, it is analogous to Structured Query Language (SQL) when dealing with databases. XQuery is an attempt to create a query structure that is independent of the surface XML schema (W3C XQuery Working Group, 2007). So, how is it different from XPath? As noted above, XPath functions by treating an XML document as a tree, where each XML tag represents a branch on the tree. XPath statements navigate these trees by calling or processing specific branches and the attributes that make up a specific tag. XQuery essentially works to solve the same problem (extracting and parsing XML data) but attempts to do it using a structured query language rather then part of an XML tree. As a result, XQuery has developed its own set of functions and methods that can be used to act upon extracted XML data, providing a very SQL-like experience when processing XML documents. In many cases, XPath or XQuery comes down to a matter of personal taste as well as support for the tools being used to process XML data. Some users will like the more structured processing language found in XQuery, while other users who are more familiar with the traditional HTML document object model (DOM) approach are likely to thrive using XPath processing. In either case, XPath and XQuery offer users the ability to process XML documents using the approach that best fits their learning styles.

XPOINTER

XPointer is methodology for dealing with XML fragments (W3C XPointer Working Group, 2002). XPointer is a technology used in conjunction with XPath in XSLT documents.

XML SCHEMA

XML Schemas represent an attempt to create a methodology for defining XML tag structures for automated processing (W3C Schema Working Group, n.d.). The use of XML Schemas is currently part of an ongoing debate on how to best structure and define XML documents. XML documents can be defined utilizing a number of methodologies, and, at present, the W3C and Dublin Core organization are taking a close look at XML Schemas to see how this technology can be used to generate Application

Profiles that allow for the automated processing of XML documents. A truly automated solution for XML documents still remains an elusive goal.

At the top of the tree, we find standardized general markup language (SGML). SGML represents the genesis of current markup languages. Ironically, SGML was initially conceived by Ed Mosher, Ray Lorie, and Charles Goldfarb in 1969, the same year that Library of Congress released the first MARC specification. Originally, Mosher, Lorie and Goldfarb, who worked for IBM at the time, set out to develop a markup language for structuring legal documents to a standardized format. The goal of the project was to create a method of structuring documents so that they could be read and acted upon by a computer. This action was mainly limited to the formatting and reformatting of data for publication, but the underlying concept would allow the documents to become more useful as new tools could be built to act upon the structured data. In 1970, IBM extended the project to encompass general text processing, and SGML was born. In the early 1990s, a group from the European Organization for Nuclear Research (CERN) developed HTML, a small subset of SGML, for the publication of linked documents on the Web. This metadata schema provided a common tag set for online publication, quickly becoming the lingua franca for publishing on the Web. Finally, in 1996, a group known as the XML Working Group was formed out of the W3C with the goal of creating a subset of SGML that would enable generic SGML objects to be processed over the Web in much the same way that HTML is now. (W3C, www.w3.org/TR/REC-xml/).

In Figure 4-1, there are a number of items located below XML. These represent a number of technologies or metadata schemas that have been developed out of the XML specification. What's important to note is that XML is, in large part, simply a markup language for data. In and of itself, XML has no inherent functionality outside of the meaning and context that it brings to the data that it describes. Now, that is a very powerful function. It gives elements within a document properties and attributes that allow one to enhance the available metadata by creating context for the document elements. What's more, XML is not a "flat" metadata structure, allowing for the creation of hierarchical relationships between elements within a document. An XML document can literately become a digital object itself. This is very different from a markup language, like MARC, that functions solely as a container for data transfer. As a "flat" data structure, MARC lacks the ability to add context to the bibliographic data that it contains. Moreover, data stored in XML has the ability to exist separately from the object that it describes and still maintain meaning given its contextual and heirarchical nature. However, as stated above, XML is, in essence, simply a fancy text file. What makes XML special and useful as a metadata schema is the ancillary technologies currently built around the XML specification that can be used to interpret meaning from the various properties and attributes of a given element. At the heart of these technologies is the XML parser. Currently, a number of different XML parsers exist, including Saxon, a Java XML/XSLT parser; libxml, the Gnome XML parsing library; and MSXML, the XML parser currently built into the Windows Operating System. These XML parsers offer users two primary methods for interacting with an XML document: DOM (document object model) and SAX (simple API for XML).

DOM

The document object model should be familiar to anyone who does Web development using JavaScript. DOM is a platform-neutral interface to the content and structure of a given XML document. Conceptually, DOM breaks down an XML document as nodes in a tree. Each tag represents a different branch, and the attributes are its leaves, if you will. Within the DOM model, the entire XML document is loaded into memory to construct the DOM tree. As a result, the DOM object model represents a very inefficient method for accessing large XML documents. While it makes data access easier and more convenient through the DOM interface, it comes at a big cost. All XML processing done using XPath, XQuery, or XSLT uses DOM processing, meaning that most XML transformations are done employing the DOM architecture.

SAX

The simple API for XML was initially developed as a Java-only processing method. Within the SAX model, the XML file is read sequentially, with events being filed as the parser enters and leaves elements within the document. The document is read sequentially, and it is much less memory intensive since only small chunks of an XML document will be loaded at any one time. However, unlike DOM, the parser does not have access to all of the elements in the XML tree, but only to the specific data that is being read at that moment.

Because of its flexibility and convenience, many XML processing technologies are built around the DOM application model. Chapter 6 takes a closer look at XSLT and how it is utilized to perform metadata crosswalking between one metadata framework to another.

Early on, a number of libraries looked to the work of the W3C and the XML Working Group as a method for bridging the access gap between print and digital resources. Many of these projects continue to play a major role in how XML-based metadata schemas are utilized today.

- The Lane Medical Library at Stanford University initiated a project in 1998 with the purpose of exploring metadata schemas that could better represent digital objects. Through the Medlane project, the Stanford group developed one of the first MARC-to-XML crosswalks and developed XML-MARC, one of the first MARC-to-XML mapping software tools. Using this tool, the Medlane library was able to test the feasibility of migrating large existing MARC databases into XML. In many respects, the work done at Stanford would be a precursor to the work that the Library of Congress would eventually undertake: creating an official MARCXML crosswalk as well as the eventual development of the MODS (Metadata Object Description Schema) metadata framework. The Lane Medical Library's project (http://xobis.stanford.edu/) continues to this day; however, the project has expanded with the development of a new bibliographic schema known as XOBIS (XML Organic Bibliography Information Schema) designed to examine new ways of structuring library bibliographic data.

- Prior to the work that the XML Working Group would eventually accomplish in 1996, the Online Archive of California (OAC) was already doing research on how SGML could be utilized to create archival finding aids. Between the years of 1993 and 1995, a full year before the XML Working Group would be established, the OAC published a prototype finding-aid syntax known then as the Berkeley Finding Aid Project. Using this prototype, the OAC developed one of the very first union databases composed primarily of encoded finding aids—showing early on some of the benefits that could be gained by using structured metadata. This prototype would eventually be developed into what we know today as EAD (Encoded Archival Description), the lingua franca of the library archival community.

Today, libraries make use of XML nearly every day. We can find XML in the ILS systems, in image management tools, and in many other facets of the library.

Figure 4-2 is an example of how one current ILS vendor, in this case Innovative Interfaces, is utilizing XML to make bibliographic metadata available directly via the Web. In Figure 4-3, we see how CONTENTdm is utilizing XML, particularly the OAI (open archive initiative) harvesting framework to make a collection's metadata available for harvesting. In both examples, the availability of the XML interfaces offers digital library developers additional opportunities for integrating information from these disparate systems. Moreover, technologies like OAI provide a way for other organizations to harvest and index the bibliographic metadata from a digital repository into local system. This opens up the possibilities for information from one's digital repository to show up in tools like Google,

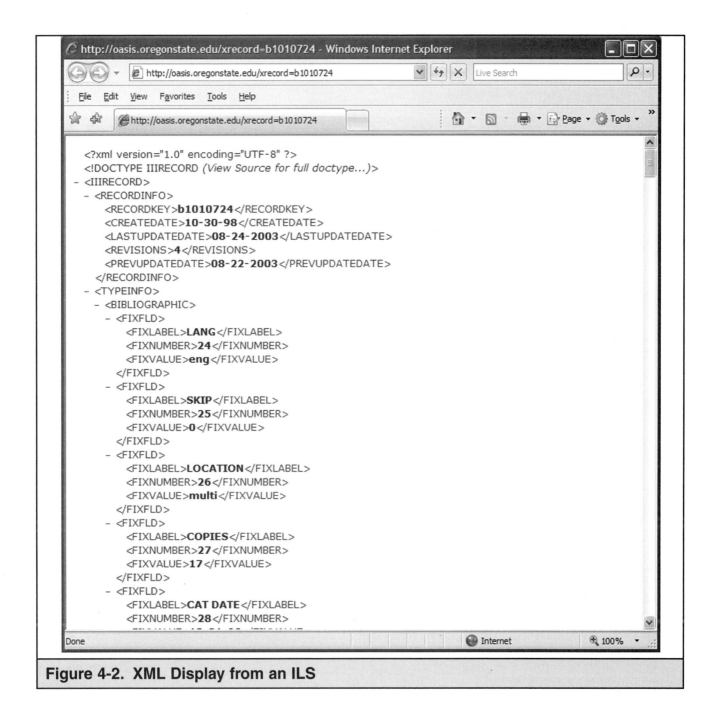

Figure 4-2. XML Display from an ILS

Yahoo!, and MSN. In fact, a recent research document published by the Institute of Electrical and Electronic Engineers (IEEE) discussed the support for the current OAI corpus of information by major search providers. The study found OAI coverage varied, with Yahoo! and Google harvesting the greatest percentage of the corpus at 65 and 45 percent respectively (McCown et al., 2006). The OAI-PMH protocol is discussed in greater

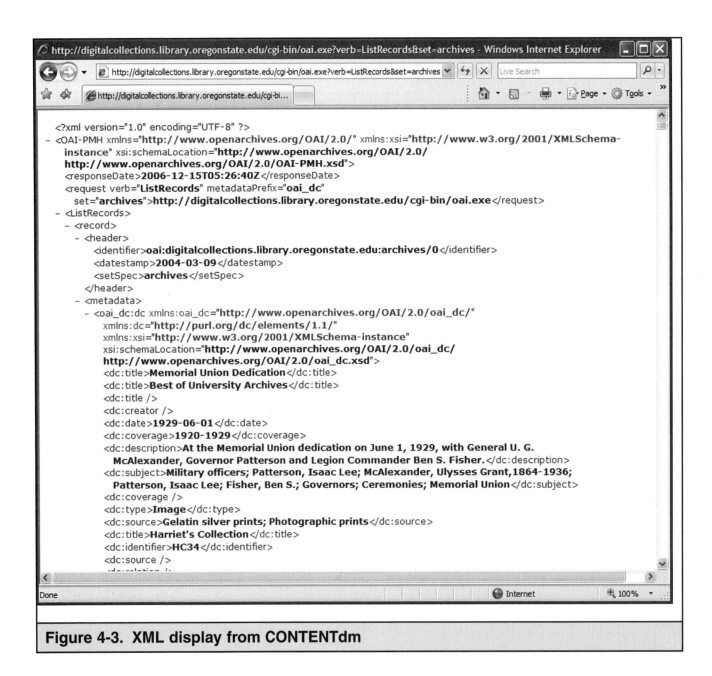

Figure 4-3. XML display from CONTENTdm

detail in Chapter 6, but the ability to provide XML-formatted data from one's digital repository is a valuable access method. When making decisions regarding a digital repository, one must look at how well the digital repository supports XML and XML-related technologies. One should ask the following questions:

1. Does the digital repository support XML-structured bibliographic and administrative metadata? Does the

digital repository support structural XML-based meta-data schemas like METS (Metadata Encoding and Transition Standard)?

2. Can the metadata be harvested or extracted? And can the data be extracted in XML?

3. Does the digital repository support SOAP or other XML query syntaxes?

4. Can my digital repository support multiple metadata formats?

Individuals should be able to answer each of the questions above about potential digital repository options. One must remember that an organization's digital repository will eventually be the store-house for many important documents and research. As such, one must ensure that the repository will make the metadata available in whatever format is needed, for the both present and the future.

WHY USE XML-BASED METADATA?

A common question that comes up during the planning stages of many digital projects is why utilize an XML-based schema at all for bibliographic description. Libraries seem to have gotten along just fine with MARC for the last 50 years—why the sudden change? Why should an organization adopt a new way of doing bibliographic description when no one sees a problem with the current one? It's a fair question and one that an organization needs to be prepared to answer. This is especially true if an organization has had no other projects using a non-MARC markup format. From the prospective of building a digital repository, here are five reasons to support such a transition.

XML IS HUMAN READABLE

One of the primary benefits associated with XML is that the generated metadata is human readable. This is very different from binary formats like PDF, MS Word, or even MARC21, which do not allow for easy inspection of data. Of course, many XML records are never meant to be read by an individual without the help of an XML reader, but this characteristic of XML (1) makes data more transparent, (2) makes the data less susceptible to data corruption, and (3) reduces the likelihood of data lockup.

Data transparency provides a number of immediate benefits. In a closed binary system, the actual document schema, or the rules that give the document meaning, are hidden from the user. In an XML-based metadata system, the document schema is always readily available. Users can inspect the data markup as well as any DTDs (document type definition) or namespace files defined within the document schema. This is a powerful aspect of XML; it opens one's data, which makes it easier for organizations or individuals to reuse the metadata with other systems. As noted, this is very different from other binary data formats, including MARC. Binary data formats, like MARC, are computer-generated formats, meaning that while they can be read with some difficulty by humans, they are not really meant to be human readable. Take the MARC record below:

01224nam 2200289Ka
45000001000900000003000600000900500170001500060019000320080041
00051035000180009204000180011004900009001280740023001370860001
70016008600170017722450132001942600133003263000004900459500000
54005085000021005625000019005835380016100602650005100763710006
3000814856004400087790700130092174837078-OCoLC-
20061102142329.0-m d f -061102s2005 dcu s f000 0 eng d-
a(GPO)99199980- aGPOcGPOdMvl- aORE1- a0431-C-65 (online)-0 aTD
4.87:H 78-0 aTD 4.87:H 78-00aFinal programmatic environmental impact
statement for horizontal launch and reentry of reentry vehiclesh[electronic
resource].- a[Washington, DC] :bDept. of Transportation, Federal Aviation
Administration, Office of Commercial Space Transportation,c[2005]- a1 v.
(various pagings) :bdigital, PDF flie.- aTitle from title screen (viewed on
Nov. 2, 2006).- a"December 2005."- a"014605.indd."- aMode of access:
Internet from the AST FAA web site. Address as of 11/2/06:
http://ast.faa.gov/files/pdf/ Final_FAA_PEIS_Dec_05.pdf; currrent access
via PURL.- 0aLaunch vehicles (Astronautics)zUnited States.-1 aUnited
States.bOffice of Commercial Space Transportation.-40uhttp:// purl.
access.gpo.gov/GPO/LPS75552- b24333487-

Figure 4-4. MARC Record

While much of this record can be read, it is itself not readable since the information in the records directory and leader must be unscrambled to determine the meaning of each data element. Likewise, this record is in MARC21, meaning that only users who are literate in MARC21 will be able to understand the encoded data found within this record. Contrast this record with the following XML representation of the same record (Figure 4-5).

```
<?xml version="1.0" encoding="utf-8"?>
<modsCollection xsi:schemaLocation="http://www.loc.gov/mods/v3
http://www.loc.gov/standards/mods/v3/mods-3-0.xsd"
xmlns="http://www.loc.gov/mods/v3"
xmlns:xsi="http://www.w3.org/2001/XMLSchema-instance">
 <mods version="3.0">
 <titleInfo>
 <title>Final programmatic environmental impact statement for horizontal
launch and reentry of reentry vehicles</title>
 </titleInfo>
 <name type="corporate">
 <namePart>United States</namePart>
 <namePart>Office of u67 ?ommercial Space Transportation
</namePart>
 </name>
 <typeOfResource>text</typeOfResource>
 <originInfo>
 <place>
 <placeTerm type="code" authority="marccountry">dcu</placeTerm>
 </place>
 <place>
 <placeTerm type="text">Washington, DC]</placeTerm>
 </place>
 <publisher>Dept. of Transportation, Federal Aviation Administration,
Office of Commercial Space Transportation</publisher>
 <dateIssued>[2005]</dateIssued>
 <dateIssued encoding="marc">2005</dateIssued>
 <issuance>monographic</issuance>
 </originInfo>
 <language>
 <languageTerm authority="iso639-2b" type="code">eng</languageTerm>
 </language>
 <physicalDescription>
 <form authority="marcform">electronic</form>
 <form authority="gmd">electronic resource</form>
 <extent>1 v. (variousÔpagings) : digital, PDF flie.</extent>
 </physicalDescription>
 <note>Title from title screen (viewed on Nov. 2, 2006).</note>
 <note>"December_2005."</note>
 <note>"014605.indd."</note>
 <note>Mode of access: Internet from the AST FAA web site. Address as
of 11/2/06: http://ast.faa.gov/files/pdf/Final_FAA_PEIS_Dec_05.pdf;
currrent access via PURL.</note>
 <subject authority="lcsh">
 <topic>Launch vehicles (Astronautics)</topic>
 <geographic>United States</geographic>
 </subject>
```

Figure 4-5. XML Representation of Figure 4-4

Continued

```
<classification authority="sudocs">TD 4.87:H_78</classification>
<classification authority="sudocs">TD 4.87:H_78</classification>
<classification authority="">TD 4.87:H_78</classification>
<classification authority="">TD 4.87:H_78</classification>
<identifier type="uri">http://purl.access. gpo.gov/GPO/ LPS75552 </identifier>
<location>
<url>http://purl.access.gpo.gov/GPO/LPS75552</url>
</location>
<recordInfo>
<recordContentSource
authority="marcorg">GPO</recordContentSource>
<recordCreationDate encoding="marc">061102</recordCreationDate>
 <recordChangeDate
encoding="iso8601">20061102142329.0</recordChangeDate>
 <recordIdentifier source="OCoLC">74837078</recordIdentifier>
</recordInfo>
</mods>
</modsCollection>
```

Figure 4-5. XML Representation of Figure 4-4 (continued)

While the XML record is admittedly more verbose, its use of human-readable tagging and hierarchical structure makes it easy for a person to read and parse it. While one could probably guess the title of the document described in the MARC record, the XML document leaves no doubt since the title is actually found in an XML tag marked *title*. This level of data transparency is a big benefit of using nonbinary data; the data format, structure, and relationships can be easily inspected and understood by experts and novices alike.

With all binary data formats, data corruption is always a big concern. Even within a digital repository, one must have systems in place to protect against data corruption of any binary data loaded into the system. Why is this an issue? Within a binary document, each byte retains a special meaning. The loss or modification of one of these bytes will invalidate the entire binary document, making it unreadable. While XML documents are susceptible to data corruption, the ability to correct an XML document if data corruption does occur should give organizations much more confidence in storing their metadata in an open format. Consider how this relates to Figure 4-4. As will be explained in Chapter 6, the MARC format utilizes fixed start positions and lengths to read field data within the record. This information is stored in the directory, that is, the first set of numerical bytes in the record. As a result, the modification of any of these bytes within the records directory, or the subtraction or addition of bytes in the record data itself (without the recalculation of the records directory), will result in an invalid or unreadable record. So, for example, with the addition of a single period to this record, after the word (online) (marked in bold in Figure 4-6), the MARC record becomes unreadable, potentially losing the stored data.

01224nam 2200289Ka
4500000100090000000030006000009005001700015006001900032008004100051035001800009204000180011004900009001280740023001370860017001600086001700177245013200194260013300326300004900459500005400508500002100562500001900583538016100602650005100763710006300814856004400087790700130092 1-74837078-OCoL
C-20061102142329.0-m d f -061102s2005 dcu s f000 0 eng
d- a(GPO)99199980- aGPOcGPOdMvl- aORE1- a0431-C-65 (online).-0
aTD 4.87:H 78-0 aTD 4.87:H 78-00aFinal programmatic environmental impact statement for horizontal launch and reentry of reentry vehiclesh[electronic resource]. a[Washington, DC]: bDept. of Transportation, Federal Aviation Administration, Office of Commercial Space Transportation, c[2005]- a1 v. (various pagings):bdigital, PDF flie. aTitle from title screen (viewed on Nov. 2, 2006).- a"December 2005." a"014605.indd."- aMode of access: Internet from the AST FAA web site. Address as of 11/2/06: http://ast.faa.gov/files/pdf/ Final_FAA_PEIS_Dec_05.pdf; currrent access via PURL.- 0aLaunch vehicles (Astronautics)zUnited States.-1 aUnited States.bOffice of Commercial Space Transportation.-40uhttp://purl.access.gpo.gov/GPO/ LPS75552- b24333487-

Figure 4-6. Unreadable MARC Record

Within an XML-encoded record, this type of data corruption isn't an issue. So long as the data continues to follow the strict XML encoding rules, the record will always be readable. Open-data XML formats ensure the long-term preservation of data since it will always be readable by the current technology. Binary formats tend to change and become obsolete through time, essentially locking up the data that they contain. Outside the library community, a number of state governments interested in preserving access to their born-digital documents are examining this. Will documents produced in products like MS Word or PDF be accessible in the future? Past experience tells us that they will not. Current versions of Adobe's PDF reader are not always compatible with its earliest formats, while MS Word struggles to open documents from much earlier versions. The difficulty with all binary documents is that data formats will become stale, and support for these older formats will disappear, "losing" the data. Open-data formats like XML ensure that a document's data is always accessible—even if only through visual inspection—preserving long-term access to information.

The benefits of an open-data structure cannot be overstated, particularly for an organization that may wish to customize or extend its digital repository software. The ability to read and understand the native metadata provides an invaluable tool for software and Web developers, in addition to preventing data from being locked or lost in unsupported binary formats.

XML OFFERS A QUICKER CATALOGING STRATEGY

In many cases, XML-based metadata schemas will lower many of the barriers organizations currently face when creating bibliographic metadata. One reason is the separation of administrative, structural, and bibliographic metadata. Administrative metadata would include the technical information about the digital object to be loaded into one's digital repository, while structural metadata stores a record of all digital objects, including metadata, that make up the "whole" record for the item. One benefit of many XML-based metadata schemas is that a number of specialized schemas exist for storing administrative metadata, separating this information from the descriptive metadata. Since many systems like DSpace and Fedora automatically generate administrative metadata for each object loaded into the repository system, the individual submitting material into a repository is only responsible for the actual description of his or her object. Moreover, unlike MARC, which is governed by AACR2, many XML-based systems provide few, if any, descriptive rules. This allows organizations to create custom metadata schemas and data dictionaries that best suit the metadata needs for a particular project. For example, at Oregon State University, the data dictionaries are utilized to define how Dublin Core elements for a particular project are to be defined and interpreted. Figure 4-7 is an example of something that might be utilized as a data dictionary for a project.

Field Label	Dublin Core	Description
Digital Collection Title	Title	"Best of the Oregon State University Archives"
Image Title	Title	First sentence of caption provided by photographer or OSU Archives staff.
Alternative Title	Title-Alternative	Used like a 740 or a 246 in MARC, this gives the cataloger the ability to provide alternate access points to a title. Use AACR2 guidelines to add when appropriate. Will display in CONTENTdm only when data is present.
Photographer/Studio	Creator	Includes the photographer or photograph studio when known.
Date	Date	Format should be [YYYY-MM-DD], so for items with years only, the format will be: 1910-00-00. Circa information should be added to the Time Period field.
Time Period	Coverage-Temporal	Selected from a control vocabulary, the time period will be used to represent the decade a particular image is from.
Date Search	NONE	This field will be used when constructing Date searches. This field will primarily be used to handle ca. dates by including 2 years before and after the ca. date. This is a hidden field.

Figure 4-7. Sample Data Dictionary

Continued

Description/Notes	Description	Includes complete caption information if not already contained in the Image Title field and any additional interpretive information.
Subject	Subject	Use LC TGM I: subject terms; available within CONTENTdm and on Cataloger's Desktop. LCSH will be used when an appropriate heading is not available in LC TGM.
Geographic Subject or Location Depicted	Coverage-Spatial	Geographic region—LC Authority File. Oregon entries, for the time being, will be entered as (Ore.) *Example: Benton County (Ore.)*
Object Type	Type	Genre—use LC TGM II. There will be several genre types for this project.
Original Collection	Source	Name of collection in which the image originated. *Example: Agriculture Photograph Collection (p. 40).*
Item Number	Identifier	Number of the image within its original collection.
Other Forms	Type	Form of image other than what was scanned—print (if neg. scanned), enlarged print, copy negative. Use LC TGM II terms.
Restrictions	Rights	"Permission to use must be obtained from the OSU Archives."
Transmission Data	Format	Provides brief information regarding the creation of the digital image. For most of the images in this project, the text should read: "Master scanned with Epson 1640XL scanner at 600 or 800 dpi. Image manipulated with Adobe Photoshop ver. 7.0."
File Name	Identifier	File names will be constructed using a 10-digit identifier constructed using the Project and image numbers. *Example: P003_00012.tif*
Project Comments & Questions	NONE	Internal note

Figure 4-7. Sample Data Dictionary (continued)

The data dictionary then defines for both the user and the submitter the necessary metadata fields, as well as the data to be used. In the case of this sample collection, one sees that a number of Dublin Core elements have been repeated, but that each element has a specific meaning within the data dictionary. Moreover, with this data dictionary, a DTD can be created to allow programmers in the library to easily interpret the metadata from this collection.

XML CAN REPRESENT MULTI-FORMATTED AND EMBEDDED DOCUMENTS

One of XML's strengths is its ability to represent hierarchical data structures and relationships. An XML record could be generated that contains information on a single document available in multiple physical formats with the unique features of each item captured within the XML data structure. Or, in the case of EAD, there is the ability to capture structured relationships between items and the collections of which they are a part.

```
<dsc id="a23" type="combined">
    <c01 level="series">
        <did>
            <unitid encodinganalog="099">Series I</unitid>
            <unittitle encodinganalog="245$a">Scientific Reports</unittitle>
            <unitdate calendar="gregorian" era="ce" encodinganalog="245$f"
                normal="1977/1992">1977-1992</unitdate>
            <physdesc><extent encodinganalog="300$a">2.5 cubic
            feet</extent><extent encodinganalog="300$a">8
boxes</extent></physdesc>
        </did>
        <scopecontent>
            <p>Series I consists of published and unpublished scientific papers on spotted owls and aspects
                of spotted owl biology, including the Mexican spotted owl; annual reports from demographic
                studies in the Pacific Northwest; and reports prepared by industry biologists, consultants, and
                scientists. Reports from committee groups are found in Series VIII. Committee Efforts. </p>
        </scopecontent>
        <c02 level="item">
            <did>
                <container type="box">1</container>
                <unitid encodinganalog="099">0001</unitid>
                <origination>
                    <persname encodinganalog="100"
role="creator">Postovit,
                        Howard</persname></origination>
                <unittitle encodinganalog="245$a">A Survey of the Spotted Owl in Northwestern Washington.
                Forest Industry Resource and Environment Program, Washington, D. C. 10 pages. (North Dakota
                State University)</unittitle>
                <unitdate era="ce" calendar="gregorian"
encodinganalog="245$f"
                    type="inclusive" normal="1977">1977</unitdate>
            </did>
            <scopecontent>
                <p>Surveys were conducted to locate spotted owls on public and private land in northwest
                    Washington during April-August 1976.</p>
                <p>report from zoology department at North Dakota State University</p>
                <p>#SCIENTIFIC REPORT; STOC MONITORING; WASHINGTON STATE</p>
            </scopecontent>
        </c02>
```

Figure 4-8. Part of an EAD Record

In the above example, we see an EAD snippet in which a series and items have been defined. This makes it possible for an EAD record to capture the structural relationships that each child has with its parent, which, in turn, offers EAD systems interesting opportunities in terms of the display and linking of elements within document. This allows the metadata object the ability to become an information object itself. This aspect allows XML metadata to exist outside of its parent systems and act almost as a surrogate for the object that it describes, making the data more meaningful to other organizations, such as libraries or search providers.

XML METADATA BECOMES "SMARTER"

How exactly does metadata get smarter? In an XML document, metadata fields can have attributes and properties that can be acted upon. Moreover, with XSLT and XPath, data can be manipulated and reordered without having to rework the source XML document. XSLT commands like xsl:sort and position(); last(); xsl:for-each; xsl:if; and xsl:when offer users the ability to act upon data within the XML document by tag, attribute, or tag contents, separating content from display. But this extends beyond simple data manipulation. The ability to illustrate relationships and interlinks between documents—the ability to store content or links to content within the metadata container—each of these options is available through XML or an XML-based system. As already noted, the document becomes an information object itself, having its own "metadata" and properties that can be leveraged both inside and outside its parent system. Systems like Dspace and Fedora, which can utilize and produce object-oriented metadata objects like METS, can be utilized outside their parent systems as surrogate items. Surrogates can then be utilized within a remote system to stand in for, and link to, the parent item. Most digital repository systems create a number of metadata objects for each document stored, creating metadata objects for structure, administration, and bibliographic data. METS-based systems use the METS format to bind these individual objects together as a cohesive whole, but in doing so, they create "smart" metadata that are their own information objects.

XML IS NOT JUST A LIBRARY STANDARD

Traditionally, libraries have had very few vendor choices for software purchases or hiring outside consulting. The main reason for this is the standards on which libraries have become reliant. MARC is a good example. No other profession uses MARC or the AACR2 descriptive framework. As a result, only a handful of "library" vendors support the creation and use of MARC data. Libraries inevitably have few ILS choices—with larger organizations essentially having to choose from two or three larger vendors. So while these "library" standards have served the library world well for a great many years, they have also perpetuated a retarding of software development within the library community. Today, library "innovation" is essentially pushed by a handful of large vendors providing expansive, monolithic systems. To a large degree, the library communities' continued reliance on MARC and AACR2 has stagnated library development into the current generation. XML promises to change some of these problems. First, XML is not a library standard. While the library and information sciences community has created XML-based schemas like MODS, METS, and Dublin Core, the fact that these schemas are in XML allows libraries to look outside the traditional library vendors to a broader development community. For the first time, libraries can truly start to leverage the larger open-source community and not simply a handful of open-source developers that happen to work in libraries. Additionally, libraries are able to leverage a much larger knowledge base, as libraries are able to look for individuals with XML experience rather than library experience in libraries.

FUTURE OF SOFTWARE DEVELOPMENT

To a large extent, the future is now, as more and more software development moves towards an XML-centric approach. Large organizations like Google and Yahoo! are increasingly making API access to their platforms available through SOAP or XML gateways. Likewise, users of these services are responding by building tools and services known as mashups around these XML-based APIs. Mashup is a relatively new term used to describe a set of Web tools or services that combine content from more than one source to create a new tool or service. Mashups have allowed users to customize how services and information are offered to them. For example, markovic.com provides a simple mashup that links eBay with Google's Mapping service. This mashup allows users who want to purchase a product to see where the individual items will be shipping from, as well as what locations have the highest concentration of auctions for an item.

Figure 4-9 shows a screen shot of this service just after January 1, 2007, looking for the number of individuals currently selling Nintendo Wiis on eBay. Not only does this service provide a map of the sellers' locations, but clicking on each item on the map pulls the title, short description, and thumbnail from eBay and renders it as a tooltip on the map. Services like this one illustrate how users who are looking for new ways to build bridges between commonly used services and the expansion of information organizations providing XML-based API are facilitating this growth.

Additionally, client applications like Open Office and Microsoft's MS Office platforms are moving away from the more traditional binary file formats to XML-based storage formats. Even within the library community, companies like OCLC have become more active in creating registry and look-up services for ILL that utilize SOAP-based interfaces and in providing metadata via OAI. The move towards standardization on XML

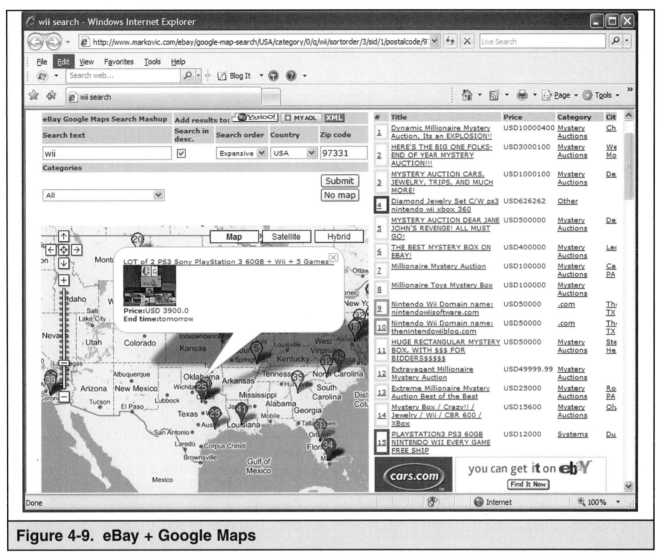

Figure 4-9. eBay + Google Maps

Source: eBay+Google search: www.markovic.com/ebay/google-map-search/

platforms has already begun—and it's up to everyone in the information community to follow.

Current-generation digital repositories offer a number of metadata options. Users wanting to make Qualified Dublin Core their primary descriptive metadata format would do well to examine DSpace, Fedora, or CONTENTdm. Each software solution offers the ability to create customized data dictionaries for discreet collections and offers the ability to batch import digital objects and metadata. DSpace and Fedora have a more formal approach, using METS importing methodology. CONTENTdm uses a tab delimited approach. What's more, each software package offers solutions for plugging new metadata schemas into the software; this means they are flexible enough to grow as standards change.

WEB SERVICES AND SOAP

Related to XML is SOAP, the Simple Object Access Protocol. SOAP is a standard method for generating API for Web-based applications. As a digital repository's content and traffic grow, users of the repository may want to access the repository's content outside the traditional user interface. Just as likely, the digital repository's parent organization will want to integrate content from the repository with other organizational information. Traditionally, this type of integration was done by exporting bibliographic data from a repository and mirroring it within an outside database. At Oregon State University, this type of process is used for many applications that utilize data from the ILS system. For example, the new books list (http://osulibrary.oregonstate.edu/new/newbooks.htm) is simply a static HTML page that is regenerated the first of each week through a static data dump from the database. Ideally, this type of process would be run directly against the ILS system, allowing the list to be built dynamically, but a lack of API access to the system hampers such development efforts. In the same way, a digital repository that lacks Web services support greatly reduces the amount of integration that an organization can accomplish with it's content. Really Simple Syndication (RSS) services and federated search services are just two tools that can benefit from a Web services API.

Web services also promote remixability, an often-neglected concept that is of vital importance when considering the development of any Web-based resource. Remixability, for the purposes of this text, is the concept associated with the ability to integrate, or mix, data with other services. The development of Web services emphasizes an organization understanding that its users will have uses for its data that they currently do not understand or anticipate. By providing Web service access and the ability to remix and reuse one's digital content, service users will find themselves able to create new tools using an organization's service offerings.

A number of different Web services techniques exist: common object broker request architecture (COBRA) or Java's remote method invocation (RMI) methodology, to name a few, but the SOAP Web services style has the most traction within the library community. SOAP is a communications protocol that runs over HTTP and uses XML as a common method of information exchange. What makes the use of SOAP advantageous is twofold. First, SOAP has become so ubiquitous that all major operating systems include all the components necessary to create and communicate with SOAP-based services. Second, SOAP's communication protocol is generally firewall-friendly since it communicates on the same port as normal Web traffic. As mentioned, within the library community, a number of SOAP-based protocols exist, the most important being search and retrieval URL (SRU). SRU is an object-oriented Web services protocol that the Library of Congress and partners are developing as a replacement for Z39.50. For example, a search of the Library of Congress's catalog for an item with the title Map of Oregon (http://z3950.loc.gov:7090/voyager?operation=searchRetrieve&version=1.1 &recordPacking=xml&startRecord=1&maximumRecords=20&query= dc.title%3D%22Map+of+oregon), would result in the following information shown in Figure 4-10.

Looking at Figure 4-10, one notices that the response is just a simple XML document made up of some container elements and the records themselves. This makes the information easily parsable for inclusion into other resources. That is essentially the power of Web services—the ability to allow individuals to utilize content outside the confines of the application in which it resides. It is a powerful tool for

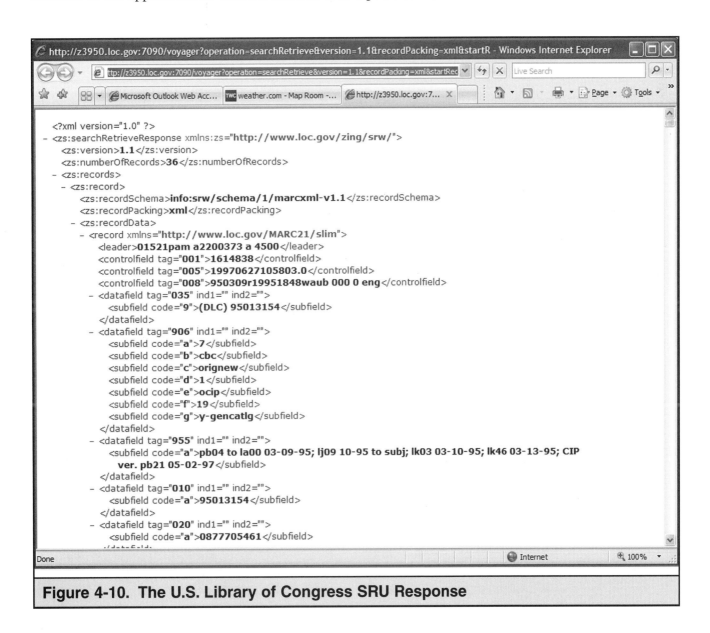

Figure 4-10. The U.S. Library of Congress SRU Response

the organization and user alike as users are free to create mashups utilizing the Web services API found in a digital repository. The net effect of this is to allow users to bring content of interest from a digital repository into their workflows, wherever that may be. Whether that means bringing images from CONTENTdm or DSpace into a personalized Web space (Figure 4-11) or using images found on the Web to play hamster sudoku (www.beckysweb.co.uk/sudoku/flickrsudoku.asp), it allows users to access information where they want it and to bring information to wherever they want to use it.

Figure 4-11. Personalized Google Home Page with CONTENTdm Widget

Building or utilizing an online Web services is a relatively simple process. In Figure 4-11, the Web service was written on top of CON-TENTdm's OAI server in PHP. In Figure 4-12, the Google Class from the script has been provided. This class takes the data pulled from the OAI server and restructures the data into the XML response format required by Google's widget service. With this small snippet of code on top of the CON-TENTdm OAI server, anyone can pull images from Oregon State University's CONTENTdm image collections onto their Google home page.

```
class Google {
function header($title, $link, $date) {
$string = '<?xml version="1.0" encoding="UTF-8"?>' . "\n" .
'<Module>' . "\n" .
'<ModulePrefs title="' . $title . '" scrolling="true" />' . "\n" .
'<Content type="html">' . "\n" .
'<![CDATA[';
return $string;
}

function footer() {
$string = ']]>' .
'</Content>' .
'</Module>';
return $string;
}

function buildItem($DCValues) {
$string = "<div>\n";
$string .= $DCValues["description"];
$string .= "</div>\n";
return $string;
}

function encodeDescription($set, $description, $title, $uri) {
$tarr = explode("/", $uri);
$parr = explode(",", $tarr[count($tarr)-1]);
$ptr = $parr[1];
$set = $parr[0];
$string = "<img src=\"" . BaseURL . "cgi-bin/getimage.exe?CISOROOT=/" .
$set . "&CISOPTR=" . $ptr .
"&DMSCALE=10.5&DMWIDTH=250&DMHEIGHT=250\" border=\"0\" /><br
/>";
$string .= "<a href=\"" . $uri . "\">$title</a>";
return $string;
}

}
```

Figure 4-12. CONTENTdm Google Widget Snippet, in PHP

Figure 4-12 gives a simple demonstration of some of the benefits of providing functionality that allows data to be remixable. In this case, a simple API is built on top of a digital image collection that provided a feed of new images to a personalized Google Home page. So what? The point of this demonstration is not to show how data can be added to Google, but to emphasize the ease with which services promoting remixability can be integrated with other tools that the service's users employ every day. Libraries are deluding themselves if they believe that users only make use of the tools and services provided by their organization. Rather, an organization's users make use of a myriad of tools and services that collect information from a variety of different sources. Blog aggregators like Bloglines or Google's Feedreader are excellent examples of how user preferences for getting information on news and entertainment are changing. RSS feedreaders allow users to pull content from hundreds of different sources and read them using a single application. To a large degree, creating digital collections that promote remixability does the same thing. It encourages users to interact with data within their own workflows. The above Google widget demonstrates this point. While this information could easily be gotten from the OSU digital collection pages, the widget makes it possible to pull this information, which is outside of that context, and insert it into the context in which other information is aggregated. In this case, that location is a personalized Google Home page; however, it could easily have been an RSS feedreader or a library portal. The underlying concept is the same: Web services promote the ability for users to interact with data on their own terms within their own workflows, encouraging greater user of library services.

Furthermore, most modern scripting and high-level programming languages make the process of consuming Web services requests a fairly simplistic process. In the case of SOAP, a Web service would expose what is known as a Web services description language (WSDL) file from the Web server. A WSDL file is basically an XML-formatted file that is then utilized by the program/scripting language to access methods exposed directly through the API. For example, in Ruby, a SOAP request would look like the following example:

```
Require 'soap/wsdlDriver'
driver = SOAP::WSDLDriverFactory.new("http://servername.com/
query/wsdl").create_rpc_driver
results = driver.Search("dc:title=Map of oregon", 1, 10)
```

Figure 4-13. Ruby WSDL Example

Current-generation programming languages continue to lower the bar, providing relatively novice users with the tools necessary to make use of developing Web services. There has been a long-standing myth that Web services or Web-based API only benefit a few übertechnical users who may understand the service. However, this is no longer the case. As Figure 4-13 illustrates, current generation programming languages are creating novice-friendly tools and frameworks that lower the accessibility barrier to formerly expert topics.

SHARING YOUR SERVICES

Given the relatively low barriers to SOAP and Web services in general, the question really comes down to how much control an organization is willing to give up when it comes to content. Organizations considering a digital repository need to ask the following questions when considering whether to offer Web services access to their systems.

1. Is the organization comfortable giving up some control over how content is utilized? This is a big question to consider since users occasionally have a quirky way of doing unexpected things. The Hamster sudoku game is a benign example of a user repurposing images in a way never intended by the content owners. However, these images could just as easily show up on a Web site that the content owners would find inappropriate. Is that something the organization can live with? If not, then it is necessary to consider carefully what types of access the organization is comfortable providing.

2. Can the organization support it? In the case of providing Web services access to one's digital repository, support will need to be twofold. First, the organization needs to be willing to provide infrastructure support. Were a digital collection to build a popular Web service, how would the additional traffic affect the quality of the service? And second, the organization needs to be willing to provide user support through the creation of documentation and other services. The two code samples in Figure 4-12 and Figure 4-13 offer relatively simple examples of how one might utilize a Web service. Can the organization provide support for these types of API usage? What kind of programming staff is currently available?

3. Can the digital repository exist outside the organization's existing information infrastructure? If the answer to this question is no, then you likely will need API

access to the digital repository. At that point, one would just need to decide whether to make that access public or private.

Each of these questions should be carefully considered and the potential pitfalls weighed against benefits to outside users. Of the three questions, the ability to give up some control over the content in one's digital repository is likely to be the most difficult. Given the care and thought that often goes into the creation of a digital repository, it is understandable for an organization to want to "protect" their brand and their content. Digital repository builders should consider, however, that this ability to provide remote access mechanisms is what the current Web 2.0 and future Web 3.0 frameworks are built on. The ability to dynamically query and repurpose content is a powerful tool for all users of a digital repository. What's more, information organizations can set an example to their commercial vendors in regards to open-access for digital information. As a whole, the information community continues to work with their vendors, that are data aggregators with traditionally closed publishing models like Lexis Nexis or Elsevier, to provide an unmediated form of access to their content. Some vendors, like OCLC, are actively undertaking projects to provide content available through SOAP services while other vendors still need some gentle nudging. The information community can be a role model of sorts by making its own data available with as few access restrictions as possible.

SUMMARY

When building or considering a digital repository platform, careful thought is needed for all aspects of the platform's implementation. As previous chapters have stated, a digital repository will require new workflows, new acquisitions models, and new responsibilities from an organization's information technology (IT) departments. And while it might be tempting to simply let the repository platform guide your decisions relating to metadata and metadata accesses, it is important to resist. Aside from the content, the metadata is the single most important part of the digital repository. And in many cases, it is likely to be the most valuable component of the digital repository, given the large investments that go into creating metadata and the value that outside users and data harvesters place on that metadata. As such, digital repository builders should weigh their available options, selecting—from the myriad metadata schemas available—the schema that best suits the needs of the organization, its users, and the bibliographic description of the repository's content.

Digital repository builders also need to consider how much access and how truly available the content of their repositories ought to be. Technologies like SOAP hold the keys to opening a digital repository beyond the walls of the application platform, allowing other services like search engines or users to search, harvest, or integrate data from one digital repository into their own context or workflow. Moreover, one must consider how Web services could enable an organization to better integrate their digital repository content into the organization's existing information architecture. And ultimately, it needs to be determined how many different access points does an organization wish to provide and what metadata schemas will be needed to support these points of access.

REFERENCES

eBay + Google Map Search. Available: www.markovic.com/ebay/google-map-search/

McCown, Frank, Xiaoming Liu, Michael L. Nelson, and Mohammad Zubair. 2006. "Search Engine Coverage of the OAI-PMH Corpus." *IEEE Computer Society* (March/April) 10, No. 2: 68.

OCLC. "WorldCat.org." Available: www.worldcat.org.

W3C Schema Working Group. "W3C XML Schema." Available: www.w3.org/XML/Schema

W3C XForms Working Group. "XForms 1.0 (2nd Ed.)" (Last updated March 14, 2006). Available: www.w3.org/TR/xforms/

W3C XHTML Working Group, "XHTML 1.0: The Extensible HyperText Markup Language (2nd edition)." (Last updated August 1, 2002). Available: www.w3.org/TR/xhtml1/

W3C XLink Working Group. "XML Linking Language (XLink) Version 1.0." (Last updated June 27, 2001). Available: www.w3.org/TR/xlink/

W3C XML Working Group. "XML Path Language." (Last updated November 16, 1999). Available: www.w3.org/TR/xpath

W3C XPointer Working Group. "XML Pointer Language (XPointer)." (Last updated August 16, 2002). Available: www.w3.org/TR/xptr/

W3C XQuery Working Group. "XQuery 1.0: An XML Query Language." (Last updated January 23, 2007). Available: www.w3.org/TR/xquery/

W3C XSLT Working Group. "XSL Transformations (XSLT)." (Last updated November 16, 1999). Available: www.w3.org/TR/xslt

5 METADATA FORMATS

When digital library platforms first started emerging, users had few options when it came to metadata frameworks for their bibliographic descriptions. Systems tended to support a single descriptive schema, like Unqualified Dublin Core or the system's own closed internal metadata schema. This situation meant that digital repository implementors had to decide upfront what metadata schema would be sufficient for use in describing the various materials that might be eventually loaded into the digital repository system. Once a digital repository system was chosen, all metadata decisions would be left to the digital repository platform, giving the implementer few options for customization or expansion. And while this approach would lead to a universal descriptive format on the digital repository platform (in many respects, emulating the ubiquity of MARC with ILS), its net effect was to create metadata that was in many cases too broad to be useful within any meaningful context.

Today, digital repository software has become much more flexible in the sharing and creation of metadata. This allows implementers to store bibliographic data in one of many current metadata schemas, creating metadata storehouses that are heterogeneous in nature and that can interoperate with a greater variety of systems. This flexibility allows organizations to take a much closer look at how they describe different material types and at the granularity of description for each item appearing in the digital repository. While this chapter will not provide a comprehensive guide for any one metadata schema, it examines a handful of metadata schemas currently used by digital repository implementers, looking at how and when specific schemas maybe used.

METADATA PRIMITIVES

Considering the significant investment organizations make in metadata creation, it seems fitting to start this chapter by looking at why the ability to utilize a heterogeneous metadata system is important. The most

117

obvious reason is that libraries function within a very homogenous environment. Since 1969, when the Library of Congress first released the specifications for the MARC framework, libraries have optimized their workflows and systems to support the creation of MARC records. Even when utilizing non-MARC formats, libraries still tend to rely on the traditional AACR2 guidelines when creating metadata. In general, librarians want to maintain the homogenous nature of their bibliographic content while experimenting with non-MARC formats. However, no single metadata element set accommodates the functional requirements of all applications, and as the Web dissolves boundaries, it becomes increasingly important to be able to also cross boundaries (Johnson, 2001). For many organizations, the digital repository represents the first significant foray into the world of non-MARC metadata. And while many may find themselves wishing that ALA or the Library of Congress would step up and create a single, universal XML metadata schema that adopts current cataloging rules (AACR2, RDA [Resource Description and Access]) (Johnson, 2001: 86), we find ourselves in a place where multiple standard formats have been developed to allow description to happen in the schema best suited for a particular material type.

In 2002, Roy Tennant wrote his now famous (or infamous, depending on your perspective) column calling for the death of the MARC metadata format (Tennant, 2002). He argued that libraries would be unable to move forward so long as MARC was being utilized as the primary descriptive metadata schema, provoking the ongoing debate between whether libraries should use MARC or XML. However, different schemas serve different purposes, so it is normally not productive to think in terms of using only MARC or only XML. In fact, much of Tennant's dismissal of MARC relates to the general rules that govern MARC record creation.

Rather than debate MARC versus XML, it would be better to ask whether AACR2 is still relevant within today's digital environment, particularly given that AACR2 was created for a print-centric world where catalogs only contained printed cards. In fact, Tennant seems to make this argument in a later article (Tennant, 2004), in which he steps back from calling for the death of MARC, arguing for a new way of thinking about bibliographic infrastructure. Today organizations like the Library of Congress question the need for traditional controlled access points (Calhoun, 2006) and the future of metadata creation (Marcum, 2004), leaving libraries to struggle with how digital materials should be described and accessed in local and remote systems. This does not mean that the current descriptive rules should not be used at all as an organization begins its digital repository efforts, but, rather, that it must recognize that the current bibliographic descriptive rules by themselves may be insufficient. However, before taking a closer look at some of the common XML metadata formats that are supported using today's digital repository software, a very brief look at the MARC metadata schema is in order.

MARC

As previously noted, MARC was originally developed in 1969 by the Library of Congress as a standard method for transferring bibliographic data between systems on electromagnetic tapes. Today, MARC is *the* language for transmitting data between ILS systems within the library community. And while very few digital repositories actually handle MARC records directly, a handful can export their bibliographic metadata in MARC or provide an easy path to the creation of MARC records for stored content.

Within the library community, MARC itself is often misunderstood. Often when librarians think of MARC, they are thinking of the fields and tags defined by the physical rules governing the input of data, like AACR2. Figure 5-1 shows a representation of a MARC21 record of an electronic thesis from Oregon State University.

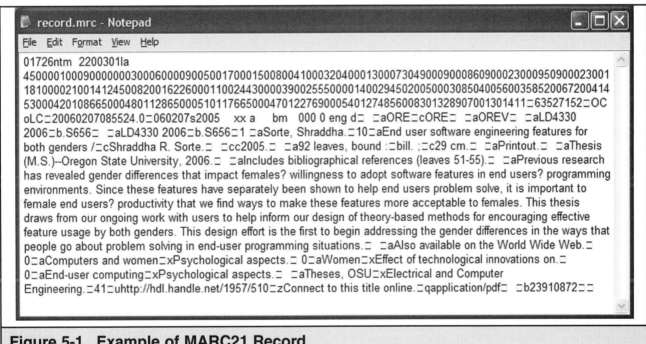

Figure 5-1. Example of MARC21 Record

These rules define what data elements can be placed within a particular MARC field, creating specific "flavors" of MARC. For example, one could find flavors for MARC21 (a merging of USMARC, CANMARC and UKMARC), CHMARC (China), FINMARC (Finland), or UNIMARC (universal). Currently, the Library of Congress recognizes approximately 40 different

MARC flavors in use around the world (U.S. Library of Congress, accessed: 2006).

Technically, MARC is nothing more than a binary data format made up of three distinct parts: (1) the leader, (2) the directory, and (3) the bibliographic data. The leader makes up the first 24 bytes and contains information about the MARC record itself. The leader includes the total length of the record, notes start position of the field data, the character encoding, record type, and encoding level of the record. Within the leader, one of MARC's most glaring limitations is made visible. A MARC record reserves just 5 bytes to define the total length of the record. This means that the length of a valid MARC record can never exceed a total length, including directory and field data, of 99,999 bytes. And it should also be noted that the length is indeed calculated against bytes, not characters—an important distinction when using Unicode scripts, since a single Unicode character is made up of multiple bytes. For example, an *e* with an acute accent (é) is a single Unicode character, but is made up of 2 distinct bytes. Within the MARC record leader and directory, this single character would need to be represented as 2 bytes for the record/field lengths to be valid. This behavior allows Unicode records to be readable, or backwards compatible, with non-Unicode-aware systems.

The dictionary, which starts at byte 25, is made up of numerous 12-byte blocks, with each block representing a single bibliographic field. Each block then contains a field label (bytes 0–2), the field length (bytes 3–6) and the position relative to the bibliographic data (bytes 7–11). Field data is limited to 9,999 bytes given that field length can only be expressed as a 4-byte value. Figure 5-1 shows the following example from the directory: 245008200162 (third line from the top, 14 characters in). This block can be broken down into the following sections:

- Field label: 245
- Field length: 0082
- Start position: 00162

This information tells a MARC parser how to extract the 245 field data from the MARC record. This same record broken into a text view (Figure 5-2), shows how a MARC parser treats this information. In the Figure 5-2 version of the record, a MARC parser has read the leader and directory and has extracted the MARC data into a more visually friendly format.

A number of technical limitations make MARC a poor choice for a digital repository. First and foremost, as a metadata schema, MARC is virtually unknown outside of the library community. This fact limits the number of available partners or vendors that can be called on to create or support systems utilizing the MARC record format. Moreover, it limits data sharing primarily to the library community. Second, the record-size restrictions limit the amount and type of bibliographic content that can be provided. Within the XML formats described later in this chapter, records

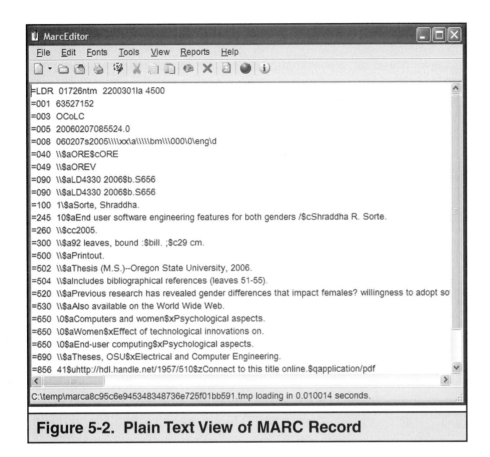

Figure 5-2. Plain Text View of MARC Record

can be created containing a much richer set of data, including large data elements like table of contents, abstracts, summaries, or even the full text of an item. In addition, within XML formats, rich content like images and documents can be embedded into the metadata records themselves, making these records information objects.

MARC21XML

MARC21XML is a lossless XML representation of MARC with one notable exception. Unlike MARC, which supports the MARC-8 character set, MARC21XML exclusively supports the UTF-8 (8-bit UCS/Unicode Transformation Format) character set, meaning that character data in MARC-8 must be rectified to UTF-8. MARC21XML was first proposed by Library of Congress in 1994 as one potential method for migrating data currently in MARC format into an XML schema. However, MARC21XML has found only sparse use within the library community: primarily as a data crosswalking mechanism for MARC between other metadata schemas. For example, MarcEdit, a free application written by Terry Reese (2006), uses MARC21XML as the control metadata schema when moving data between differing library metadata schemas. Figure 5-3, for example, is a MARC21XML representation of the sample record found in Figure 5-1. This representative record was generated using MarcEdit.

Figure 5-3. MARC21XML Record

Looking at Figure 5-3, one can see that MARC21XML is an XML-based metadata format; because of this, few of the technical restrictions in MARC are inherently present with MARC21XML. For example, MARC21XML has no predefined record-size limit, which means that users could embed large data elements into the XML-record. Moreover, like all XML-based metadata schemas, MARC21XML can have data such as images or documents embedded directly into the metadata.

While MARC21XML does not contain the same limitations of MARC at the technical level, these limitations do exist. However, they are limitations imposed because MARC21XML is required to be a lossless representation of MARC. For MARC21XML to be utilized as initially conceived, it must inherit the same technical limitations as the MARC framework if compatibility between the two formats is to remain.

DUBLIN CORE

Serendipity can be a funny thing. Small decisions or discussions can have a lasting effect on the world around you. For example, in 1980–1981, David J. Bradley, a computer engineer at IBM, wrote a few lines of code that would forever change the way that people interact with present-day computers. Writing the code as an "Easter egg," or backdoor, for computer developers, Bradley introduced the three-key sequence combination, CTRL+ALT+DEL. In what Bradley would later describe in an interview as "not a memorable event," his few lines of code were designed specifically to give developers a set of escape sequences to do administrative functions before powering down a computer and was never meant to be seen by the general public (Bradley, accessed: 2006). However, this three-key sequence has become one of the primary methods that computer users today perform the actions of logging on/off, locking, and powering down. In much the same way, Dublin Core has surprisingly become one of the most important metadata frameworks within the library community and beyond.

HISTORY

The history of Dublin Core goes back to the Second International WWW Conference in 1994. During the conference, Yuri Rubinsky (SoftQuad), Stuart Weibel, Eric Miller, Terry Noreault of OCLC (Online Computer Library Center) and Joseph Hardin of the National Center for Supercomputing Applications (NCSA) had a hallway conversation focusing on the current difficulties of finding materials on the Internet (Caplan, 2003). As a result of that conversation, OCLC and the NCSA decided to team up and collectively look for a solution to this growing problem. So, in 1995, in Dublin, Ohio, OCLC and the NCSA led a joint workshop called the OCLC/NCSA Metadata Workshop. The workshop was to focus on three primary goals:

1. Decide what descriptive elements would be needed to promote findability of all documents on the Web.
2. Explore how to create a solution that would be flexible for past, present, and future online publication on the Web.
3. Explore how to promote the usage of such a solution if it exists.

Outside of this meeting, the participants were able to produce an agreed-upon set of descriptive elements: 15 general descriptive terms that could be universally applied to virtually any resource available on the Web at the time. From those initial 15 elements, the Dublin Core Initiative was born.

Originally, the Dublin Core schema was defined primarily as a method for describing Web documents, like Web sites, through the use of meta tags within a documents header. These tags would then provide a reliable mechanism for search engines to harvest and index materials since metadata elements like titles, descriptions, authors, and even subject access points could be easily identifiable. A number of tools were created to help users wishing to markup their Web documents (Powell, accessed 2006).

Figure 5-4 provides a simple illustration of how Dublin Core was to be used on the Web. Prior to the Dublin Core specification, Web-page developers had few options when it came to tagging documents for indexing by

```
<link rel="schema.DC" href="http://purl.org/dc/elements/1.1/">
<meta name="DC.title" lang="en" content="Dublin Core Meta tags – Test
  Document">
<meta name="DC.creator" content="Terry Reese">
<meta name="DC.subject" lang="en" content="DCMI; Dublin Core
  Metadata Initiative; DC META Tags">
<meta name="DC.description" lang="en" content="Examples of Dublin
  Core META Tags.">
<meta name="DC.publisher" content="Terry Reese">
<meta name="DC.contributor" content="DCMI Dublin Core Metadata
  Initiative">
<meta name="DC.date" scheme="W3CDTF" content="2004-01-01">
<meta name="DC.type" scheme="DCMIType" content="Text">
<meta name="DC.format" scheme="IMT" content="text/html">
<meta name="DC.identifier" content="http://oregonstate.edu/
  meta-tags/dublin/">
<meta name="DC.source" content="http://oregonstate.edu/meta-tags/">
<meta name="DC.language" scheme="RFC1766" content="en">
<meta name="DC.relation" content="http://oregonstate.edu/meta-tags/">
<meta name="DC.coverage" content="World">
<meta name="DC.rights"
  content="http://oregonstate.edu/about/disclaim.htm">
```

Figure 5-4. Dublin Core Meta Tag Example

search systems. Dublin Core's syntax made this possible by giving Web developers a standard set of tags that could be used to create uniform metadata for documents published on the Web. At the same time, this gave search providers a standard set of metadata from which to harvest and index. However, in general, this concept wasn't very successful, because search engines tended to ignore meta tagging as a result of tag abuse. Approved by the American National Standards Institute (ANSI) (2001), the Dublin Core Initiative schema has since been accepted as an ANSI standard (Z39.85 2001) and an ISO (International Standards Organization) standard (15836) and has been adopted for formal use by a number of national governments (Australia, UK, Canada, etc.).

ELEMENTS

The Dublin Core itself is made up of 15 central, unqualified elements known as Unqualified Dublin Core. These elements represent the 15 agreed-upon core descriptive elements shared by all published documents. The core elements provide document publishers with a known set of metadata values that can be applied to create minimal-level metadata records that can then be utilized by any system that is Dublin Core aware. However, this comes at a cost. Unqualified Dublin Core metadata suffers from a low level of granularity—much of the contextual information about the data within a record is retained only at the most basic level.

Figure 5-5 shows the Dublin Core equivalent to the MARC record found in Figure 5-1. Initially, it should be easy to see how the record has been flattened, as information relating to subjects and classification have been removed from the sample record. At present, Unqualified Dublin Core defines the following 15 elements (Dublin Core Metadata Initiative, accessed: 2006):

- **Title**
  Stores all title information about a piece. When working with Unqualified Dublin Core, the title field can store the primary title as well as alternate titles.

- **Creator**
  Notes all individuals or organizations responsible for the creation of a document.

- **Contributor**
  Notes individuals, organizations, and the like that contributed to the publication of a document. This could include editors and sponsoring organizations. For individuals with a background in AACR2, the contributor field is often a difficult one since it has no clear equivalent in MARC. For this reason, the contributor field is often ignored when crosswalking Dublin Core data into MARC.

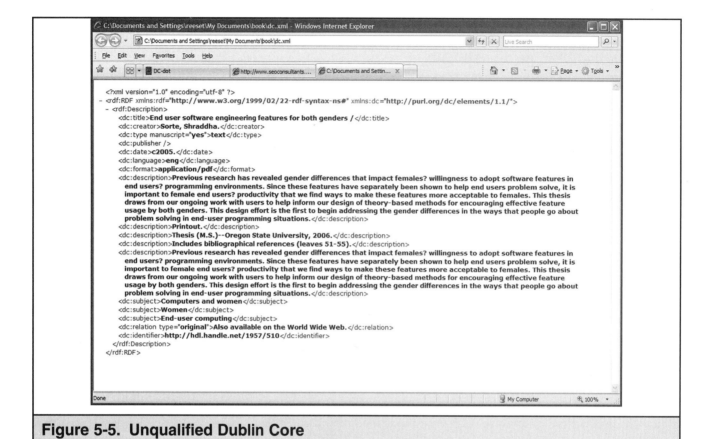

Figure 5-5. Unqualified Dublin Core

- **Description**

  Stores information about an item. This includes information like notes, abstracts, table of contents, summaries, and the like. For all practical purposes, the description element is a free-text element where any information about an item can be stored.

- **Date**

  Stores temporal information relating to the life cycle of the document. This includes information about the publication, creation, or modification of the document.

- **Subject**

  Stores topical information about a document. This includes information like keywords, phrases, controlled vocabularies, or classification codes.

- **Coverage**

  Stores contextual information about a document as it relates to spatial and temporal information. For example, coverage could be utilized to store the time period that a document's content covers or note the spatial area of a document's study area.

- **Publisher**
  Notes the individual, organization, or entity responsible for the publication of the described resource.

- **Rights**
  Identifies any licenses, restrictions, or copyright statements covering the described resource or relating to the accessibility of the described resource.

- **Format**
  Identifies the physical or digital aspects of the described resource. This includes the dimensions and material type for a physical item or a description of the digital resources type.

- **Language**
  Notes the language or languages used in the described resource.

- **Relation**
  Used to note materials related to the described resource.

- **Source**
  Used primarily for reproductions or for resources created from a larger work. The source element notes the parent document from which the described resource was derived.

- **Type**
  Notes the document's type. This field traditionally references a controlled vocabulary like DCMITYPE to provide a known list of available document types. For example, the DCMITYPE list defines resource types like moving images, image, and text.

- **Identifier**
  Specifies a unique identifier like a URI, control number, or classification number that can uniquely identify the resource.

Another element, audience, was added later and placed outside of the core element set. While many consider audience to be the unofficial sixteenth core element, it technically exists as a refinement to the original set. Within many of these elements, the Dublin Core has made available a set of refinements, attributes that can be utilized to refine the meaning of a specific element and to provide additional context. This is known as Qualified Dublin Core. For example, a qualifier exists for title, so one can note if a title is an alternative title or not. Likewise, a number of qualifiers exist for the date element for noting the creation and modification date. The qualifiers allow metadata creators to create documents with a greater level of metadata granularity than would be found in an Unqualified Dublin Core record without breaking compatibility with most Dublin Core data parsers.

STRENGTHS

Today, Dublin Core is one of the most widely used metadata schemas within the library community. Many digital repository platforms, like DSpace and CONTENTdm, utilize Dublin Core as their primary metadata language. The reason Dublin Core has been so successful is its greatest strength, which is flexibility. Dublin Core recognizes that it does not cover the potential needs of all users and is not sufficient for purposes other than simple resource discovery, so the metadata schema itself has been designed to allow for the creation of local extensions to meet local needs. However, unlike many other metadata schemas, the addition of these local extensions does not cause compatibility problems for Dublin Core because metadata elements can always be reduced down to the core 15 unqualified elements. This allows metadata implementers to customize the Dublin Core schema for their own local usage without sacrificing the ability to share metadata between other systems. For example, within DSpace, Qualified Dublin Core is utilized in metadata

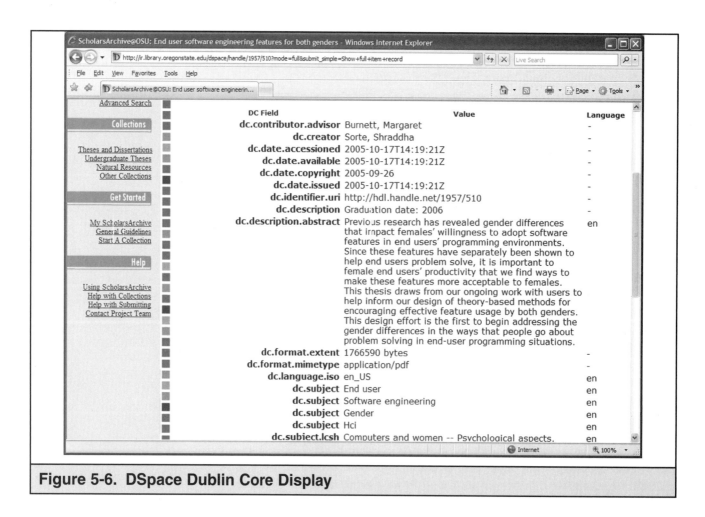

Figure 5-6. DSpace Dublin Core Display

creation so that information can be captured at the highest level of granularity that Dublin Core provides.

Figure 5-6 provides a screenshot of a record in the Oregon State University DSpace repository. Within the metadata, one can see how elements, like date, are being utilized with refinements to provide additional contextual information about the metadata located within the attribute. For example, dc.date.created indicates to the user when the item was created. Moreover, within DSpace, a number of local refinements have been defined to provide additional context to controlled vocabularies, like water basins or OSU departments. However, since many of these refinements would have little value outside of the Oregon State digital repository, they are removed when metadata is provided for public consumption through the Open Archives Initiative (OAI), allowing users to harvest metadata in Unqualified Dublin Core.

The importance of the Dublin Core community itself can hardly be overstated. This community is a large international body that is helping evolve the Dublin Core by worldwide consensus. This has allowed the Dublin Core schema to tackle areas such as semantic interpretability and multilingualism on a global scale. Likewise, the community provides strong leadership in the shape of the Dublin Core Initiative and promotes Dublin Core as an extensible standard both within the library community and beyond.

Additionally, the simplistic nature of Dublin Core has allowed for quick adoption by a number of digital library providers, as well as standards providers from various fields and disiplines. Within the library community, protocols like OAI, SRU (Search and Retrieval URL) and Z39.50 (the ANSI/NISO Z39.50. Information Retrieval Protocol) all provide standard methods for utilizing Dublin Core as the metadata capture language, which makes sense given that a Dublin Core element will mean the same thing across disciplines. Metadata creation also can be greatly simplified with Dublin Core, since metadata can be created at varying levels of granularity, encouraging the use of automated metadata creation methods.

CHALLENGES

Dublin Core's simplicity is also its greatest weakness. Unqualified Dublin Core was purposefully designed as the lowest common denominator language in order to preserve the highest level of semantic interoperability—but it has come at a high cost. It simply isn't as granular as many other specialty metadata formats, like MARC. This means that a great deal of data, both real and contextual, is lost when data needs to be moved between metadata formats. Given the low costs of the implementation of Unqualified Dublin Core, many early digital repository systems implemented systems supporting only Unqualified Dublin Core, causing many to loathe the overly simplistic nature of the metadata produced.

In this same vein, librarians tend to view the Dublin Core's lack of formalized input standards as a cause for great concern. Given the rigid set of rules for traditional library metadata creation (e.g., AACR2), the lack of such standardization for entering information like controlled names, keywords, and subjects has been seen in the library community as one of Dublin Core's major deficiencies relating to its use. Groups such as the Greater Western States Metadata Group have sought to fill that void for libraries by creating more formal standards to govern the input of data into Dublin Core (Collaborative Digitization Project, accessed: 2006), but this level of flexibility is still viewed as a fundamental weakness of the schema.

MODS (METADATA OBJECT DESCRIPTION SCHEMA)

Given the large quantity of metadata, workflows, and knowledge tied up in the development of bibliographic data such as MARC, an important question is how these legacy records and systems will be moved toward a more XML-centric metadata schema. In the mid-1990s, the Library of Congress made an important first step by offering an XML version of MARC in MARC21XML. As noted above, MARC21XML was developed to be MARC, but also in XML. It represented a lossless XML format for MARC data, with many of the benefits of XML, although still inhibited by the technical limitations of MARC.

HISTORY

Unfortunately, MARC21XML has not been widely adopted by the metadata community. While benefits exist to using MARC21XML over traditional MARC, few library systems have made the move to support MARC21XML as an ingestible metadata format. As such, the usage of MARC21XML has been primarily by library developers creating custom applications for their own local use.

In part, it is likely that MARC21XML did not catch on as a popular library metadata format precisely because it was so closely tied to traditional MARC. For many, MARC and the rules governing it had simply become too archaic. MARC was developed for the time when bibliographic data was printed on catalog cards. The move to an XML-based metadata schema represented a chance to break away from that bibliographic model.

For its part, the Library of Congress recognized the need within the library community for a metadata schema that would be compatible with the library community's legacy MARC data while at the same time providing a new way of representing and grouping bibliographic data. These efforts led to the development of the Metadata Object Description Schema (MODS) metadata format. MODS represents the next natural step in the evolution of MARC into XML. MODS represents a much simpler alternative that retains its compatibility with MARC. Developed as a subset of the current MARC21 specification, MODS was created as a richer alternative to other metadata schemas like Dublin Core. However, unlike MARC21XML, which faithfully transferred MARC structures into XML, the structure of MODS allowed for metadata elements to be regrouped and reorganized within a metadata record.

As seen in Figure 5-7, another major difference between MODS and MARC/MARC21XML is the use of textual field labels rather than numeric fields. This change allows MODS records to be more readable than traditional MARC or MARC21XML records and promotes a design

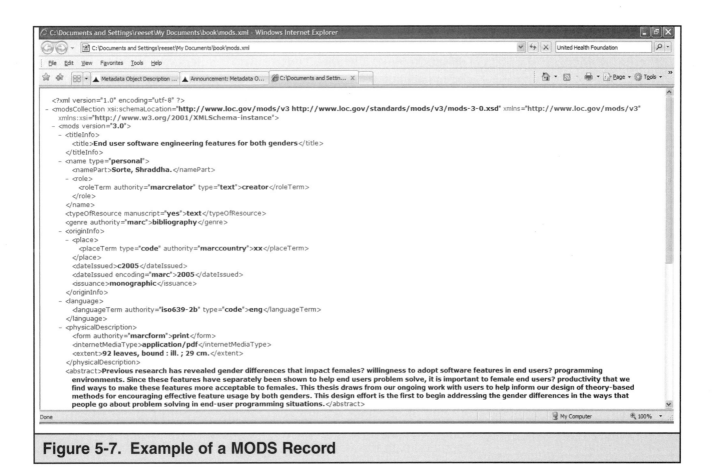

Figure 5-7. Example of a MODS Record

that allows for element descriptions that can be reused throughout the metadata schema. A number of digital library efforts are looking at formalizing MODS support to either replace or augment Dublin Core-only metadata systems. Likewise, groups like the Digital Library Federation have started recommending that organizations and software designers provide MODS-based OAI harvesting capability to allow for a higher level of metadata granularity. E-print systems like DSpace have looked at ways of utilizing MODS either as an internal storage format or as a supported OAI protocol, while digital repositories like Fedora currently utilize a MODS-like metadata schema as the internal storage schema. Furthermore, interest has grown in using MODS for ILS development. This is due in large part to the open-source development work being done by the Georgia Public Library System on Evergreen, an open-source ILS built around MODS.

Finally, MODS was not developed in a vacuum or as a one-time alternative to MARC. MODS was developed as a subset of a number of larger ongoing metadata initiatives at the Library of Congress. While MODS offered the library community many potential benefits, it was developed, in part, as an extension format to the Metadata Encoding and Transmission Standard (METS) to provide a MARC-like bibliographic metadata component for METS-generated records. Likewise, the MODS schema was tapped as one of the registered metadata formats for SRU/SRW (Search/Retrieve URL/Search/Retrieve Web Service), the next-generation communication format designed as a replacement for Z39.50. So, while MODS was created to work as a stand-alone metadata format that could be used for original record creation, translating MARC data into XML, or facilitating the harvesting of library materials, it was also created as part of a larger ongoing strategy at the U.S. Library of Congress to create a set of more diverse, lightweight XML formats that could be used with the library community's current legacy data.

STRENGTHS

As mentioned earlier in the chapter, MODS has a number of advantages over other general purpose metadata schemas, like Dublin Core, when one considers the current library community environment. While applications like digital repositories tend to avoid using MARC for bibliographic description, the reality is that MARC still dominates the metadata landscape within the library community. Nearly all major ILS vendors currently support MARC as their de facto metadata schema, leading to thousands of MARC-filled databases. The ability of MODS to provide an element set already compatible with the existing bibliographic descriptions within these large MARC databases provides a clear migration path for users to an XML-based schema. This is very different from schemas, like Dublin Core, which lacks the granularity of elements to provide a clear migration path away from something like MARC. By providing this compatibility, MODS is able to provide a bridge as the metadata continues to evolve. This increased granularity also allows MODS records to provide richer descriptions than those found in a Dublin Core record. MODS utilizes an expanded element set (~20 high-level elements, coupled with multiple refinements) to encourage richer bibliographic description, and, as a result, it is well suited for the hierarchical nature of the METS framework.

MODS introduces the ability to utilize hierarchies within the bibliographic description of an item. This is very different from MARC and even Dublin Core, which are flat metadata schemas, meaning that descriptions are limited to the item that they are describing. MODS provides the capability for users to describe an idea as well as the parts that make up that item, arranging the bibliographic description hierarchically within the record. This allows MODS objects to create "actions" around the various levels of hierarchy and encourages software designers to utilize these hierarchical elements in displaying relationships within, to, and from an individual resource.

CHALLENGES

Like Dublin Core, MODS's biggest challenge is a result of its biggest asset. While MODS does not prescribe any set of input rules upon the metadata framework, its close relationship to MARC emphasizes the type of data that is best suited for this format. The Library of Congress has attempted to position MODS as a general metadata format, but its need to maintain compatibility with the library community's MARC legacy data does raise barriers to general mainstream adoption outside the library community.

Moreover, unlike Dublin Core, MODS is an internal metadata schema created for the Library of Congress. While the Library of Congress has accepted a leadership role within the library community and has committed to continued development of MODS to meet the needs of the library community as a whole, it lacks the large community input and oversight that supports Dublin Core. Though a large community is currently working with and providing feedback to the Library of Congress regarding the MODS implementation, the schema lacks the support of a multi-organizational maintenance body. MODS is developed primarily by the Network Development and MARC Standards Office at the Library of Congress—which may ultimately limit the growth and scope of the MODS framework as it goes forward. Obviously, within today's global environment, a more multinational metadata schema like Dublin Core presents a number of distinct advantages over a schema developed primarily for the purposes of a single nation or organization.

METS (METADATA ENCODING AND TRANSMISSION STANDARD)

Unlike other metadata formats discussed within this chapter, METS is not a metadata format utilized for bibliographic description of objects. Dublin Core, MODS, and even MARC/MARC21XML all share the same primary purpose of providing a vehicle for the description of bibliographic data. While each metadata format has its own advantages and disadvantages that can help a digital repository developer select one metadata format over another, they still share the same goal. Ultimately, each of the discussed metadata formats function to provide various levels of bibliographic description of a digital object. The same, however, cannot be said of METS. METS is a very different animal, in that it acts as a container object for the many pieces of metadata needed to describe a single digital object. Within a digital repository, a number of pieces of metadata are attached to each digital object. While the individual who submitted the digital object may only be responsible for adding information to the bibliographic metadata, the digital repository itself is generating metadata related to the structural information of the digital object, that is, assembling information about the files that make up the entire digital object (metadata, attached items, etc.). METS provides a method for binding these objects together so that they can be transferred to other systems or utilized within the local digital repository system as part of a larger application profile.

HISTORY

The history of METS is closely tied to the history of MODS. In the late 1990s, the Library of Congress began exploring avenues for moving locally created digital collections to an XML-based platform. During this period of exploration, only two general purpose XML metadata formats existed: MARC21XML and Dublin Core. Each of these two formats would prove to be undesirable for different reasons (Dublin Core due to its inability to capture metadata at a fine enough granularity, and MARC21XML due to its reliance on MARC structures and rules). The Library of Congress then developed MODS, a simpler subset of MARC that could produce rich descriptions at the desired level of granularity. However, while MODS provided a robust format for bibliographic metadata description, a method still needed to be developed that would bind together the administrative, structural, and bibliographic metadata of a digital object. Moreover, loading digital objects into a digital repository and exporting them would need to include this information as well. In other words, the digital object must be able to retain its metadata, in all its forms, to be useful outside of the host system. So, in essence, METS was created to be this glue for digital objects, binding together all relevant metadata on item structure, description, and administration.

The Library of Congress started experimenting with the mixing of METS and MODS almost immediately after releasing the specifications in 2002. Later that year, the Library of Congress started work on the Digital Audio-Visual Preservation Prototyping project (Cundiff, accessed: 2006), which combined the use of MODS as the bibliographic description framework and METS as the digital object framework. Since then, the Library of Congress has produced a wide variety of projects utilizing the MODS/METS combination.

METS AT A GLANCE

Before taking a look at how METS is being used within current digital repository efforts, it helps to take a quick look at what makes up a METS document. Obviously, this is by no means comprehensive. The current METS documentation spans hundreds of pages and examples, but the following should provide an adequate overview of what makes up a METS document and how those elements tie the various pieces of a digital object together. There are currently seven sections to a METS document (Tingle, accessed: 2006).

- **metsHdr**
  METS Header: This tag group stores information about the METS document itself, not the digital object that it describes.
- **dmdSec**
  Descriptive metadata section: This tag group stores all the descriptive metadata for all items referenced by the METS document.
- **amdSec**
  Administrative metadata section: This tag group stores all the administrative metadata for all items referenced by the METS document.
- **fileSec**
  Content file section: This tag group stores information on all files referenced by the METS document.
- **structMap**
  Structural map: This tag group stores the hierarchical arrangement of items referenced by the digital object.
- **structLink**
  Structural map linking: This tag group stores linking information between referenced items in the structural map section.
- **behaviorSec**
  Behavior section: This tag group defines behaviors associated with the referenced items in a METS document. (i.e., executable behaviors, etc.)

Figure 5-7 illustrates a very basic METS document utilized at Oregon State University for archiving structural information about digitized text. In this example, one can see that OSU has chosen to use Dublin Core rather than MODS for embedding its bibliographic descriptive data. This decision was made primarily because OSU uses DSpace, which stores metadata in Dublin Core. So, in the interest of repurposing the metadata, Dublin Core was chosen as the descriptive metadata language. However, this example demonstrates the flexibility of the METS container. While METS was developed in concert with MODS, its greatest strength lies in its ability to accommodate any descriptive metadata format. This allows users take advantage of the METS framework while still utilizing the metadata schema best suited for their materials or infrastructure. The U.S. Library of Congress provides access to a number of additional sample METS documents at the METS homepage (www.loc.gov/mets).

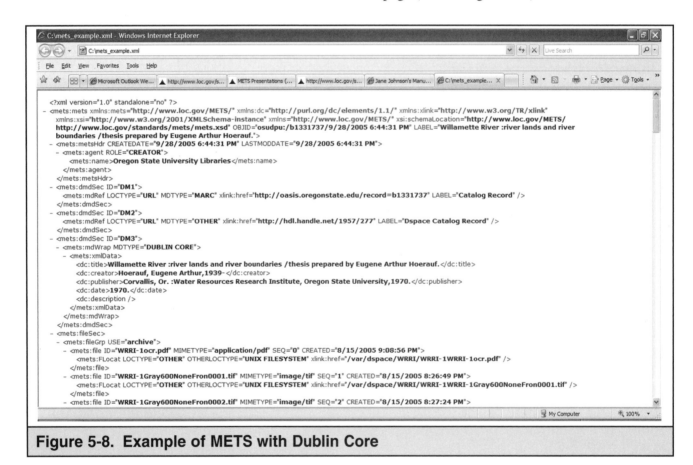

Figure 5-8. Example of METS with Dublin Core

APPLICATIONS

Since METS is not a bibliographic description format in the same sense as Dublin Core or MODS, a look at the format in terms of challenges or strengths seems moot. METS' primary strength is its ability to bind objects together for use on or outside the host system. This is very different from other metadata schemas covered in this chapter. More interesting for the purpose of this book is examining the actual applications of METS in the real world, particularly as it relates to digital repositories. As such, this section will focus on two real-world cases.

Page-Turning Applications

Surprisingly, emulating simple page turning of a document has been a difficult task in many digital library systems. METS offers the ability to overcome this obstacle by providing access to the structural map of a document. One of the first examples of utilizing METS to build a page-turning application come from Indiana University's (IU) digital library program. IU developed a small software application called the METS Navigator, which would provide a method for taking a METS document and constructing a publicly viewable Web object that could perform the simple task of turning a page (IU Digital Library Program, accessed: 2006b).

The IU software provided a demonstration of how the structural information found in METS could power more intelligent document delivery systems. Figure 5-9 shows one sample object taken from the IU digital

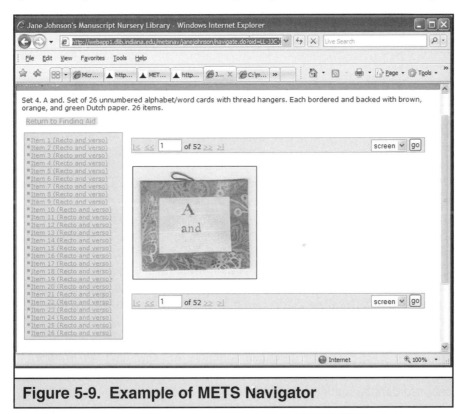

Figure 5-9. Example of METS Navigator

Source: Indiana University Digital Library Program (a). "Jane Johnson's Manuscript Nursery Library." Available: http://webapp1.dlib.indiana.edu/metsnav.janejohnson/navigate.do?oid=LL-JJC-04&pn=1&size=screen (accessed November 25, 2006).

repository. Using a METS document, the METS Navigator is able to construct a full index of the document, providing links to the individual pages or the ability to turn the individual pages of the document. Had bibliographic metadata been provided to each individual item, a software application like the METS Navigator could easily expose it, thanks to the METS document structure.

Importing Digital Objects

As a transmission format, METS provides digital repository designers with a simple structure that can be supported to facilitate the batch import of digital objects. For systems that do not natively support METS, like CONTENTdm, batch importing tends to be done with simple tab-delimited files for flat objects or the file system to preserve document hierarchy. (At the time of publication, DiMeMia's CONTENTdm software offered no METS support for the import or export of digital objects.) However, this type of importing tends to be problematic as it assumes that metadata is clean, has been delineated correctly, and is laid out on the file system in a very specific structure. Digital library systems (like DSpace and Fedora) that provide native support for METS objects greatly simplify the import process by utilizing a highly structured metadata framework in which all metadata about the object is self-contained.

SEMANTIC WEB

It becomes very apparent when one starts working with digital repositories and their content that one has a wide range of metadata choices to choose from. This chapter merely discusses the most widely used general metadata frameworks, but others like Federal Geographic Data Committee (FGDC) for geographic information systems (GIS) data, Visual Resource Core (VRC) for visual items, Encoded Archival Description (EAD) for finding aids, Metadata Authority Description Schema (MADS) for authority data, ONIX (Online Information Exchange) for publishers data, and others, all provide specialized metadata forms that a digital library program may need to integrate into their digital and metadata architecture. Given the wide range of metadata schemas and the need for libraries to interoperate with entities outside of the library community, how can this encoded data be made more transparent?

The answer, at least for now, is it can't. Data interoperability between formats and communities will continue for the immediate future to be governed primarily through the use of data crosswalks to normalize the metadata from one community into a format that can be understood by another. With that said, the W3C has proposed a number of recommendations directly related to the creation of a common framework that can be used to enable the interoperability of data across community boundaries. This work, commonly known as the "semantic Web," seeks to create a framework that will allow machines to understand the relationships between interconnected data.

Browsing the Web has become second nature for most individuals, but even new users with very little Web experience are able to quickly view and make decisions regarding the content they find. When browsing Web content, human beings are easily able to understand the difference between advertisements and content and can unconsciously filter the advertisement out of their mind's eye. Likewise, when one considers library metadata, a cataloger with any experience can quickly determine the primarily control number found on a MARC record, allowing them to interpret not only the metadata record but the rules necessary to place said metadata into alternative formats. Machines simply do not have that ability at this point in time. Automated machine processes require the presence of rules and schemas to inform the software application what relationships exist between data. A machine would have a very difficult time identifying an advertisement from content simply by examining the content. In part, this is why the pop-up blockers and advertisement scrubbers found in Web browsers today work primarily through the use of blacklists and known advertising content providers to determine the relations between the elements of a document. In reality, automated advertisement-blocking software is primarily making its best guess regarding the nature of the examined content. For catalogers, the problem is the same. Automated bibliographic creation/editing processes still require a great deal of human intervention to create the necessary rules for a machine to interpret a metadata set. Without these rules, a machine could certainly parse a metadata set but would have no way of building or interpreting the relationships of this bibliographic data to other metadata content.

The semantic Web, then, is about connecting these dots to allow machine processes to determine and infer relationships and meaning about the data that it describes. If this sounds a lot like metadata for one's metadata, you would be essentially right. The Resource Description Framework (RDF), is one of the cornerstones of the semantic Web initiative. RDF is being created as the de facto descriptive language of the semantic Web framework. The framework is made up of a number of parts. There is RDF/XML, which is an XML metadata schema for describing RDF vocabularies and documents, as well as RDF Semantics and RDF concepts documents that define the data models, inference rules, and abstract syntax. In theory, when taken as a whole, RDF provides a common descriptive framework that can "wrap" an existing set of metadata or data to provide the missing information needed to allow machine processes to draw relationships between heterogeneous data sets. RDF, coupled with Web Ontology Language (OWL), the make up two major components of the semantic Web framework designed to bring out the relationships between data on the Web.

So what does this look like? The Dublin Core community is currently the most active community utilizing RDF as part of its metadata description. In April 2007, the Dublin Core Metadata Initiative produced a draft document titled "Expressing Dublin Core Metadata Using the Resource Description Framework (RDF)" providing its most detailed document to date discussing how Dublin Core metadata can be expressed within the RDF metadata framework. The document illustrates how Dublin Core can be encoded to ensure that nonhuman processes can understand the important concepts related to the metadata record—for example, details relating to classification, ontologies, and relationships (both hierarchical and relational) to other items (Dublin Core Metadata Initiative, 2007). At its simplest, RDF/XML encoding of Dublin Core data can look something like Figure 5-10.

```xml
<?xml version="1.0" encoding="utf-8" ?>
<rdf:RDF xmlns:rdf="http://www.w3.org/1999/02/22-rdf-syntax-ns#" xmlns:
  dc="http://purl.org/dc/elements/1.1/" xmlns:dcam="http://purl.org/dc/rdf/">
    <rdf:Description>
      <dc:title>Report of the exploring expedition to the Rocky
          Mountains in the year 1842 : and to Oregon and north
          California in the years 1843-44 /</dc:title>
      <dc:creator>
        <rdf:Description>
          <dcam:memberOf rdf:resource="http://authorities.loc.gov/" />
          <rdf:value>Frémont, John Charles,1813-1890.<rdf:value>
        </rdf:Description>
      </dc:creator>
      <dc:creator>
        <rdf:Description>
          <dcam:memberOf rdf:resource="http://authorities.loc.gov/" />
          <rdf:value>Torrey, John,1796-1873.</rdf:value>
        </rdf:Description>
      </dc:creator>
      <dc:creator>
        <rdf:Description>
          <dcam:memberOf rdf:resource="http://authorities.loc.gov/" />
          <rdf:value>Hall, James,1811-1898.</rdf:value>
        </rdf:Description>
      </dc:creator>
      <dc:creator>
```

Figure 5-10. Example of RDF/XML Encoding of Dublin Core Data

Continued

```
        <rdf:Description>
            <dcam:memberOf rdf:resource="http://authorities.loc.gov/" />
            <rdf:value>United States.Army.Corps of Engineers.</rdf:value>
        </rdf:Description>
    </dc:creator>
    <dc:type>text</dc:type>
    <dc:publisher>Washington : Blair and Rives, Printers,</dc:publisher>
    <dc:date>1845.</dc:date>
    <dc:language>eng</dc:language>
    <dc:description>The Astronomical and Meteorological
        observations of the 1842 expedition, which form p. 585-693 of
        the Senate edition (Senate ex. doc. 174) are not included in
        this.</dc:description>
    <dc:subject>
        <rdf:Description>
            <dcam:memberOf rdf:resource="http://www.loc.gov/" />
            <rdf:value>Discoveries in geography</rdf:value>
        </rdf:Description>
    </dc:subject>
    <dc:subject>
        <rdf:Description>
            <dcam:memberOf rdf:resource="http://www.loc.gov/" />
            <rdf:value>Paleontology</rdf:value>
        </rdf:Description>
    </dc:subject>
    <dc:subject>
        <rdf:Description>
            <dcam:memberOf rdf:resource="http://www.loc.gov/" />
            <rdf:value>Botany</rdf:value>
        </rdf:Description>
    </dc:subject>
    </rdf:Description>
</rdf:RDF>
```

Figure 5-10. Example of RDF/XML Encoding of Dublin Core Data (continued)

In Figure 5-10, RDF/XML elements are used to define the ontologies used by the controlled terms found within the record. In this example, there are representative universal resource identifiers (URI) identifying the creator and subject elements. So while the URIs provided will not resolve to anything meaningful, they capture the idea behind the RDF/XML markup. Ideally, the rdf:resource URIs would resolve to the ontology, which could then be parsed to build relationships between the terms in this record and the terms found within the ontology. Of course, this is just a simple example of how RDF/XML could be used to represent a Dublin Core record. The recent Dublin Core draft paper goes into much more detail, illustrating the many different levels of RDF encoding that can be supported and recommended for use.

The big question is, why do we care? By all accounts, the adoption of semantic Web concepts is still somewhere out in the distant future. Current generation digital content is being developed within the constructs of a "Web 2.0" information architecture—an architecture that is still very much in a stage of development and flux. And within the library community, the adoption of "Web 2.0" methodologies is still a relatively hot-button issue. Given the current adoption of second-generation data practices, it seems unlikely that semantic Web design, or "Web 3.0," as it's already being called, will become widespread in the next five or even ten years. However, there are a number of things that data providers can be doing today to help encourage the development of semantic Web-based technologies.

1. Start encoding data in RDF. While there are few technologies today that can fully utilize RDF-encoded documents, the presence of RDF-encoded data has no adverse affect on how current-generation tools and parsers utilize our data. In large part, the vision of the semantic Web will only be realized if and when the data on the Web has been encoded to allow for these connections to be made. With that in mind, digital repository program managers would be well served to investigate their own software platforms so they understand the issues and dependencies needed to produce their own RDF-encoded content. By working to create semantic Web-capable data today, we are encouraging the continued development for tomorrow.

2. Begin using OWL for the encoding of ontologies and ontological data. RDF-encoded data represents only one part of the semantic Web equation. In addition to data encoded within a common framework, the information about that data must be made parsable, as well. The semantic Web promises to provide interoperability between heterogeneous datasets and, in part, the ability to determine how ontologies relate and can be incorporated into diverse systems.

APPLICATION PROFILES

Given the wide range of metadata formats available, only a few of which have been discussed here, it becomes apparent that each metadata schema has its own strengths and weaknesses. It is very unlikely that one metadata schema will be able to fulfill all the needs of an organization. In part, this is because most metadata schemas will be heavy-laden with domain-specific element sets that allow the schema to meet the needs of a particular community. However, the ability to mix and match metadata formats would seem to have a tremendous amount of value, as one could essentially pull metadata elements from different schemas—though the resulting frankenschema would likely have many interoperability issues, particularly within a large-scale operation or across domains.

For semantic Web developers, this is where application profiles come in. Application profiles (AP) promise the ability to mix and match metadata schemas, but in a way so that standard machine processes can determine namespace requirements and treat the embedded element set as part of the standard schema. In writing about APs, Rachel Heery and Manjula Patel noted that "Application profiles are useful as they allow the implementer to declare how they are using standard schemas. In the context of working applications... there is often a difference between the schema in use and the 'standard' namespace schema" (Heery and Patel, 2000). In essence, application profiles represent the Holy Grail for metadata interoperability and dissemination as metadata frameworks could easily "borrow" between XML namespaces without the fear of introducing interoperability issues. RDF offers one option for building such an application profile. As seen in the RDF/XML example (Figure 5-10), RDF makes it possible to embed definable elements into an XML document. In part, this is a feature of the RDF conceptual model, which utilizes an RDF triple to fully define an object. Each RDF triple is made up of three components (Dublin Core Metadata Initiative, 2007):

- the subject, which defines the RDF URI reference
- the predicate, an RDF URI reference
- the object, an RDF URI reference, node or literal

These components make up a date model that allow an RDF object to both document and define the behavior and properties of a given object. Using this method, an RDF object could be easily created using metadata elements from other XML schemas, given that the RDF object contained the necessary reference information needed to document and integrate the foreign element sets.

However, the full realization of this potential is still a "Holy Grail" many years into the future. As noted by the Dublin Core Usage Board Review of Application Profiles, application profiles are currently utilized primarily as a means of documentation, while "it is hoped that in the longer-term, machine-processable version of such APs based on data models such as RDF will provide a basis for automating metadata interoperability functions..."

(Baker, 2003). While many communities, including the RDF and METS communities, are spending a great deal of time researching and developing frameworks and tools to encourage application profiles, the current reality is that the inability to realize the AP's full potential will continue to temper widespread adoption of the concept until available tools are able to handle these complex data types.

SUMMARY

This chapter covers only a small number of the metadata frameworks currently available to digital library designers. We focused on the three metadata frameworks that are most prevalently used on today's digital repository platforms, but many more exist. Frameworks targeting geographic content (FGDC, www.fgdc.gov), images (VRA, www.vraweb.org/vracore3.htm), textual documents (TEI, www.tei-c.org) and archival finding aids (EAD, www.loc.gov/ead/) all provide metadata frameworks for the rich description of specific material types. When choosing a digital repository, implementers should take stock of the types of materials that will likely be stored within the resource and ask some of the following questions:

- Who will be creating metadata within my digital repository?
- What level of granularity will I require?
- Should my system support batch importing and exporting of its digital objects?
- What role will legacy metadata play in my digital library programs?
- Will my organization use a single monolithic system, or will my digital repository system be made up of many heterogeneous components?

Obviously, how one answers these questions will indicate what metadata framework would likely be best suited for one's digital library system. For example, will materials be entered by technical services staff or will metadata be submitted by faculty and students? If the latter, utilizing a metadata framework like Dublin Core, which provides a set of generally understandable elements, would likely reduce metadata creation as a barrier for submission. However, each of these choices must be weighed by the individual institution while factoring in current workflows, expertise, and system infrastructure.

REFERENCES

American National Standards Institute. 2001. "The Dublin Core Metadata Element Set." Available: www.niso.org/standards/resources/Z39-85.pdf

Baker, Thomas. 2003. "DCMI Usage Board Review of Application Profile." Available: http://dublincore.org/usage/documents/profiles/

Bradley, David. "Unattributed Interview." Available: www.youtube.com/watch?v=TVRMrxF9BkQ (accessed November 21, 2006).

Calhoun, Karen. "The Changing Nature of the Catalog and Its Integration with Other Discovery Tools." (Last updated March 2006). Available: www.loc.gov/catdir/calhoun-report-final.pdf (accessed October 23, 2006).

Caplan, Priscilla. 2003. *Metadata Fundamentals for All Librarians.* Chicago: American Library Association.

Collaborative Digitization Project. "CDP Dublin Core Best Practices." Available: www.cdpheritage.org/cdp/documents/CDPDCMBP.pdf (accessed November 30, 2006).

Cundiff, Morgan. "Using METS and MODS to Create an XML Standards-based Digital Library Application." Available: www.loc.gov/standards/mets/presentations/Digital_Future_Cundiff.ppt#7 (accessed December 1, 2006).

Dublin Core Metadata Initiative. "DCMI Metadata Terms." Available: www.dublincore.org/documents/dcmi-terms/ (accessed November 25, 2006).

Dublin Core Metadata Initative. "Expressing Dublin Core Metadata Using the Resource Description Framework (RDF)." (Last updated 2007). Available: www.dublincore.org/documents/2007/04/02/dc-rdf/

Heery, Rachel, and Manjula Patel. 2000. "Application Profiles: Mixing and Matching Metadata Schemas." *Ariadne* 25 (September 24). Available: www.ariadne.ac.uk/issue25/app-profiles/intro.html

Indiana University Digital Library Program (a). "Jane Johnson's Manuscript Library." Available: http://webapp1.dlib.indiana.edu/metsnav/janejohnson/navigate.do?oid=L-JJC-04&pn=1&size=screen (accessed November 25, 2006).

Indiana University Digital Library Program (b). "METS Navigator." Available: http://metsnavigator.sourceforge.net/ (accessed December 1, 2006).

Johnson, Bruce. 2001. "XML and MARC: Which Is 'Right'?" *Cataloging & Classification Quarterly* 32, no. 1: 81-90.

Marcum, Deanna B. *Future of Cataloging.* Address to the EBSCO Leadership Seminar, January 16, 2004. Available: www.loc.gov/library/reports/CatalogingSpeech.pdf (accessed October 20, 2006).

Powell, Andy. "Dublin Core Metadata Editor." Available: www.ukoln.ac.uk/metadata/dcdot/ (accessed December 5, 2006).

Reese, Terry. "MarcEdit." Available: http://oregonstate.edu/~reeset/marcedit/ (accessed December 5, 2006).

Tennant, Roy. 2004. "Building a New Bibliographic Infrastructure." *Library Journal* 129, no. 1: 38.

Tennant, Roy. 2002. "MARC Must Die." *Library Journal* 127, no. 17: 26-28.

Tingle, Brian. "METS Schema 1.5 Documentation." Available: www.loc.gov/standards/mets/docs/mets.v1-5.html (accessed December 1, 2006).

United States Library of Congress. "MARC Code List: Part V: Format Sources." Available: www.loc.gov/marc/relators/relaform.html (accessed November 1, 2006).

SHARING DATA: METADATA HARVESTING AND DISTRIBUTION

The library community has traditionally championed the sharing and distribution of metadata in all forms. This sharing is a large part of the legacy of the library community as a whole. OCLC, for example, is built around the concept of shared metadata. OCLC organizes a global information system for bibliographic metadata distribution and has helped facilitate a process of cross-institutional borrowing of physical materials. What's more, the creation of protocols like Z39.50 and, more recently, Search and Retrieve via URL/Search and Retrieve via Web (SRU/SRW), continues to demonstrate the library community's commitment toward information sharing.

However, the advent of digital repositories has brought about a curious shift in the library community. For many organizations, building a digital repository includes the construction of barriers to that information. These barriers can come in the form of intellectual property restrictions, copyright provisions, or metadata restrictions interrupting the normal distribution of information into the current information ecosystem. While open access to information may not always be possible, digital repository implementers should consider how these barriers affect their place in the current information ecosystem. Since the authors of this book feel strongly that digital repositories should strive to be open-access repositories, this chapter will focus primarily on why and how digital repositories can support the distribution of their metadata.

THE EVOLVING ROLE OF LIBRARIES

The library community traditionally has been early technology adopters when it comes to the world of information distribution. As the current information ecosystem has evolved, so too has the library community's role within that ecosystem. In the not too distant past, the library community was the information ecosystem, representing the central location for trusted content within its user community. The library was a warehouse of information, its physical materials being its single largest tangible asset. The value of that asset was, however, dependant on the size of one's library—meaning that user communities were served unequally depending on the health of the community's library. Interlibrary loan changed this paradigm, as libraries made materials available for inter-institutional borrowing. Interlibrary loan effectively made every small library a giant by providing its users access to various research collections around the world. Moreover, as new digital capture technologies developed, libraries have been able to integrate these new processes to speed document delivery and provide new and exciting levels of access. Throughout each of these changes, the library remained its users' central repository for information.

So what changed? The rise of search engines like AltaVista, Lycos, Yahoo! and now Google have done for many users something that the library community was never able to do—provide the illusion of order to the chaos of the World Wide Web. Web search engines offered users a method of querying millions or billions of pieces of data, returning what is theoretically the most relevant information. For many user communities, a search engine has replaced the library as the primary source of trusted information and changed the information ecosystem. Libraries no longer reside in the center of this ecosystem, but now co-exist as equal partners with other information providers.

The fact that the role of libraries has evolved with the changes in technology is nothing new. This has been a central theme for hundreds of years, as libraries have adapted to meet its users' needs as technology changes have spurred changes in the publication and distribution process. What makes today's evolution different from previous changes is the realization that the library is no longer its community's primary source for trusted information. The library has been slowly edged out of the central role in the current information ecosystem. The library still retains a prominent place within this ecosystem, particularly within the research community, but it is now simply a small fish in an otherwise growing pond.

But is this evolution a negative one for users? Not necessarily. It simply is part of the maturing process of today's information infrastructure. What's more, it shows the success that libraries have had in helping mature the current information ecosystem. The library community has traditionally cultivated a rich and diverse information community, and this community simply grew up, allowing the library be one of many members of the information community rather than having to be *the* information community.

For the library community, this means learning a new language and new rules without losing some of the core library values. "Web 2.0" concepts such as socially driven content, social networking, social bookmarking, resource personalization, and recommender services need to become a part of the library communities vocabulary and tool kits. Digital repository developers need to come to an understanding that library services need to be transparent. Unlike commercial information providers, the library is most successful when it connects users with information in the most unobtrusive method. A good example would be the current generation of OpenURL resolvers. Most current-generation OpenURL resolvers will not link users directly to resources, but instead redirect users to a branded page that contains the links to a resource. Digital library developers should work to do a better job of not tripping over their own technology and work to find ways to remove obtrusive branding when applicable and provide more direct paths to information. In some cases, this may mean looking outside the library community for usable or compatible technologies. Protocols like OpenSearch (to be discussed in Chapter 7) provide a low-cost, high-return method of exposing a digital repository to users, developers, and services outside of the library community.

Unfortunately, as the library community slowly comes to grips with its new role within today's information infrastructure, some community members have taken to actively restricting access to their digital assets and metadata. As digital repository softwares continue to evolve, developers have actively developed protocols like Open Archives Initative (OAI), Search and Retrieve URL (SRU), and OpenSearch into repository platforms to encourage interoperability efforts within the library community. These efforts are sometimes wasted, however, as some organizations have actively moved to restrict access to an institution's bibliographic metadata. Some restrict access to "protect" an organization's digital assets while others are uncertain of the resources necessary to allow data harvesting. Ironically, the library community is often the first to take the publishing and vending community to task for the lack of transparency in their products. Complaints about the openness of the integrated library system (ILS), availability of electronic journal metadata, interoperability with commercial search engines, and interoperability with federated search tools remain hot topics within the library community. At the same time, some organizations within the library community are building up similar restrictions around their own digital content and metadata, filtering access to content through a handful of "approved" interfaces. In order for the library community to fully participate with the vendor community within this new information ecosystem, a new reciprocal relationship must evolve in which both sides work to lift the barriers preventing interchange of information. For the library community, this may be difficult since it will also mean giving up a measure of control over collection metadata and how that metadata is used and integrated into other products.

METADATA WANTS TO BE FREE

The library community has historically promoted the idea that metadata should be freely accessible between systems. The Z39.50 protocol represented one such manifestation of this belief, as it allowed organizations the ability to query and retrieve metadata from remote systems. Using this one protocol, the library community has built a number of tools and services. For example, citation services like EndNote have traditionally utilized Z39.50 to extract citation information from remote systems. More recently, Z39.50 has been used as a primary connection point for organizations looked to build federated search systems. (Federated searching and some of the pertinent protocols supporting that effort will be discussed in greater detail in Chapter 8.) But in each of these cases, the services were made available only through recognition that (1) metadata is a valuable commodity and (2) unfettered access and the ability to re-use, disassemble, and merge one's metadata is a good thing. And if that last point sounds a lot like the concept behind mashups, you're right. Mashups, applications that are a mixture of content or elements taken from multiple sources (Computer Language Company, 2006), have become more prevalent in recent years as other communities have realized the value in providing a method to access a system's metadata. In this regard, the library community happened to be ahead of the curve with the development of Z39.50 and having the foresight to see how metadata from other systems could be used to enhance local services.

Over the last decade, many information providers have "freed" their metadata, embracing the mashup concept either as a business model or as a user service. Large information providers like search engines (Google, Yahoo!, MSN) or social networking services like Flickr and del.icio.us have moved to offer API (application programming interface) to provide easier remote-system access and encourage use of their services from remote users. Mapping software, like Google Maps, MapQuest, or MSN Live Mapping service, are good examples of resources that have created friendly access points so that users can embed or mix cartographic information in a number of different contexts. And the users of these services have seemed to respond. Type into your favorite search engine keywords like "Google Maps mashups" or "MSN Live Maps mashups," and you will receive 3,980,000 (Google, accessed: 2007) and 172,456 (MSN Live, accessed: 2007) number of hits respectively.

The growing trend towards mashups and system interoperability is not new. Many system and application developers have called for this type of interoperability for a number of years. However, what's different now is that it is the users themselves, not the application developers, that are driving the mashup trend. What can this tell us? It points to the real need to make information available in ways that users can access within their various workflows. At this juncture, the library community could learn a great deal from the Googles and Flickrs of the world. While many digital repository platforms do provide metadata harvesting methods and possibly RSS (really simple syndication), few provide a useable API that end users could utilize to work with library metadata. Within the current information ecosystem, digital repository developers should be encouraged to develop more robust and real-time API access into systems to encourage the same "mashup" culture with library users as is found outside the library community.

SHARING METADATA

Fortunately, nearly all digital repository platforms provide some method of sharing metadata within the larger user community. While this generally is not a real-time solution as found with a more robust SOAP-based API, the ability to harvest and utilize metadata from remote systems locally is a powerful tool that is often underutilized. Since current generation digital repository platforms primarily support harvesting as a methodology for metadata distribution, the remainder of this chapter will focus on tools, methods, and protocols necessary to crosswalk harvested content to different metadata schemas, issues related to metadata crosswalking, and protocols used to support metadata harvesting on current digital repository platforms.

XSLT (EXTENSIBLE STYLESHEET TRANSFORMATION)

In XML metadata crosswalking, very likely one will be working with XSLT (eXtensible Stylesheet Transformation). XSLT is a W3C technology designed to work with XSL (eXtensible Stylesheet Language), which is essentially a style-sheet language for XML. XSLT was originally designed and is used primarily for the transformation of an XML document from one XML document language to another. On the Web, XSLT is utilized to transform XML documents to HTML documents for public display.

XSLT itself defines a list of functions and vocabularies that can be utilized to manipulate an XML document. By itself, an XSLT style sheet is no more than an XML document. Transformation commands are constructed as tags within the document, utilizing XPath to extract and reformat individual data nodes to be processed. XSLT processing instructions are defined through a namespace. Within an XML document, the namespace is used to define a set of tags through the use of an identifying URI. XSLT defines the following namespace URI: http://www.w3.org/1999/XSL/Transform to define for the XML/XSLT parser a valid set of processing instructions that can perform an XSLT transformation.

XSLT offers a simple method for transforming an XML document to other formats, be it another XML document or a document of another type like HTML. With XSLT one can separate the display or transformation instructions from the bibliographic content, allowing the bibliographic content to be clearer and more portable. Figure 6-1 shows a very simple XML document and how this document might be transformed using XSLT.

```
<?xml version="1.0" encoding="utf-8" ?>
<ZooTrip>
      <photo title="Standing at the Elephant's pen"
filename="http://oregonstate.edu/~reeset/presentations/xml/look_elephant.jpg">
            <animals />
            <people>
                  <name>Kenny Reese, Terry Reese</name>
            </people>
      </photo>
      <photo title="Walking Elephant"
filename="http://oregonstate.edu/~reeset/presentations/xml/elephant_boy.jpg">
            <animals>
                  <name>Elephant</name>
            </animals>
            <people>
                  <name>Kenny Reese, Terry Reese</name>
            </people>
      </photo>
      <photo title="Feeding the birds"
filename="http://oregonstate.edu/~reeset/presentations/xml/bird1.jpg">
            <animals>
                  <name>Lorikeets</name>
            </animals>
            <people>
                  <name>Kenny Reese, Terry Reese</name>
            </people>
      </photo>
      <photo title="Driving in the Savannah"
filename="http://oregonstate.edu/~reeset/presentations/xml/truck.jpg">
            <animals />
            <people>
                  <name>Kenny Reese, Terry Reese</name>
            </people>
      </photo>
</ZooTrip>
```

Figure 6-1. XML Document Transformed Using XSLT

Figure 6-1 is a simple marked-up document detailing a trip to the zoo. In the document, each object is grouped using a *photo* tag, which is enhanced with attributes providing information about the title and filename of the photo. Beneath the *photo* tag are children elements that provide some additional information about the content of the photo, specifically the animals and people in the pictures. Using this document, a number of XSLT transformations could be applied to generate different displays for this document. For example, if one wanted to generate an HTML document sorted by title from this XML source, one would need to utilize an XSLT document like the following:

```
<?xml version="1.0" encoding="UTF-8" ?>
<xsl:stylesheet version="1.0"
xmlns:xsl="http://www.w3.org/1999/XSL/Transform">
<xsl:template match="/">
<html>
<head>
<title>Kenny's trip to the Zoo</title>
</head>
<body>
<table>
 <xsl:for-each select="ZooTrip/photo">
   <xsl:sort select="@title"/>
   <tr>
     <td>
       <table>
         <tr>
           <td valign="top">
             <xsl:call-template name="print_image">
               <xsl:with-param name="filename" select="@filename"/>
             </xsl:call-template>
             <br/>
             <xsl:call-template name="print_title">
               <xsl:with-param name="title" select="@title"/>
             </xsl:call-template>
             <xsl:call-template name="print_animals">
               <xsl:with-param name="name" select="animals/name"/>
             </xsl:call-template>
             <xsl:call-template name="print_people">
               <xsl:with-param name="name" select="people/name"/>
             </xsl:call-template>
           </td>
         </tr>
       </table>
     </td>
   </tr>
 </xsl:for-each>
</table>
</body>
</html>
</xsl:template>
<xsl:template name="print_image">
<xsl:param name="filename"/>
```

Figure 6-2. Using XSLT to Transform an XML Document to HTML Sorted by Title

Continued

```
<img>
<xsl:attribute name="src">
<xsl:value-of select="$filename"/>
</xsl:attribute>
<xsl:attribute name="style">zoom:15%</xsl:attribute>
</img>
</xsl:template>
<xsl:template name="print_title">
<xsl:param name="title" />
<b>Title:</b>
<xsl:value-of select="$title" />
<br />
</xsl:template>
<xsl:template name="print_animals">
<xsl:param name="name" />
<b>Animals:</b>
<xsl:value-of select="$name" />
<br />
</xsl:template>
<xsl:template name="print_people">
<xsl:param name="name" />
<b>People:</b>
<xsl:value-of select="$name" />
<br />
</xsl:template>
</xsl:stylesheet>
```

Figure 6-2. Using XSLT to Transform an XML Document to HTML Sorted by Title (continued)

In the XSLT sample document in Figure 6-2, a number of common XSLT processing elements are used. First, the xsl:template element. This creates a capsulized set of processing instructions that are reused whenever a specific set of criteria is met. In this case, the template is run when the root node is encountered. One can get a better idea how this is utilized by looking at the print_title, print_animal, and print_people templates. Sorting is accomplised with the xsl:sort command and identifying the sort element. In this case, the sort element is the title attribute. Applying this XSLT to the source XML document produces the following HTML output.

The display in Figure 6-1 could be changed quickly by making minor modifications to the XSLT document. For example, if one wanted to re-sort by a different element, one would simply need to modify the xsl:sort tag or add a conditional to print-only items that had elephants. And while this is only a simple XSLT example, it demonstrates the primary purpose for which it was developed: to transform XML structures to new and useful documents.

So how does this relate to digital repositories and its metadata? Since most digital repositories utilize XML-based data structures, XSLT can be

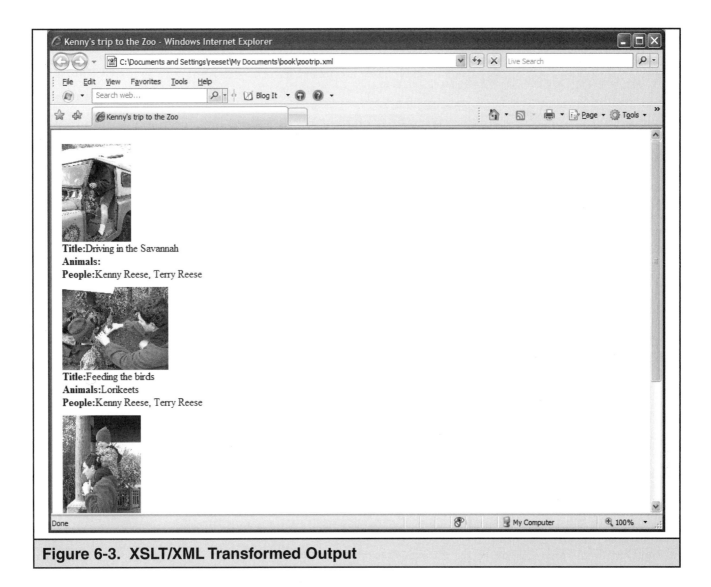

Figure 6-3. XSLT/XML Transformed Output

the method for moving data into an out of different metadata schemas or to create new displays. The earlier examples presented a very simplistic view of XSLT—but how could that be used to translation metadata from one format to another? The answer is that the translation gets more complicated.

The XSLT snippet in Figure 6-4 comes from a larger XSLT document capable of transforming Dublin Core metadata to MARC21XML. Looking at this snippet, a number of things become apparent. First, the XSLT document itself is a valid XML document with a number of namespaces defined at the top of the file. A valid XSLT file must define all namespaces that will be utilized during the process, and, therefore, we see namespaces defined for xsl, dc (Dublin Core) and MARC21XML, which is defined as the primary namespace. Within the file, conditional operations like xsl:for-each and xsl:if, are used to evaluate the current document being transformed.

```xml
<?xml version="1.0" encoding="UTF-8"?>
<xsl:stylesheet version="1.0" xmlns:dc="http://purl.org/dc/elements/1.1/"
xmlns="http://www.loc.gov/MARC21/slim"
xmlns:xsl="http://www.w3.org/1999/XSL/Transform" exclude-result-
prefixes="dc">
  <xsl:output method="xml" indent="yes"/>
    <xsl:template match="/">
    <record xmlns:xsi="http://www.w3.org/2001/XMLSchema-instance"
xsi:schemaLocation="http://www.loc.gov/MARC21/slim
http://www.loc.gov/standards/marcxml/schema/MARC21slim.xsd" >
        <xsl:element name="leader">
          <xsl:variable name="type" select="dc:type"/>
          <xsl:variable name="leader06">
            <xsl:choose>
                <xsl:when test="$type='collection'">p</xsl:when>
                <xsl:when test="$type='dataset'">m</xsl:when>
                <xsl:when test="$type='event'">r</xsl:when>
                <xsl:when test="$type='image'">k</xsl:when>
                <xsl:when test="$type='interactive resource'">m</xsl:when>
                <xsl:when test="$type='service'">m</xsl:when>
                <xsl:when test="$type='software'">m</xsl:when>
                <xsl:when test="$type='sound'">i</xsl:when>
                <xsl:when test="$type='text'">a</xsl:when>
                <xsl:otherwise>a</xsl:otherwise>
            </xsl:choose>
          </xsl:variable>
          <xsl:variable name="leader07">
            <xsl:choose>
                <xsl:when test="$type='collection'">c</xsl:when>
<xsl:otherwise>m</xsl:otherwise>
            </xsl:choose>
          </xsl:variable>
          <xsl:value-of select="concat('',$leader06,$leader07,' 3u')"/>
        </xsl:element>
        <xsl:for-each select="//dc:title[1]">
          <datafield tag="245" ind1="0" ind2="0">
            <subfield code="a">
                <xsl:value-of select="."/>
            </subfield>
          </datafield>
        </xsl:for-each>
        <xsl:for-each select="//dc:title[position()>1]">
          <datafield tag="246" ind1="3" ind2="3">
            <subfield code="a">
                <xsl:value-of select="."/>
            </subfield>
          </datafield>
        </xsl:for-each>
```

Figure 6-4. XSLT Excerpt from a Larger XSLT Document

Currently, XSLT can be used with two control vocabularies, version 1.0 and version 2.0 of the XSLT language. The difference between the two syntaxes is primarily the richness of the feature set. XSLT version 1.0 had mainly control elements for managing information flow. Rudimentary functionality relating to string, date, and math manipulations were available, but spartan. In many cases, XSLT style sheets would be designed to utilize some of these convenience functions, extensions to the XSLT language, found within the XSLT parser. Unfortunately, these extensions were not portable between parsers, making these types of solutions useful only in a local context. Version 2.0 of the XSLT language provides a richer vocabulary set, providing functionality for grouping, matching, and enhanced string, math, and date manipulation. However, not all XSLT parsers support XSLT version 2.0, limiting solutions utilizing this vocabulary's portability as well.

However, as noted, an XSLT document is at its core a specially crafted XML file. For this file to have meaning, one must utilize an XSLT parser. Most current generation Web browsers, like Firefox, Internet Explorer, Opera and Safari, provide a built-in XSLT parser making it possible to run an XSLT transformation within a Web browser. The XML file treeview interface, standard in all versions of Internet Explorer for example, is merely an XSLT-translated display copy of the original XML file. However, for actual XML/XSLT development, a native XSLT parser is recommended. Fortunately, again, XML has become so ubiquitous that XML/XSLT parsers are built into most operating systems, including Linux, Microsoft Windows 98–present, and Mac OS X. Likewise, a number of very good custom XSLT parsers like Saxon, libxml, and xerces are available for developers who want an XSLT parser with a specific set of custom extensions.

Furthermore, as noted, XSLT is becoming more widely utilized for creating user interface development within digital library projects. At present, XML-driven user interface (UI) projects are in active development, with institutional repository software projects leading many of these efforts. One example of such an ongoing project is found at Texas Tech University, where researchers are working to replace the traditional java server page interface found in Dspace with a more flexible XML-driven UI uses XSLT to generate unique collection interfaces. This project, known as Manakin, is an effort to utilize the inherent flexibility found in XML and XSLT to simplify the DSpace UI generation process and provide additional flexibility (Phillips et al., 2005). However, these are by no means the only projects working with XML-generated interfaces. A number of vendor and open-source projects are moving to XML-generated UI to enable more rapid prototyping of services and enable potential integration opportunities with other projects.

METADATA CROSSWALKING

The crosswalking of metadata is a process in which an XML document is transformed from one schema to another. During the crosswalking process, user defines XSLT style sheets to facilitate the movement of metadata between two formats. This process requires a number of decisions about how metadata elements from one schema relate to another. Metadata crosswalks are developed by examining the similarities and differences between differing schemas. Are they one-to-one relationships, that is, do elements share like meanings, or will the data need to be interpreted? Will the conversions be lossless, and, if not, what level of data loss will be acceptable? These decisions are actually some of the most important in the crosswalking process as they will ultimately affect the quality of the final product.

So why build metadata crosswalks? If crosswalking of metadata could result in the loss of metadata granularity, why not just create all metadata in the desired format to begin with? Well, metadata crosswalking is done for a variety of reasons, though few as important as interoperability. Information systems today have to be able to ingest various types of metadata from remote sources. Since the metadata found on remote servers may be different from that of the host system, the captured metadata must be crosswalked into a format that the local system can understand. Today, metadata crosswalking remains the primary mechanism by which different systems interoperate with each other. The crosswalking process removes data transfer barriers, allowing heterogeneous systems to successfully share data. Within the library community, this has manifested itself in federated search systems, which ingest metadata in various formats and provide a standardized search syntax between resources.

In addition to system interoperability, metadata crosswalking can be used to move data from an obsolete metadata schema. This type of data crosswalking has been done for decades when dealing with binary formats. Organizations routinely need to migrate image or document data from obsoleted file formats. Like binary formats, metadata formats change and become obsolete with time. As formats are phased out, crosswalks can be created to provide an upgrade path for obsolete metadata schemas.

Crosswalking Challenges

In many ways, moving bibliographic data between various metadata schemas is like trying to fit a square peg into a round hole. In the end, a crosswalk is simply a process of trying to round the square peg so that it makes for an easier fit. Fortunately, crosswalking challenges can generally be broken down into four categories:

1. metadata consistency
2. schema granularity
3. the "spare parts"
4. dealing with localisms

1. Metadata Consistency

When crosswalking metadata, consistency is the rule. The crosswalking process must assume that metadata in one format has been consistency created in order to develop rules about how that information should be represented in other metadata formats. Given the algorithmic nature of the crosswalking process and digital interoperability efforts in general, data consistency remains the key to these efforts (Gill and Miller, 2002). Without data consistency, crosswalking processes would need to be overly complex to deal with various data and very likely require human interaction during or after the process. Ideally, interoperability efforts should be fully automatic, requiring few exceptions for variations in the data. However, when dealing with interoperability, the issue of data consistency is often a large hidden cost. Within organizations, metadata practices tend to change over time. XML-based metadata formats have exasperated this problem in that institutions may change a metadata element's definition over time or by project. These types of changes, while possibly advantageous within a local system, prevent an organization from participating in larger interoperability efforts.

2. Schema Granularity

Very rarely does crosswalking occur between two metadata schemas that share the same level of granularity. In part, this is the nature of descriptive formats; they tend to be created to meet a specific need and capture specific types of descriptive information. As a result, the crosswalking of metadata becomes a process of (1) deciphering how metadata elements are related and (2) ascertaining if the crosswalk will result in a loss of data granularity. In the best-case scenario, metadata crosswalkers are looking for metadata elements that have one-to-one matches. For example, a title in one schema that matches the title element in another schema exactly. In this case, metadata can be directly mapped from one element to another. This would be a lossless crosswalk: something really only achieved when moving data between MARC21XML and MARC. More likely, metadata crosswalkers will need to match one element to many potential matches. This means one metadata element in one schema matches the definition of multiple metadata elements in a different schema—for example, moving data between Dublin Core and MARC21. As noted in past chapters, Dublin Core is a relatively low granular format with only 15 core metadata elements. When crosswalking between Dublin Core and MARC, there are a number of instances in which a single Dublin Core field maps to multiple MARC fields.

Taking a closer look at the Dublin Core creator field, it is clear how granularity can affect metadata crosswalking. The Dublin Core creator element, by definition, stores information about the publishers of a work. This means that any individual or organization responsible for the creation of the document should be tagged as a creator in the Dublin Core schema. In MARC21, entities are tagged according to the type of entity (personal, corporate, etc.)

Dublin Core	MARC21
Creator	100, 110, 111, 700, 710, 711, 720

Figure 6-5. Dublin Core to MARC21 Author Crosswalk

and their relation to the work—for example, as the main entry or contributor to a work. As such, the Dublin Core creator element could theoretically map into one of seven different metadata elements within MARC21. What's more, since Dublin Core doesn't capture the entity's type or relevance to the work, any mapping into MARC21 would be prone to tagging errors or be overly generalized. Would a crosswalk of this nature be useful? It would depend on the application. Within a federated search tool, where metadata tends to be interpreted broadly, this mapping would likely be good enough. Within a more formalized metadata management system that utilizes the tagged granularity to index data, this mapping would be of minimal use.

3. Dealing with "Spare Parts"

Because metadata crosswalking is rarely a lossless process, one often has to decide what information is "lost" during the crosswalking process. Moreover, data loss isn't limited strictly to the loss of descriptive metadata, but the contextual metadata as well. Going back to the example in Figure 6-6, metadata being crosswalked from MARC21 to Dublin Core could be transferred in a lossless manner since all data could be placed into the creator element. However, while bibliographic data would not be lost, the contextual metadata relating to the entity type of the creator (whether it's a personal or corporate author), as well as information relating to the entity tagged as the main entry, would not be kept. So in this case, the data loss would be primarily contextual.

One of the primary tasks associated with creating a metadata crosswalk is how one deals with the "spare parts," the unmappable data that cannot be carried through the crosswalk. For example, Encoded Archival Description (EAD) is a very hierarchical metadata schema with bibliographic data on both a collection- and item-level. This type of hierarchical structure is very difficult to crosswalk between metadata schemas and, in most cases, will just be dropped. In these cases, metadata experts need to decide what information must be preserved and try to work within the crosswalking parameters.

4. Dealing with Localisms

Lastly, metadata crosswalking must constantly be conscious of what one might call *localisms*—data added to the metadata to enable data to sort or display a specific way within a local system. Within digital repository software, many of these localisms will exist. At Oregon State University, a number of these localisms can be found within the library's image repository system. When the university first started adding images to its digital repository, a great deal of care was put into defining how the metadata should be displayed to the user. In order to normalize the metadata displayed to the user, HTML elements were embedded into the bibliographic metadata to insert line breaks, attach styles to data elements, or insert JavaScript into the user display to control specific layout elements. Within the local content system, these localisms did provide users with a normalized experience. However, harvesting this metadata for indexing outside of the local system consistently proved to be a challenge until the localisms were eventually removed.

OPEN ARCHIVES IMITATIVE PROTOCOL FOR METADATA HARVESTING (OAI-PMH)

Once an item has made it into a digital repository, how is it to be shared? Contributors are likely to want their work to reach the broadest audience; at the same time, digital repository administrators want to expose data in a way that will maximize its exposure at a relatively low cost. Can the repository be crawled by search engines or can the metadata be accessed by remote systems? In our shared information climate, digital repository software must be able to provide a straightforward method for sharing metadata about the items that it houses.

Fortunately, such a method exists in all major digital repository services. Open Archives Imitative Protocol for Metadata Harvesting (OAI-PMH) is simply a HTTP-based protocol that can be used to make digital repository's metadata available for harvest. The protocol works over a normal HTTP Get request allowing metadata to be harvested by the construction of a simple URL. For example, the following URL, http://digitalcollections.library. oregonstate.edu/cgi-bin/oai.exe?verb=ListRecords&metadataPrefix=oai_dc& set=bracero, will harvest all metadata items from the Oregon State University Libraries' Bracero collection. The protocol utilizes a limited set of verbs, limiting its functionality primarily to metadata harvesting and the querying of information about a specific collection or collections on the server. To simplify the OAI-PMH, the protocol requires the support of Unqualified Dublin Core. This is what is known as the compatibility schema, so no matter what OAI-PMH repository is harvested, one can be guaranteed that the metadata will be available in Dublin Core. However, this doesn't limit an OAI-PMH repository from supporting other metadata formats. In fact, quite the contrary. OAI-PMH implementers are encouraged to support multiple metadata formats, so that the repositories' metadata can be provided in various levels of granularity.

The OAI-PMH protocol recognizes five actions, or requests, that can be made to an OAI-PMH server. Attached to these actions is a limited set of arguments that can be set to limit the range of data to be harvested by date or set as well as request the harvested metadata in a specific schema. Harvesting limits are set primarily by identifying a range of dates from which to harvest using the *from* and *until* OAI-PMH arguments. Within the OAI-PMH server, date ranges limit the OAI-PMH response to items whose metadata timestamp has been modified within the specified date range. The *from* and *until* argument can be used as pairs or separately to selectively harvest metadata from an OAI-PMH repository. Additional arguments that can be found in an OAI-PMH request are set, resumptionToken, and metadataPrefix. The set argument is used to selectively harvest metadata from defined sets, or collections, of items on the OAI-PMH server. The metadataPrefix, on the other hand, specifies the OAI-PMH response metadata schema. Finally, OAI-PMH allows for the use of a resumptionToken as a method to control data flow. Many OAI-PMH servers will return a maximum number of records per request. If more metadata records exist within a given OAI-PMH request, the server will provide a resumptionToken that can be used to retrieve additional requested items.

OAI-PMH VERBS

- **GetRecord**
  This verb retrieves an individual metadata record from a repository. The GetRecord verb requires the use of the identifier and the metadataPrefix arguments. To request a record with the following id: oai:digitalcollections.library.oregon state.edu:bracero/37 from the Oregon State University Libraries' Bracero collection in Dublin Core format, one would submit the following request: http://digitalcollections .library.oregonstate.edu/cgi-bin/ oai.exe?verb=GetRecord& identifier=oai:digitalcollections.library.oregonstate.edu: bracero/37&metadataPrefix=oai_dc. This request would return the response in Figure 6-6.

- **Identify**
  This verb retrieves information about the repository. Sending an Identify request to an OAI-PMH server will return information such as the repository's name, the

```
<?xml version="1.0" encoding="UTF-8"?>
<OAI-PMH xmlns="http://www.openarchives.org/OAI/2.0/"
       xmlns:xsi="http://www.w3.org/2001/XMLSchema-instance"
       xsi:schemaLocation="http://www.openarchives.org/OAI/2.0/
       http://www.openarchives.org/OAI/2.0/OAI-PMH.xsd">
```

Figure 6-6. Response to a Get Record Request

Continued

```
    <responseDate>2006-12-10T21:36:58Z</responseDate>
    <request verb="GetRecord" metadataPrefix="oai_dc"
identifier="oai:digitalcollections.library.oregonstate.edu:bracero/37">http://
digitalcollections.library.oregonstate.edu/cgi-bin/oai.exe</request>
    <GetRecord>
      <record>
      <header>
<identifier>oai:digitalcollections.library.oregonstate.edu:bracero/37</identifier>
      <datestamp>2004-03-17</datestamp>
      <setSpec>bracero</setSpec>
      </header>
      <metadata>
      <oai_dc:dc
      xmlns:oai_dc="http://www.openarchives.org/OAI/2.0/oai_dc/"
      xmlns:dc="http://purl.org/dc/elements/1.1/"
      xmlns:xsi="http://www.w3.org/2001/XMLSchema-instance"
      xsi:schemaLocation="http://www.openarchives.org/OAI/2.0/oai_dc/
      http://www.openarchives.org/OAI/2.0/oai_dc.xsd">
      <dc:title>Washing &amp; ironing clothes.</dc:title>
      <dc:title>Braceros in Oregon Photograph Collection.</dc:title>
      <dc:creator></dc:creator>
      <dc:date>ca. 1942</dc:date>
      <dc:description>Mexican workers washing and ironing clothes. </dc:
description>
      <dc:subject>Agricultural laborers--Mexican--Oregon; Agricultural
laborers--Housing--Oregon; Laundry</dc:subject>
      <dc:coverage></dc:coverage>
      <dc:type>Image</dc:type>
      <dc:source>Silver gelatin prints</dc:source>
      <dc:title>Extension Bulletin Illustrations Photograph Collection
(P20)</dc:title>
      <dc:identifier>P20:1069</dc:identifier>
      <dc:source>Copy negative.</dc:source>
      <dc:rights>Permission to use must be obtained from OSU
Archives.</dc:rights>
      <dc:description>Master scanned with Epson 1640XL scanner at 600
or 800 dpi. Image manipulated with Adobe Photoshop ver.
7.0.</dc:description>
      <dc:identifier>P020_1069.</dc:identifier>
<dc:identifier>http://digitalcollections.library.oregonstate.edu/u?/bracero,37
</dc:identifier>
      </oai_dc:dc>
    </metadata>
    </record>
  </GetRecord>
</OAI-PMH>
```

Figure 6-6. Response to a Get Record Request (continued)

repository administrator's e-mail address, the base URL of the repository, the version of OAI-PMH supported, the timestamp of the first record placed into the repository, how it handles deleted records, and the harvesting granularity supported by the server. In regard to harvesting granularity, this doesn't refer to the metadata schemas supported by the OAI-PMH server, but rather granularity relating to an item's timestamp within the repository. Granularity for harvesting can be set to any valid ISO8601 combination. Most commonly, digital repositories utilize a day as the level of harvesting granularity, meaning requests would come in YYYY-MM-DD format, but could be extended to allow the specification of hours, minutes, seconds, and so forth. An example of an Identify request on the Oregon State University Libraries' OAI-PMH server would look like this: http://digital collections.library.oregonstate.edu/cgi-bin/oai.exe? verb=Identify and would return the response in Figure 6-7.

```
<?xml version="1.0" encoding="UTF-8"?>
<OAI-PMH xmlns="http://www.openarchives.org/OAI/2.0/"
      xmlns:xsi="http://www.w3.org/2001/XMLSchema-instance"
      xsi:schemaLocation="http://www.openarchives.org/OAI/2.0/
      http://www.openarchives.org/OAI/2.0/OAI-PMH.xsd">
<responseDate>2006-12-10T21:57:57Z</responseDate>
<request verb="Identify">http://digitalcollections.library.oregonstate.
edu/cgi-bin/oai.exe</request>
<Identify>
      <repositoryName>OSU Valley Library CONTENTdm Server
Respository</repositoryName>
      <baseURL>http://digitalcollections.library.oregonstate.edu/
cgi-bin/oai.exe</baseURL>
      <protocolVersion>2.0</protocolVersion>
      <adminEmail>systems@library.oregonstate.edu</adminEmail>
      <earliestDatestamp>2002-10-14</earliestDatestamp>
      <deletedRecord>transient</deletedRecord>
      <granularity>YYYY-MM-DD</granularity>
   </Identify>
</OAI-PMH>
```

Figure 6-7. Response to an Identify Request

- **ListMetadataFormats**

  This verb is retrieves the supported metadata schemas from an OAI-PMH server. This allows OAI-PMH harvesters to see if an OAI-PMH server supports a more granular metadata schema than the required Unqualified

Dublin Core. An example of a ListMetadataFormats request on the Oregon State University Libraries' OAI-PMH server would look like this: http://digitalcollections.library. oregonstate.edu/cgi-bin/oai.exe?verb=ListMetadata Formats. It would return the following response.

```
<?xml version="1.0" encoding="UTF-8"?>
<OAI-PMH xmlns="http://www.openarchives.org/OAI/2.0/"
        xmlns:xsi="http://www.w3.org/2001/XMLSchema-instance"
        xsi:schemaLocation="http://www.openarchives.org/OAI/2.0/
        http://www.openarchives.org/OAI/2.0/OAI-PMH.xsd">
    <responseDate>2006-12-10T22:05:33Z</responseDate>
    <request verb="ListMetadataFormats">http://digitalcollections.library.
oregonstate.edu/cgi-bin/oai.exe</request>
    <ListMetadataFormats>
      <metadataFormat>
        <metadataPrefix>oai_dc</metadataPrefix>

<schema>http://www.openarchives.org/OAI/2.0/oai_dc.xsd</schema>
<metadataNamespace>http://www.openarchives.org/OAI/2.0/oai_dc/</me
tadataNamespace>
      </metadataFormat>
      <metadataFormat>
        <metadataPrefix>qdc</metadataPrefix>
        <schema>http://epubs.cclrc.ac.uk/xsd/qdc.xsd</schema>
<metadataNamespace>http://epubs.cclrc.ac.uk/xmlns/qdc/</metadataNa
mespace>
      </metadataFormat>
    </ListMetadataFormats>
</OAI-PMH>
```

Figure 6-8. Response to a Request Using List Metadata Formats

Note in the *request* that multiple metadata formats are supported on this server. In this case, the server supports the standard oai_dc metadata Prefix (Unqualified Dublin Core) as well as the qdc metadataPrefix—or in this case, Qualified Dublin Core.

- **ListIdentifiers**
  This verb is used to return the identifiers of a set of items in an OAI-PMH repository. A request utilizing this verb can be paired with arguments setting a date range (from and until), a metadataPrefix, a limit by set, or the use of a resumptionToken for long requests. ListIdentifier requests do not return any other metadata about the items in a repository except the identifier, which could later be used

by the GetRecord verb to retrieve a specific item's full metadata record. An example of a ListIdentifiers request on the Oregon State University Libraries' OAI-PMH repository would look like this: http://digitalcollections. library.oregonstate.edu/cgi-bin/oai.exe?verb=ListIdentifiers &set=bracero&metadataPrefix=oai_dc. It would return the (truncated) response shown in Figure 6-9.

```
<?xml version="1.0" encoding="UTF-8"?>
<OAI-PMH xmlns="http://www.openarchives.org/OAI/2.0/"
        xmlns:xsi="http://www.w3.org/2001/XMLSchema-instance"
        xsi:schemaLocation="http://www.openarchives.org/OAI/2.0/
        http://www.openarchives.org/OAI/2.0/OAI-PMH.xsd">
  <responseDate>2006-12-10T22:13:16Z</responseDate>
  <request verb="ListIdentifiers" metadataPrefix="oai_dc"
set="bracero">http://digitalcollections.library.oregonstate.edu/
cgi-bin/oai.exe</request>
  <ListIdentifiers>
    <header>
<identifier>oai:digitalcollections.library.oregonstate.edu:bracero/37</identifier>
      <datestamp>2004-03-17</datestamp>
      <setSpec>bracero</setSpec>
    </header>
    <header>
<identifier>oai:digitalcollections.library.oregonstate.edu:bracero/38</identifier>
      <datestamp>2004-03-17</datestamp>
      <setSpec>bracero</setSpec>
    </header>
    <header>
<identifier>oai:digitalcollections.library.oregonstate.edu:bracero/39</identifier>
      <datestamp>2004-03-17</datestamp>
      <setSpec>bracero</setSpec>
    </header>
```

Figure 6-9. Response (Truncated) to a Request Using List Identifiers

- **ListRecords**

  This verb is used to harvest a list of full metadata records from an OAI-PMH server. This verb can be paired with arguments limiting the records to be harvested by date (until and from) or by set, as well as arguments setting the metadata preference (metadataPrefix) a resumptionToken when harvesting large data sets. In general, the ListRecords request looks identical to the ListIdentifiers request, save for the different variable usage and that the response to this request looks similar to the Get Record response format. An example of such a request for records in the Braceros collection on the Oregon State University Libraries' OAI-PMH server would look like this: http://digitalcollections.library.oregonstate.edu/cgi-bin/oai.exe?verb=ListRecords&metadataPrefix=oai_dc&set=bracero. The returning (truncated) response is shown in Figure 6-10.

```
<?xml version="1.0" encoding="UTF-8"?>
<OAI-PMH xmlns="http://www.openarchives.org/OAI/2.0/"
        xmlns:xsi="http://www.w3.org/2001/XMLSchema-instance"
        xsi:schemaLocation="http://www.openarchives.org/OAI/2.0/
        http://www.openarchives.org/OAI/2.0/OAI-PMH.xsd">
 <responseDate>2006-12-10T22:22:49Z</responseDate>
 <request verb="ListRecords" metadataPrefix="oai_dc"
set="bracero">http://digitalcollections.library.oregonstate.edu/
cgi-bin/oai.exe</request>
 <ListRecords>
   <record>
    <header>
<identifier>oai:digitalcollections.library.oregonstate.edu:bracero/37</identifier>
        <datestamp>2004-03-17</datestamp>
        <setSpec>bracero</setSpec>
    </header>
    <metadata>
      <oai_dc:dc
        xmlns:oai_dc="http://www.openarchives.org/OAI/2.0/oai_dc/"
        xmlns:dc="http://purl.org/dc/elements/1.1/"
        xmlns:xsi="http://www.w3.org/2001/XMLSchema-instance"
        xsi:schemaLocation="http://www.openarchives.org/OAI/2.0/oai_dc/
        http://www.openarchives.org/OAI/2.0/oai_dc.xsd">
        <dc:title>Washing &amp; ironing clothes.</dc:title>
        <dc:title>Braceros in Oregon Photograph Collection.</dc:title>
        <dc:creator></dc:creator>
        <dc:date>ca. 1942</dc:date>
        <dc:description>Mexican workers washing and ironing clothes.
</dc:description>
        <dc:subject>Agricultural laborers--Mexican--Oregon;
Agricultural laborers--Housing--Oregon; Laundry</dc:subject>
        <dc:coverage></dc:coverage>
        <dc:type>Image</dc:type>
        <dc:source>Silver gelatin prints</dc:source>
        <dc:title>Extension Bulletin Illustrations Photograph Collection
(P20)</dc:title>
        <dc:identifier>P20:1069</dc:identifier>
        <dc:source>Copy negative.</dc:source>
        <dc:rights>Permission to use must be obtained from OSU
```

Figure 6-10. Response to a Request Using List Records

Continued

```
Archives.</dc:rights>
        <dc:description>Master scanned with Epson 1640XL scanner
at 600 or 800 dpi. Image manipulated with Adobe Photoshop ver.
7.0.</dc:description>
        <dc:identifier>P020_1069.</dc:identifier>
<dc:identifier>http://digitalcollections.library.oregonstate.edu/u?/bracero,37
</dc:identifier>
     </oai_dc:dc>
     </metadata>
    </record>
```

Figure 6-10. Response to a Request Using List Records (continued)

- **ListSets**

  This verb is used to identify the current list of collections, or sets, registered on an OAI-PMH server. Only the resumptionToken argument can be paired with this verb—and only when a resumptonToken is necessary to complete a ListSets request. A sample ListSets request would look like the following: http://digitalcollections.library.oregon state.edu/cgi-bin/oai.exe?verb=ListSets. It would return the response in Figure 6-11.

```
<?xml version="1.0" encoding="UTF-8"?>
<OAI-PMH xmlns="http://www.openarchives.org/OAI/2.0/"
        xmlns:xsi="http://www.w3.org/2001/XMLSchema-instance"
        xsi:schemaLocation="http://www.openarchives.org/OAI/2.0/
        http://www.openarchives.org/OAI/2.0/OAI-PMH.xsd">
    <responseDate>2006-12-10T22:28:31Z</responseDate>
    <request verb= "ListSets">
http://digitalcollections.library.oregonstate.edu/cgi-bin/oai.exe </request>
    <ListSets>
      <set>
        <setSpec>bracero</setSpec>
        <setName>Braceros in Oregon Photograph Collection</setName>
      </set>
      <set>
        <setSpec>archives</setSpec>
        <setName>Archives</setName>
      </set>
      <set>
        <setSpec>streamsurvey</setSpec>
        <setName>NW Stream Survey</setName>
```

Figure 6-11. Response to a Request Using List Sets

Continued

```
    </set>
    <set>
      <setSpec>dna</setSpec>
      <setName>DNA</setName>
    </set>
    <set>
      <setSpec>pawardsmedals</setSpec>
      <setName>Pauling's Awards and Medals</setName>
    </set>
    <set>
      <setSpec>chembond</setSpec>
      <setName>Nature of the Chemical Bond</setName>
    </set>
    <set>
      <setSpec>plaserfiche</setSpec>
      <setName>Plaserfiche</setName>
    </set>
  </ListSets>
</OAI-PMH>
```

Figure 6-11. Response to a Request Using List Sets (continued)

OAI-PMH APPLICATION

With only five verbs and a limited set of arguments, OAI-PMH presents a low-barrier method for digital repositories to make their metadata harvestable to the world. And while many, including the authors, feel that digital repositories should make their metadata harvestable to the outside world, the obvious question for digital repository implementers is, what's in it for me? Obviously, metadata harvesting requires the allocation of resources to the harvesting process, as the harvesting of large repositories could mean the transfer of hundreds of megabytes of data. The Oregon State University institutional repository, for example, requires the transfer of about 50 megabytes of data if one were to harvest all available metadata. This type of data transfer could very easily start to consume significant resources if harvesting was done regularly by multiple institutions. So while harvestable metadata may make one a good neighbor within the current information ecosystem, it does come at a real cost. So what benefits can an organization glean from supporting an OAI-PMH server?

FACILITATING THIRD-PARTY INDEXING

First and foremost, organizations that support OAI-PMH have a greater likelihood of having their digital repositories indexed by the major commercial search providers. Search providers like Google, Yahoo!, and MSN all utilize OAI-PMH to crawl and index digital repositories. With a protocol like OAI-PMH, items within a database-driven application like a digital repository are hidden from a search provider's crawler. Search providers require static URLs to reliably crawl material, and database-driven applications utilize dynamic URLs that are constructed when an action, like data submission, is completed. This creates an invisible Web of documents that search providers simply can never index. Without this indexing, a digital repository severely limits the number of access points to the materials stored in that repository and to the repository's user interface. With only one access point, items in the repository will be underutilized and likely grow stale since they will be outside the normal discovery process.

OAI-PMH digital repositories offer a solution by making their metadata visible. In March 2006, Frank McCown, Xiaoming Liu, Michael L. Nelson, and Mohammad Zubair published a paper entitled, "Search Engine Coverage of the OAI-PMH Corpus" (McCown et al., 2006). In this report, the authors examined how the three current search providers, Google, Yahoo!, and MSN, handled automatic discovery of OAI-PMH materials. The researchers set out to discover what percentage of known OAI-PMH servers were being regularly harvested by the major search providers. To conduct the survey, the researchers downloaded ~10 million records from 776 OAI-PMH providers and extracted a sample set of ~3.3 million records (McCown et al., 2006). Using this corpus, researchers examined how often these items were indexed within the major search providers and where they would be returned within the results. What they found was that search providers Yahoo! and Google were actively harvesting materials from OAI-PMH providers, capturing 65% and 45% respectively of the items queried and finding that only 21% of the items were not indexed by any search provider (McCown et al., 2006). What the study showed was that search providers are already starting to utilize OAI-PMH as a method for harvesting academic content. Thus, digital repositories that expose the metadata using that protocol stand a higher chance of being indexed through a search provider's normal indexing process.

METADATA REPURPOSING

Digital repositories that support OAI-PMH also offer an organization a number of opportunities to repurpose metadata between various systems. Within the library community, many organizations still create MARC records for items housed in their digital repository for indexing with their ILS (integrated library system). This often means that organizations are creating duplicate copies of a metadata record: an original record created in MARC and a record created within the digital repository. However, by using a OAI-PMH server, organizations can reduce the need for duplicate metadata creation by simply deriving all metadata surrogates from the metadata stored within the digital repository.

OSU ELECTRONIC THESES PROCESS

Like many organizations, Oregon State University requires graduate students to submit their theses into the libraries' institutional repository (IR). The IR is where the primary metadata record for an individual thesis is created; however, a MARC metadata record still must be created for indexing into OCLC's WorldCat database and OSU' local ILS. Previously, library technical services staff would simply recreate the MARC records manually using the metadata from the IR as a template. While this process took only a handful of minutes to complete, when multiplied for 50–100 documents, it was found that a significant number of resources were being spent recreating these metadata records.

In order to streamline generation of MARC metadata, a process was developed that allowed technical services staff to use the OAI-PMH server to output an item's metadata and automatically generate the necessary MARC records. Moreover, given the ability to harvest sets of records in one-month increments, the harvesting process would only need to be done at the end of each month, or 12 times during the year.

To develop the process, OSU developed a custom XSLT crosswalk specific to the electronic theses collection (see http://hdl.handle.net/1957/6300) and MarcEdit's built-in OAI-PMH harvester (Reese, 2007). Utilizing MarcEdit, library staff simply initialize the built-in OAI-PMH harvester and it provides the necessary harvesting information.

Using the MarcEdit OAI-PMH Harvester, technical services staff are able to set the harvesting range and the desired characterset of the MARC records. In Figure 6-12, one can see that MarcEdit's OAI-PMH Harvester

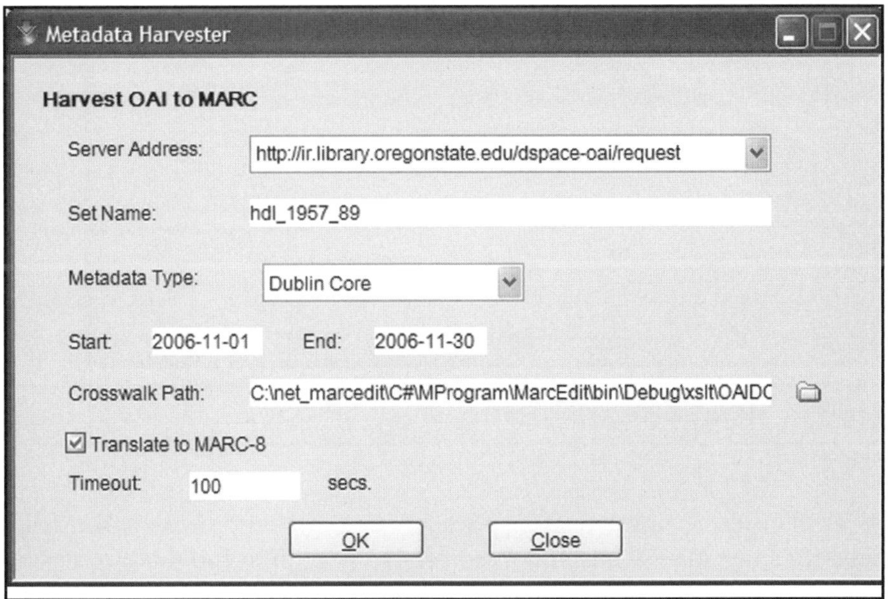

Figure 6-12. MarcEdit OAI-PMH Harvester

offers the user the ability to harvest from multiple known metadata types as well as convert XML data encoded in UTF-8 (Unicode) character set into the more traditional MARC-8 character set. With the options set, staff simply run the harvester which returns a file of generated MARC records.

Once generated, files are loaded into a MarcEditor as seen in Figure 6-13. Files harvested from the IR present a number of challenges, since metadata is only available in Unqualified Dublin Core. The prob-

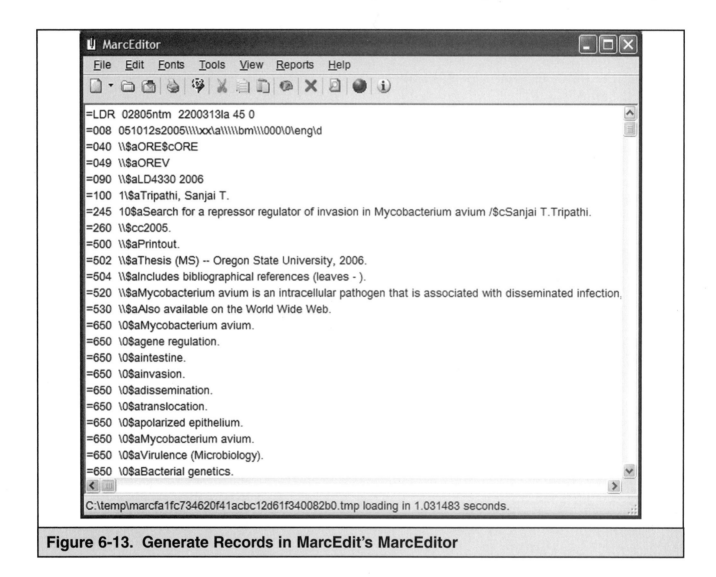

Figure 6-13. Generate Records in MarcEdit's MarcEditor

lems manifest themselves in two ways: (1) a system process will modify an item's metadata timestamp incorrectly, marking it for harvest; and (2) both controlled and uncontrolled subject terms are stored in the same Unqualified Dublin Core element. Once within the MarcEditor, staff have the ability to edit records individually or globally using one of a number of built-in tools. At OSU, staff have chosen to use MarcEdit's built-in macro language to generate a script that can remove the superfluous metadata and remove incorrectly harvested item metadata from the record set. Once the script has been completed, staff are left with a set of MARC records ready to be shared with other MARC systems. This process generates the necessary MARC records, which can be then loaded directly into OCLC and the library's ILS. The process requires staff to perform minimal record editing, significantly reducing the time needed to process materials.

MICROFORMATS

Microformats are a relatively new phenomenon in digital computing. They are built on the premise of coupling semantic data within an HTML (or XHTML) container. Unlike many methods for marking up data, which are primarily designed to make machine-to-machine communications easier, microformats are designed with humans, rather than computers, in mind. Microformats provide marked up data that is primarily human readable, but exist in an open and standard format, allowing machine processes to perform actions upon them. Microformats are designed to loosely embed semantic information into a host document. For example, hCalendar, a microformat specification that defines how calendar information can be marked up and embedded within an HTML (or XHTML) document, utilizes existing markup rules first to display information, but then to enable machine-capture of information. So within an HTML/XHTML document, an hCalendar entry may look like Figure 6-14.

```
<span class="vevent">
  <a class="url" href="http://www.innovativeusers.org/">
    <span class="summary">15th Annual IUG Usergroup</span>:
    <abbr class="dtstart" title="2007-05-14">May 14</abbr>-
    <abbr class="dtend" title="2007-05-17">May 17</abbr>,
  at the <span class="location">Hilton Hotel, San Francisco, CA</span>
  </a>
</span>
```

Figure 6-14. hCalendar Entry in an HTML/XHTML Document

This entry makes it easy to see how microformats work. The hCalendar document is embedded within a set of span tags that identify it as an event because of its class. Within the span tag group, each additional tag utilizes the class attribute to define an aspect of the event. When rendered, the HTML (XHTML) document would render the following information:

15th Annual IUG Usergroup: May 14-May 17, at the Hilton Hotel, San Francisco, CA

The embedded microformat actually generates a Web link that includes all the information for the event. Here, the microformat fulfills its primary role, which is to provide formatted data for human interaction. One could easily change how this data renders without affecting the data encoded within the microformat. This content has been made harvestable or actionable by utilizing the microformat as well; machine processes "reading" this content can now easily extract the event information.

So how are microformats used? Microformats are designed around the idea of the Web browser as a platform development tool. They work best when plug-ins or widgets can be embedded within the browser, allowing users to interact with content that appears on the page, but they also can be acted upon by pages utilizing AJAX Web techniques. This makes microformat development ideal for definable communities, as plug-ins and support networks can be developed among users. The library community, for example, while large, represents a definable population that could benefit from greater use of microformats in their digital collections and their library catalogs to help share information between institutions. Likewise, as a group, users can develop shared tools for the community. Outside of these definable communities however, microformats have less of an impact, since most Web browsers don't offer native support for many microformat specifications. This means that, in most cases, microformats have yet to obtain mainstream support, but niche developers are filling in these gaps. Examples of this exist within the library community, for example, tools like Zotero (content management Firefox plug-in utilizing COinS, or ContextObjects in Spans, www.zotero.org) and Openly's OpenURL Referrer (OpenURL Firefox plug-in utilizing COinS, http://openly.oclc.org/openurlref/) being made freely available to the research community.

What exactly do microformats do for a digital library? This is a good question, specifically when one considers that many microformats do indeed lack mainstream support for Web browsers and many library vendors in general. The answer comes back to data remixability and simplification. Microformats represent a low barrier method of adding attributes to documents or links that they describe. Since microformats are simply an HTML span tag marked with a special class element, they can be embedded with little to no effort. And while they may lack mainstream support within Web browsers, the library community has created a number of tools and browser extensions specifically designed to support specific microformats.

Second, microformats assign attributes to the objects that they are describing. Within a digital library system, these attributes become invaluable because they allow individuals and organizations the ability to develop tools that can then work between projects, domains, and groups. A good example of digital library projects using microformats is the routing of users to full-text documents. OpenURL, a protocol discussed in more detail in Chapter 7, provides a standard for linking individuals with documents. Organizations that implement an OpenURL resolver utilize a special linking syntax that directs users through the OpenURL resolver to the direct link to a full-text resource. However, since organizations have licensed access to different resources, users searching from one organization might not have access to resources through another. For example, a user from the University of Oregon may have access to a full-text item that a user from Oregon State University might not. Using the OpenURL resolution model, a University of Oregon student would be unable to retrieve the full-text information if he or she were searching the Oregon State University system. This is because the links generated to the OpenURL resolver would be generating links to items available specifically to Oregon State University patrons. However, using microforms, the OpenURL information could be decoupled from the link to the OpenURL server, allowing browser tools to autogenerate article links through the user's home OpenURL resolver. This would allow patrons to search for resources from any system but still have access to items held by their own institutions by using the microformat information to dynamically build access-links to the items. Fortunately, such a microformat exists—it's called COinS.

COINS

COinS, or ContextsObjects in Spans, represents one of the library community's first and most successful development and implementation of a microformat standard. COinS was developed on the heels of OpenURL (see Chapter 7), a protocol developed to solve the many problems with the discovery and linking to periodical content. COinS was developed as a method of embedding OpenURL information into an HTML/XHTML Web document. Traditionally, OpenURLs are generated as static URIs that link to a particular organization's OpenURL resolver for resolution. COinS provides a method for embedding OpenURL information onto a page without linking the content to a particular resolver.

Like the hCalendar example above, COinS are embedded within a span tag, however, in the case of COinS, it is a single span tag. For example, the West Midland Bird Club makes use of COinS to provide information about books or articles linked from its page. Looking at the page www.westmidlandbirdclub.com/biblio/NBotWM.htm in Firefox with the Openly OpenURL Referrer generates the text in Figure 6-15.

Figure 6-16 highlights a link that does not actually exist on the Web page. This link is generated by the Openly OpenURL Referrer utilizing a COinS that it found on the page. In this case, the COinS object in question is information about a book embedded within the document.

Figure 6-15. COinS in the Browser

```
<p class="center"><a href="http:
//en.wikipedia.org/w/index.php?title=Special:Booksources&amp;
isbn=0950788120" title="Book sources">ISBN 0 9507881-2-0 <img
src="../images/icons/external.gif" class="external" alt="*"></a>. <span
class="Z3988" title="ctx_ver=Z39.88-
2004&amp;rft_val_fmt=info%3Aofi%2Ffmt%3Akev%3Amtx%3Abook&amp
;rfr_id=info%3Asid%2Focoins.info%3Agenerator&amp;rft.genre=book&am
p;rft.btitle=The+New+Birds+of+the+West+Midlands&amp;rft.title=The+Ne
w+Birds+of+the+West+Midlands&amp;rft.isbn=0+9507881-2-
0&amp;rft.au=Graham+Harrison&amp;rft.au=Janet+Harrison&amp;rft.
date=2005&amp;rft.pub=West+Midland+Bird+Club&amp;rft.place=Studley
%2C+Warwickshire%2C+England"> </span></p>
```

Figure 6-16. Code with COinS Object for a Book Embedded

A quick inspection of the HTML code shows this to be true. Embedded within the block of code in Figure 6-16 is the COinS object for the book. The object is found in Figure 6-17.

```
<span class="Z3988" title="ctx_ver=Z39.88-
2004&amp;rft_val_fmt=info%3Aofi%2Ffmt%3Akev%3Amtx%3Abook&amp
;rfr_id=info%3Asid%2Focoins.info%3Agenerator&amp;rft.genre=book&am
p;rft.btitle=The+New+Birds+of+the+West+Midlands&amp;rft.title=The+Ne
w+Birds+of+the+West+Midlands&amp;rft.isbn=0+9507881-2-0&amp;rft.
au=Graham+Harrison&amp;rft.au=Janet+Harrison&amp;rft.date=2005&a
mp;rft.pub=West+Midland+Bird+Club&amp;rft.place=Studley%2C+Warwic
kshire%2C+England"> </span>
```

Figure 6-17. Code with COinS Object

From the information found within this span tag, the Openly plug-in was able to construct a link on the Web page directing me, the user, to the resources currently available at Oregon State University. This allows developers to capture the OpenURL information and link the user to the available content. Tools like Openly's OpenURL Referrer were developed to take advantage of COinS placed within documents, giving users a seamless way to get to content.

UNAPI

While COinS provides an embedded linking mechanism in a Web page, UNAPI (http://unapi.info/specs/), seeks to address the issue of copying rich objects on the Web. The UNAPI specification was developed primarily by the library community as a method for copying the rich content found within current digital collections between systems. The goal with UNAPI is to make data portable in a way that has not yet been realized in the library digital community. And like COinS, UNAPI was defined as a microformat utilizing an HTTP response API.

Within the UNAPI specification, document identifiers are encoded in the HTML ABBR tag block. The identifiers are used to query advertised UNAPI services. A UNAPI call for example, might look like Figure 6-18.

```
<abbr class="unapi-id" title="urn:isbn:0321154916"> The C# programming
language; ISBN: 0-32115-491-6</abbr>
```

Figure 6-18. UNAPI Call

In embedding identifier information, UNAPI opens up the possibility for tools to download and capture packages of rich content for local use. Consider UNAPI within the context of a personal digital library or research service. Users would be able to copy not just a link to the materials, but the documents themselves, for local usage.

UNAPI services respond using HTTP response codes to relay status information about the item and service, in addition to an XML wrapper providing information about an action or event. Currently, the documentation utilizes a number of predefined HTTP response codes, associating responses to each. At present, UNAPI servers utilizing the following response codes (UNAPI Spec., 2006)

- 300 Multiple Choices, for the UNAPI?id=IDENTIFIER function
- 302 Found, for responses to the UNAPI?id=IDENTIFIER &format=FORMAT function that redirect
- 404 Not Found, for requests for an identifier that is not available on the server
- 406 Not Acceptable, for requests for an identifier that is available on the server in a format that is not available for that identifier

Using a combination of response codes and XML response data, UNAPI designers have sought to create a simple set of codes to utilize specifications that can be implemented at a very low cost. And while the UNAPI format is new, the library community seems to be showing strong support for it. Popular repository software applications like DSpace and Fedora have implemented, or are planning to implement, UNAPI support within their respective platforms. Likewise, library developers have started porting UNAPI support into popular open-source software like WordPress, Evergreen, and WikiD.

SUMMARY

Digital repositories offer the library community an opportunity to interact with a growing number of information providers within today's information ecosystem. This offers the library community an opportunity to build upon its shared legacy of data sharing and serve as an example for other members of the information community. This means providing the technical support needed to enable metadata harvesting, as well as giving up control over how that metadata is used once it has been harvested. Of course, organizations benefit from this data sharing as well, because more of their repository's content will be made available to a global audience through multiple access points. The library community and digital repository implementers should be moving in a direction that will enable users to access content within their chosen workflow. Finding ways to free one's metadata from the confines of its digital repository or content management system offers a first step towards that goal.

REFERENCES

Computer Language Company. 2006. "Computer Desktop Encyclopedia." Answers.com (last updated December 8, 2006). Available: www.answers.com/topic/mashup-web-application-hybrid

Gill, Tony, and Paul Miller. 2002. "Re-inventing the Wheel? Standards, Interoperability and Digital Cultural Content." *DLIB* 8, no.1 (January). Available: www.dlib.org/dlib/january02/gill/01gill.html

Google. Available: www.google.com (accessed September 15, 2007).

McCown, Frank, Xiaoming Liu, Michael L. Nelson, and Mohammed Zubair. 2006. "Search Engine Coverage of the OAI-PMH Corpus." *IEEE Internet Computing* 10, no. 2 (March/April): 66-73

Microformats.org. "hCalendar." Available: http://microformats.org/wiki/hcalendar

Microsoft MSN Live. Available: www.live.com (accessed September 15, 2007).

Open Archives Initiative. "The Open Archives Initiative Protocol for Metadata Harvesting," (Last updated June 14, 2002). Available: www.openarchives.org/OAI/openarchivesprotocol.html

Phillips, Scott, Cody Green, John Leggett, Alexey Maslov, Adam Mikeal, and Brian Surratt. "'Manakin' XML UI Project." A&M University Libraries (last updated October 2005). Available: http://svn.di.tamu.edu/svn/xmlui/trunk/docs/ManakinDevelopersGuide.doc

Reese, Terry. "MarcEdit 5.0." (Last updated 2007). Available: http://oregonstate.edu/~reeset/marcedit

UNAPI Spec. (Last updated June 23, 2006). Available: http://unapi.info/specs/

7 FEDERATED SEARCHING OF REPOSITORIES

The overall success of a digital repository will ultimately be tied to the repository's ability to build content and facilitate discovery. Earlier chapters have discussed the necessity of having a cohesive collection development policy in place to ensure a logical development of collections within the digital repository. This ensures that the digital repository doesn't become a virtual attic full of stale materials, but rather is constantly being refreshed and weeded as the collection continues to grow.

In the same manner, responsible digital repository administrators need to consider what level of discovery their digital repository will support. In Chapter 6, a great deal of attention was given to the development of services around a digital repository and the benefits associated with allowing the harvesting of one's repository's metadata. The sharing of metadata goes a long way towards promoting the open-access culture that the library community continues to cultivate—but doesn't relate directly to discovery. In many cases, individuals will harvest and reindex metadata to create new research tools or services. Yes, this offers a different set of access points, but it provides the content within a different contextual framework. Ultimately, allowing the sharing and harvesting of metadata requires organizations to give up some level of control of the metadata and content as individuals mix and mash their services with other materials.

Discovery is a different animal altogether. While metadata harvesting does promote discovery of materials within different contexts and services, it's not explicitly used, nor should it be solely relied upon, for outside discovery. Successful digital repositories offer a multiplicity of discovery avenues, allowing users the ability to choose from different searching methodologies. Digital repository administrators need to consider what additional searching protocols they are willing to support to provide the necessary access points for both users and what we today refer to as federated searching. In some cases, support for library protocols like SRU/W or OpenURL may be provided by the digital repository software platform—but if not, what and how is support added? Likewise, does the organization wish to support emerging search protocols from outside the library community, like OpenSearch, and what benefits will adding such support give the repository and its users? How does a digital repository administrator decide what legacy protocols to continue to support and when legacy protocols should be deemed obsolete? Repository administrators have a wide range of potential protocols and search standards that could be supported by their repository software. This means that an evaluation should be conducted of who should search the repository and how. This chapter will highlight a number of the protocols most often supported within the library community and the current crop of federated search software packages.

WHAT IS FEDERATED SEARCHING?

Before jumping too far into this chapter, the sticky issue of federated search needs to be dealt with. Within the current literature, the terms federated search, metasearching, integrated searching, cross-database searching, parallel searching, and many other terms are all used to represent the same set of like concepts. For the purpose of this book, metasearch and federated search will be used interchangeably to represent the same set of technologies and concepts. So what is a federated search?

Baeza-Yates and Ribeiro-Neto (1999) give this definition for federated search:

Support for finding items that are scattered among a distributed collection of information sources or services, typically involving sending queries to a number of servers and then merging the results to present in an integrated, consistent, coordinated format.

Federated search systems provide a normalized method for searching multiple databases through a single query. It's important to note that conceptually federated search systems have been available for a very long time. Since the late 1990s, a number of federated search systems have been found within the library community and outside the library community. Early examples of federated search tools include library resources like Federated Searcher, a Java-based application used for federated searching of theses (1998), Stanford's START project (1997), Virginia Tech Federated Search (1998), and OCLC's Site Search; as well as non-library tools such as the Federal Geospatial Data Committee's 1996 Z39.50-based search portal for geospatial data. Federated search tools like OCLC's Site-Search and search engine metasearch tools like Metacrawler are good examples of these early federated search tools. These tools served as a searching portal, allowing users to query a large number of resources through a single interface.

Figure 7-1 shows a diagram of a traditional federated search system. These systems utilize a single query form that sits on top of the actual federated search engine. This engine handles the actual communication

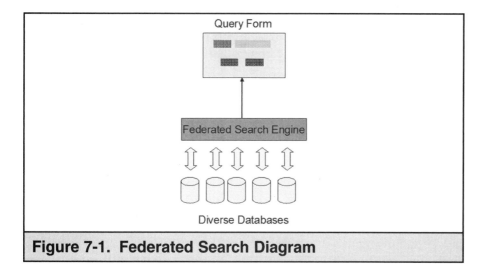

Figure 7-1. Federated Search Diagram

with the various databases to be queried. Moreover, this engine will traditionally handle tasks related to normalizing the resulting information from the various databases. This would include handling tasks like sorting, merging, and deduping results from various databases. Today, this diagram has changed slightly. With the advent of the Open Archive Initiative (OAI) and other metadata harvesting protocols, many federated search systems have become hybrid search systems—harvesting, normalizing, and locally indexing metadata for some systems—while maintaining the broadcasting search components for resources that cannot be harvested.

Hybrid federated search systems, as diagrammed in Figure 7-2, utilize a local data store to improve indexing and response time. These systems

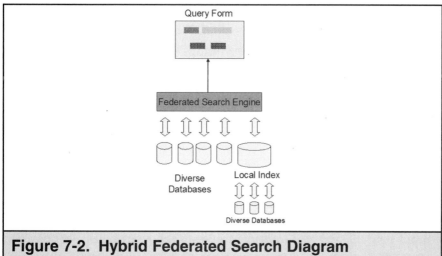

Figure 7-2. Hybrid Federated Search Diagram

utilize a just-in-case philosophy, harvesting, indexing, and normalizing metadata from a set of diverse databases prior to the user's query, much the same way a Web search engine crawls and indexes the Web.

FEDERATED SEARCH AND DIGITAL LIBRARIES

How federated search fits into the larger picture of digital libraries may not be readily apparent at first glance. For the staff of most organizations, the question of how a federated search product will interact with their digital repository infrastructure is likely to be the farthest thing from their minds. But not considering this question puts a digital collection at a distinct disadvantage and ultimately shortchanges users' overall experience.

Federated search tools are often thought of only in relation to electronic serial content. Organizations purchase access to thousands of journals online. Since 2000, federated search tools have begun springing up, promising to provide single search interface for all these resources. However, as a digital repository program develops, collections and projects will often become siloed. The development of these information silos are often unintended and tend to be a result of funding sources or software platform choices. For example, an organization may utilize DSpace for their electronic theses collection, CONTENTdm for their archival image collection, and a homegrown database application to store their Encoded Archival Description (EAD) content. Separated by software platform, each of these projects represents a separate interface that a user would need to query in order to locate content. These separate interfaces would marginalize these collections by placing them outside of the organization's mainstream query interface. What's more, this would represent three new query interfaces existing on top of a library's traditional search tools, like the integrated library system and electronic journal pages. In all, a user might have to search eight to ten different locations just to cast a net broad enough to query most of the important organizational resources for a particular topic.

While federated search tools certainly have the ability to provide a more unified search interface for vended serial content, they are probably best suited for uniting discovery for locally developed digital collections. This in large part due to the fact that an organization has the ability to control how outside resources interact with the local tools. This can give institutions the ability to create or support standard Web services API to enable better integration with their federated search software. Likewise, local digital projects are more likely to accommodate local data harvesting, allowing tools to harvest collections into a single repository for a faster search.

Digital repository programs can also take advantage of a federated search program to expand acquisition and collection development resources. Many digital repository developers will often make the mistake of considering only their organizations' digital content and projects as "collectable" digital resources. However, a good federated search program allows an organization to fully utilize digital collections not just from their own digital resources but also digital resources from other organizations, removing the barriers of organizational ownership and distance for patrons. This means users at one organization can query resources from not only their institution, but from selected digital collections from other institutions. In this way, an organization could potentially leverage the U.S. Library of Congress's American Memory Project (http://memory.loc.gov/ammem/index.html) and Oaister (www.oaister.org) alongside local and vended content. Finally, federated search tools offer organizations the ability to provide value-added services for users. Federated search tools can allow organizations to capture search history and document click counts to augment ranking algorithms and provide context to search results.

FEDERATED SEARCH VERSUS TRADITIONAL SEARCH ENGINES

Given the improvements made by search engines like Google, Yahoo!, and MSN, one is left to wonder if federated searching is still relevant today. Within the library community, federated search tools have traditionally been used to link vendor content with other resources, which to some degree is starting to happen at the search engine level through the Google Scholar and MSN Academic search sites. Given the development of these portals, should federated search even be a consideration for digital repository administrators? At this point, the answer would be yes. While traditional search engines are moving to harvest more and more academic content, the vended content still eludes indexing. Large content aggregators like EBSCOHost, Lexis Nexis, and others still shield their materials from indexing by the major search engines. What's more, most integrated library systems (ILS), local database-driven applications, and repositories will probably never be indexed by traditional search engines. This leaves a significant pool of resources from which a federated search system could benefit.

CURRENT RESEARCH

While the concept of federated searching is not new, its acceptance as a mainstream technology by the larger library community is a more recent event. As recently as 2003, nearly all federated search packages in use were developed and maintained through local library development efforts, with commercial vendors like WebFeat providing service to a handful of libraries that outsourced these services. This has changed. By and large, libraries have abandoned their own development efforts in favor of larger vendor-supported software packages that have allowed federated search to move into the mainstream. This movement has highlighted a number of areas of research that is still needed in the federated search community.

RECOMMENDER/COLLABORATIVE FILTERING

Current federated search services query preselected or user-selected groups of information. This assumes that the user community making use of a particular tool are expert users or are familiar with the resources being queried. One of the weaknesses of federated search is the ability to serendipitously discover information within larger datasets, something that the current crop of federated search tools do poorly. Within the federated search community, there is currently a drive to understand how collaborative filtering of results and databases can lead to a better understanding of how target databases could be transparently selected or recommended to the user based on query terms. Computer science researchers like Jon Herlocker of Oregon State University have been studying collaborative filtering techniques for the past 10 years. Herlocker has recently started working with the Oregon State University Valley Libraries to see how this research can be applied to a digital library (Webster, Jung and Herlocker, 2004).

DEDUPLICATION OF RESULTS

Most of the current generation of federated search tools currently provide some form of deduplication of items from a given results set. However, the way in which each tool provides that deduplication service varies in both technique and effectiveness. Given the varied nature of data recovery from target databases, deduplication techniques based solely on titles, dates, or authors are prone to be spotty at best. Federated search developers continue to research better and more normalized methods for providing better deduplication of resources and ways of displaying duplicate results.

KNOWLEDGE-BASE MANAGEMENT

Before vendor federated search systems became mainstream, a number of larger academic institutions, like the University of California system, created and managed their own federated search tools. In many ways, these early search tools remain superior to the current crop of federated search platforms due to their high level of customizability and integration with other local services. However, many of these tools have since been abandoned precisely because that management of the federated search knowledge-base, that is, the connection information required by the federated search engine was often difficult to create and expensive to maintain. Vendor-based solutions provided a method to outsource much of the technical knowledge-base management to a third-party. Even with this outsourcing, knowledge-base management still consumes a great deal of time for organizations, making this an area that federated search vendors are constantly looking to improve. Within the open-source community, this issue is also getting attention, as researchers trying to develop community-oriented federated search tools are looking at methods to create shared knowledge-base systems to reduce management tasks for all users (Reese, 2006).

AUTOMATIC DATA CLASSIFICATION

As hybrid federated search systems become more widely utilized, a growing need for the automated classification of resources will continue to develop. Given the varied nature of access points, vocabulary, and classification, research on the normalization and automatic classification of items based on concepts is a growing field. Ongoing research projects, like Emory State University's MetaCombine Project, seek to better understand how materials within a specific corpus can be automatically classified to aid local indexing and construction of faceted results sets.

RANKING SYSTEMS

All federated search systems provide some methodology for doing some relevance ranking of items within a result set. However, this ranking is often user-initiated and carried out after the items have been queried. Given the inherent speed limitations built into a broadcast search system, federated systems traditionally print results as they are returned from target databases. In other words, unlike traditional search engines, which provide the most relevant items at the beginning of a results set, federated search systems require user interaction to replicate that ranking. What's more, given the varied nature of the data returned by target resources, ranking items themselves within a larger result set can be a challenge in and of itself and continue to be fertile ground for continued research and discovery.

NEED FOR SPEED

The mainstreaming of federated search has also highlighted a number of inherent weaknesses within the current federated search infrastructure, the greatest of these being the overall time needed to complete a search. Current-generation federated search systems are built around the concept of broadcast searching. Upon receiving a user request, the federated search engine makes separate search requests to each of the target databases selected for search. System latency varies by the number of resources queried. A higher number of database targets increases system latency as the federated search tool must perform more searches before the result set can be completed. Additionally, the federated search engine must perform the varied set of normalization, ranking, ordering, and classification tasks necessary to prepare the data for presentation to the user.

Adding to the built-in inefficiencies is the lack of standardization by data providers. Often federated search developers must develop special normalization routines for specific data providers due to data structure or implementation of non-standard protocols. Until 2006, neither the National Information Standards Organization (NISO), the W3C, or the American Library Association (ALA) offered vendors guidance on the implementation of protocols or data standards for federated searching. This changed in August 2006 with the release of NISO RP-2006-02, the NISO Metasearch XML Gateway Implementers Guide. NISO RP-2006-02 provides data aggregators for the first time with guidance for the development of search gateways for federated search systems (National Information Standards Organization, 2006). As data aggregators begin to implement these emerging standards, issues relating to data normalization should become less important, and the current state of federated searching should improve. Though federated searching will never be able to provide the instant response time that a traditional search engine gives, improvements to the current federated search infrastructure should eventually lead to noticeable improvements in speed and scalability.

SEARCHING PROTOCOLS

As the library community has become more dependant on new and emerging technologies to deliver and maintain services, so too have they become more dependant on specific technical metadata standards and protocols. Chapters 4 and 5 discussed the library community's reliance on XML and XML-based metadata schemas within current-generation digital repositories for bibliographic description. These chapters discussed the various ways in which XML-centric metadata systems are changing the way that systems and individuals can interact with their descriptive data. They also discuss the major technologies currently being utilized in conjunction with these XML-centric descriptive systems. The library community has also come to rely on a specific set of communication protocols to allow remote searching of local systems.

Since the late 1990s, the library community has seen an explosion in the number of available communication protocols for library services. Protocols like LDAP for authentication, OAI for data harvesting, OpenURL and DOI for linking are playing a major role in the way the library of the twenty-first century interacts with its users. Furthermore, for the first time, the library community isn't just looking to its own community, but is looking outside the library community for communication and data transfer protocols that are easy to implement and can provide a robust level of search and integration. Digital repository administrators need to carefully consider what communication protocols they wish to support, and for each protocol, they must decide what is needed to support real-time federated search of their content. Given the girth of protocols available, this analysis will focus on the three search protocols that enjoy the widest support within the library community and beyond: Z39.50, SRU/W, and OpenSearch. Though other protocols exist, these are almost universally supported by federated search systems, and provide a great deal of flexibility in terms of query support and metadata formats.

Z39.50

Z39.50 is the grandfather of federated search protocols in the library community. Its roots go back to the early 1970s, when it was a way for large bibliographic databases like the U.S. Library of Congress and OCLC to share bibliographic data between systems. In 1979, a NISO committee was formed to investigate the development of a standard data protocol that could facilitate bibliographic data sharing. These efforts culminated in the development of Z39.50-1988, or Z39.50 Version 1. As documented later by Clifford Lynch, one of the original members of the committee, Version 1 was, in effect, a theoretical concept draft that was virtually unimplementable. In retrospect, Lynch would call the first Z39.50 draft an utter fiasco that should have never been approved by the committee (Lynch, 1997). Following the approval of Version 1, the Library of Congress was appointed as the maintenance agency for the protocol.

The protocol was subsequently revised again in 1992 (Z39.50-1992), expanding the protocols' capabilities and borrowing heavily from work being done internationally published by the International Organization for Standardization (ISO) as ISO 10162/10163. However, like the previous version of the protocol, Z39.50 was still tied to the Open System Interconnection (OSI) framework. The OSI model is a seven-layered conceptual model that describes how information moves from the application level in one environment, through the network level, and to the application level of a target.

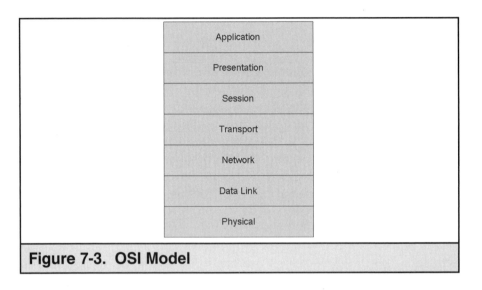

Figure 7-3. OSI Model

For practical purposes, the Z39.50-1992 draft was also unimplementable due to its continued reliance on the OSI framework—particularly a desire to make use of the presentation layer within the OSI model. This coupling hamstrung developers and continued to be a barrier for implementation. Recounting his work with the Z39.50 community, Clifford Lynch notes:

> By 1992, it was already clear to most implementers that OSI had failed, but this was not yet a politically acceptable statement within international standards bodies or certain U.S. government and library circles. There was at least one OSI-based implementation of Z39.50-1992, which was developed but never really much exercised because there was nobody to talk to—and no way of talking to anyone. In order to move Z39.50 from theory to practice it was necessary to move it into the TCP/IP based environment of the Internet, despite the political controversy that this would entail (Lynch, 1997).

Given the OSI's failure to gain traction, the Coalition for Networked Information (CNI) initiated the development of Z39.50 over a TCP/IP connection, leading to Version 3 in 1995. Z39.50-1995 (Version 3) expanded the available attribute set for searching and provided guidelines for implementing Z39.50 over a TCP/IP connection (Lynch, 1997). These changes allowed Z39.50 for the first time to be widely deployed by library software and content developers alike. Z39.50-1995 was quickly adopted by the major library ILS vendors and became the standard by which records could be shared and contributed to remote library systems. Content providers would later provide support for Z39.50 as a means for building citation applications and facilitating basic levels of remote searching into their content repositories. Citation software like EndNote would later be developed as a robust citation management application using Z39.50 to query and retrieve metadata about specific titles in a database.

So what is Z39.50? It is a stateful connection between client (or origin) and a server (target). Z39.50 supports two levels of search known as a SCAN and a SEARCH. SCAN requests retrieve result sets containing minimal metadata, basically an item's title. These requests provide a quick mechanism for retrieving a results list within a selected target. Once an item has been selected, a request for the item's full metadata can be made on the server. The second type of request is SEARCH. SEARCH differs from a SCAN request in that the data is made available within the results set. Unlike a SCAN request, which returns a list of item titles, a SEARCH request returns the entire metadata record for each item within the results set.

Given the nearly universal support for the Z39.50 protocol in the library community, one would think that the protocol was a stunning success—but that's not necessarily the case. While Z39.50 is widely supported within the library community, the protocol itself has failed to realize its full potential. Even in the absence of viable alternatives, Z39.50 has remained more of a fringe protocol, supported primarily in response to perceived need within the library community to have such a protocol rather than the presence of compelling use cases. In part, this is due to the complexity of the protocol itself. In the not too distant past, adding Z39.50 support required the development of a Z39.50 server, including components for encoding and decoding/encoding ASN.1/BER (Abstract Syntax Notation One/Basic Encoding Rules) messages between the host and target. Given the obscure nature of the protocol (i.e., it was utilized primarily by the library community), this process was often a major barrier to implementation. Only a handful of individuals outside of the vendor community knew how to actually create the necessary components to utilize the protocol. What's more, the protocol itself is expensive in terms of system resources. With that said, Z39.50 has enjoyed a re-awakening of sorts, though this time, outside of the library community. In the geographic information systems (GIS) community, the Z39.50 protocol is being used to build shared information networks like the Federal Geographic Data Committee (FGDC) (www.fgdc.gov) and create small organizational networks through GIS software solutions with Z39.50 as the networking protocol (ESRI, 2002).

While issues related to the relatively expensive nature of the Z39.50 protocol have not been overcome, adding support for the protocol has no longer become the primary barrier to implementation. This is thanks largely to the open-source library community and the development of a number of toolkits designed specifically for the integration of Z39.50. Much of the credit towards the simplification of the Z39.50 protocol goes to the Z39.50 Object-Oriented Model (ZOOM) initiative. Started in 2001, the ZOOM initiative defined a set of object-oriented Application Programming Interface (API) that has been adapted and ported to a wide variety of development languages. Toolkits such as YAZ (yet another Z39.50 component) have provided the open-source community with professional tools for creating or interacting with a Z39.50 server (Index Data, accessed: 2006). Code examples utilizing these components can be found in numerous languages like PHP, Ruby, PERL, and C#. Digital repository administrators looking to implement Z39.50 support into their repositories now have a simple set of toolkits that can be plugged into their repository software allowing quick Z39.50 integration. Of course, today one must evaluate if Z39.50 support is still valuable to his or her user community as more Internet-friendly protocols have begun to emerge and find footing within the library community.

SRU/SRW (SEARCH/RETRIEVAL/URL AND SEARCH/RETRIEVAL WEB SERVICE)

While Z39.50 has and continues to be an important protocol within the library and digital library communities, the protocol's reliance on the ASN.1/BER encoding makes it incompatible with the various XML-based systems being developed today. And while federated search tools continue to support and rely primarily on Z39.50, the execution and processing of the protocol is disruptive because these resources cannot be fully integrated into an XML-based system. Moreover, while Z39.50 does include authentication control mechanisms, they pale in comparison to authentication methodology currently being developed and deployed within today's current generation Web services. In response, the Z39.50 International Maintenance Agency began the development of ZING, the next generation of Z39.50. ZING was to be an XML-based, object-oriented form of Z39.50 that could be utilized with today's Web services infrastructure. Originally developed as a Web services protocol, ZING eventually expanded and was renamed SRU/SRW.

Although Search/Retrieval via URL (SRU) and Search/Retrieval Web Service (SRW) represent the next generation in Z39.50 development, it's important to note that SRU/SRW was not intended to supersede Z39.50, but to provide a protocol that allowed users and developers easier access to bibliographic data. SRU/SRW continues to share a number of concepts with Z39.50, most notably the EXPLAIN, SEARCH, and SCAN services, as well as retaining data in results sets.

- *EXPLAIN*
  The SRU/SRW EXPLAIN protocol provides developers an avenue for querying a server for the type of metadata schemas and query methods currently supported by that server. Moreover, this option provides users with administrative information about the server, contact informa-

tion, and information about the current configuration of the SRU/SRW instance. While this command set can be utilized by developers attempting to design a service around an SRU/SRW server, its greatest use is as an automatic discovery method for machine-to-machine processing. Since SRU/SRW utilizes a form response structure, automated processes, much like a Web crawler used by search engines, could be used to automatically capture and utilize an SRU/SRW server's configuration information for current and future queries.

- *SCAN*

   The SCAN command is a holdover from Z39.50, providing access to a quick hits list. A SCAN search returns minimal metadata (primarily title and creator) as well as information regarding the number of items in the SCAN list. In Z39.50, the SCAN command provided a lightweight mechanism for querying a Z39.50 server for fast results, forgoing the delay and the research-intensive process of retrieving actual datasets. However, in the SRU/SRW context, the SCAN command's value is lessened because of the inexpensive nature of the request coupled with the absence of a significant performance penalty for retrieving an item's full metadata.

- *SEARCH*

   Like the SCAN command, the SEARCH command is analogous to the Z39.50 SEARCH command. Like Z39.50, the SRU/SRW SEARCH command returns a recordset with access to the item's full bibliographic metadata. Unlike Z39.50, SRU/SRW allows for a finer granularity of control over how metadata is returned to the user in terms of the recordset's size and the number of records. What's more, SRU/SRW is a stateless protocol by virtue of its reliance on the HTTP communication protocol, meaning that recordsets are created dynamically on each SRU/SRW request.

However, unlike Z39.50, SRU is a fully XML-based protocol returning XML encoded data. Queries within SRU are made as string queries using textual tags to represent indices as defined by a supported context set. A context set works essentially like a namespace in an XML document: it defines the list of indices available for search. Currently, SRU/SRW recognizes a number of common context sets, including Common Query Language (CQL), Dublin Core (DC), and Z39.50 Bath Profile (bath), but does not restrict SRU/SRW only to the use of these common context sets

(U.S. Library of Congress, 2004). SRU/SRW allows the server to define the context sets that it will support.

The greatest difference between Z39.50 and SRU/SRW is the method of communication. Unlike Z39.50, SRU/SRW's primarily communicates between the client and server over an HTTP connection. SRW provides a more robust version of the protocol by encoding responses between the client and server using Simple Object Access Protocol (SOAP) messages, while SRU simplifies the communication process by utilizing simple URLs (HTTP GET requests) to issue queries and retrieve results in XML. For example, a developer wanting to use an SRU/SRW server would make an initial request to the server asking for an explanation of the services supported. Using SRU, this request can be made through the use of a simple URL. Utilizing U.S. Library of Congress's catalog, one can send the following explain request to the server to discover the supported services: http://z3950.loc.gov:7090/voyager. The response is shown in Figure 7-4.

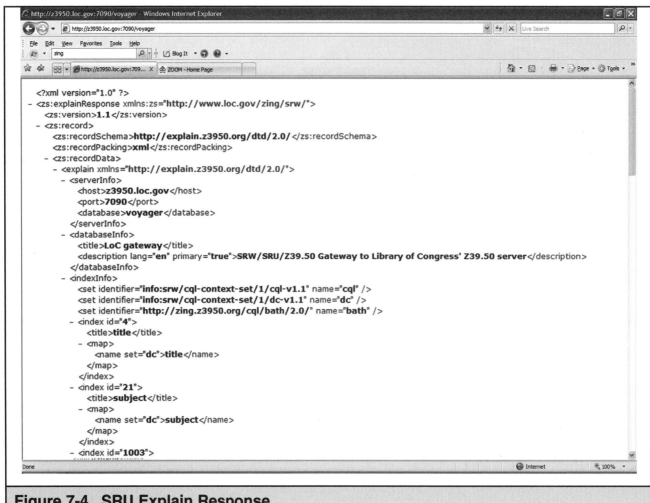

Figure 7-4. SRU Explain Response

From the response, one can discern a number of things about the Library of Congress's SRU/SRW service. First, the server supports a number of different context sets. The following is found in the IndexInfo tag.

<set identifier="**info:srw/cql-context-set/1/cql-v1.1**" name="**cql**" />
<set identifier="**info:srw/cql-context-set/1/dc-v1.1**" name="**dc**" />
<set identifier="**http://zing.z3950.org/cql/bath/2.0/**" name="**bath**" />

These tags define the context sets that will be used for query. Further examination of the explain request shows how these context sets are defined. In the explain response, a "subject" index has been defined.

<index id="**21**">
<title>**subject**</title>
<map>
<name set="**dc**">**subject**</name>
</map>
</index>

Here, each of the context sets have been defined. Searches using the bath context set would use the numeric index 21, which is mapped to the title element, while searches using the cql context set would use search, and queries using the Dublin Core context set would use dc:subject. Therefore, a subject query to the Library of Congress's SRU/SRW server could be made with any of these three context sets. For example, a subject query of "Corvallis Oregon" could use any of the following searches:

1. CQL Query http://z3950.loc.gov:7090/voyager? version=1.1&operation=searchRetrieve&query= subject="Corvallis%20Oregon"&maximum Records=1&recordSchema=marcxml

2. Dublin Core Query http://z3950.loc.gov:7090/ voyager?version=1.1&operation=searchRetrieve&query= dc.subject="Corvallis%20Oregon"&maximum Records=1&recordSchema=marcxml

3. Bath Query http://z3950.loc.gov:7090/voyager? version=1.1&operation=searchRetrieve&query=bath. subject="Corvallis%20Oregon"&maximum Records=1&recordSchema=marcxml

In all three cases, the subject request would return the record in Figure 7-5. One may notice as well, that the record in Figure 7-5 is in MARCXML. This is defined through the use of the recordSchema argument in the query URL. Like the context sets, the supported record schemas are also defined in the explain request. In the case of the Library

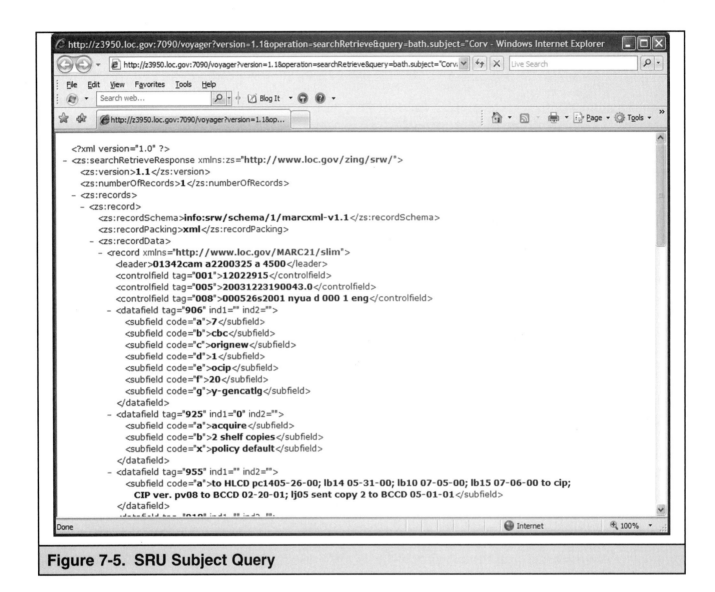

Figure 7-5. SRU Subject Query

of Congress' SRU server, the following recordSchemas are supported: marcxml, dc, mods2 and mods.

```
<schemaInfo>
  <schema identifier="info:srw/schema/1/marcxml-v1.1" sort=
    "false" name="marcxml">
  <title>MARCXML</title>
  </schema>
  <schema identifier="info:srw/schema/1/dc-v1.1" sort="false"
    name="dc">
  <title>Dublin Core</title>
  </schema>
```

```
    <schema identifier="http://www.loc.gov/mods" sort="false"
      name="mods2">
    <title>MODS v2</title>
    </schema>
    <schema identifier="info:srw/schema/1/mods-v3.0" sort=
      "false" name="mods">
    <title>MODS v3</title>
    </schema>
  </schemaInfo>
```

The development and implementation of SRU/SRW continues to hold a lot of promise for digital library developers. At the time of this writing, few organizations have made the move to utilize SRU/SRW within their production systems, but the number has been steadily growing as more tools and services are being developed. Currently, the U.S. Library of Congress hosts a Web page of known SRU servers (www.loc.gov/standards/sru/servers.html) and tools, but many more exist as digital repository software like DSpace and Fedora provide SRU functionality as either plugins or extensions to the products. Moreover, the past few years have seen SRU/SRW benefit the federated search space, with the most ambitious example being the European Digital Library (www.theeuropeanlibrary.org/), a virtual library exclusively using SRU/SRW to connect various digital collections around Europe through a single search portal. Judging from the current rate of adoption by major federated search vendors and data aggregators, SRU/SRW's future prospects continue to look promising.

OPENSEARCH

OpenSearch is an intriguing protocol when one considers how quickly it has been adopted by developers outside the library community. OpenSearch was developed in early 2004 by Amazon.com to allow resources to be integrated into its A9 search engine. However, the simplicity of the search and response syntax has led to a very quick adoption within the corporate community. So ubiquitous has OpenSearch become that Microsoft's latest browser, Internet Explorer 7, integrated OpenSearch as the methodology for adding new search targets to the software.

As a protocol, OpenSearch functions very much like SRU/SRW in that it works over an HTTP GET connection using a very simple URL query structure. What makes OpenSearch different is the response format. OpenSearch utilizes Really Simple Syndication (RSS) and Atom Syndication formats as the response formats. By utilizing these two formats, OpenSearch has been able to successfully leverage tools traditionally used for blogging to quickly develop tools and services that can serve and understand an OpenSearch query and response. Like SRU, OpenSearch utilizes a simple to understand query syntax that can be expresses through a URL.

Probably OpenSearch's biggest strength is the ease with which the protocol can be implemented. Utilizing a minimalist approach, OpenSearch uses a minimal number of arguments for query. Couple this with the known RSS/Atom response format, and most systems can be retrofit to support OpenSearch queries and responses in the course of a couple hours. For example, at Oregon State University, there was a desire to implement OpenSearch functionality within the organization's CONTENTdm software platform. Currently, Oregon State University utilizes CONTENTdm as its primary image management tool. Providing an OpenSearch interface would effectively have two desirable outcomes: (1) the resource could be integrated in the A9 search engine for broader research discovery; and (2) the collection could be natively searched by OpenSearch-aware software applications (like many current generation Web browsers). Implementing the protocol proved to be simpler than initially expected, in part due to the minimalist specifications (www.opensearch.org/Specifications/OpenSearch/1.1/Draft_3) and the wide variety of example codes currently available showing OpenSearch integration into other applications. In all, the process took about 30 minutes to produce the plugin in Figure 7-6.

```php
<?php
/**
 * Version 1.0
 * - initial version
 * - supports OpenSearch 1.0, http://opensearch.a9.com
 *
 * @Based on the WordPress opensearch plugin
 * @http://williamsburger.com/wb/archives/opensearch-v-1-0
 */
function extract_description($s, $max) {
$words = explode(" ", htmlspecialchars($s));
if (count($words)>$max) {
 return implode(' ',array_slice($words, 0, $max-1)) . "[...]";
} else {
 return $s;
}
}

//config.php includes link to DMSystem.php
require ("config.php");

//Constants
define("CONST_TITLE", "title");
define("CONST_DESCRIPT", "descri");
```

Figure 7-6. Example of Plugin

Continued

```
define("CONST_SUBJECT", "subjec");
define("CONST_CREATOR", "creato");

if (isset($_GET["searchTerms"])) { $searchTerms =
    $_GET["searchTerms"]; } else { $searchTerms = ""; }
if (isset($_GET["startIndex"])) { $startIndex =
    $_GET["startIndex"]; } else { $startIndex = 1; }
if (isset($_GET["startPage"])) { $startPage =
    $_GET["startPage"]; } else { $startPage = 1; }
if (isset($_GET["count"])) { $count = $_GET["count"]; }
    else { $count = 10; }
$records = array();

if (!empty($searchTerms)) {
    $total = 0;
    $alias = array("all");
    $field = array(CONST_TITLE, CONST_DESCRIPT,
CONST_SUBJECT, CONST_CREATOR);

    $searchstring = array();
    $searchstring[0]["field"] = "CISOSEARCHALL";
    $searchstring[0]["string"] = $searchTerms;
    $searchstring[0]["mode"] = "all";
    $sortby = array();
    $sortby[0] = "title";

    $records = &dmQuery($alias, $searchstring, $field, $sortby,
        $count, $startPage, $total);
}
?>

<?php header( "Content-type: text/xml;\n\n" , true ); ?>
<?php echo '<?xml version="1.0" encoding="utf-8" ?' . '>'; ?>
<rss version="2.0"
xmlns:content="http://purl.org/rss/1.0/modules/content/"
xmlns:wfw="http://wellformedweb.org/CommentAPI/"
xmlns:dc="http://purl.org/dc/elements/1.1/"
xmlns:openSearch="http://a9.com/-/spec/opensearchrss/1.0/"
>
<channel>
<title><?=OPENSEARCH_SERVER_TITLE?></title>
<link><?=OPENSEARCH_SERVER_LINK?></link><description>
  <?=OPENSEARCH_SERVER_DESCRIPTION?></description>
<pubDate><?php echo date( 'D, d M Y H:i:s +0000'); ?></pubDate>
<generator><?=OPENSEARCH_SERVER_GENERATOR?></generator>
<language><?=OPENSEARCH_SERVER_LANGUAGE?></language>
```

Figure 7-6. Example of Plugin

Continued

```
<openSearch:totalResults><?=$totalResults?></openSearch:totalResults>
<openSearch:startIndex><?=$startIndex?></openSearch:startIndex>
<openSearch:itemsPerPage><?=$count?></openSearch:itemsPerPage>

<?php if ( $records ) {
$items_count = 1; ?>
<?php foreach ( $records as $record ) {?>
 <item>
 <title><?=$record[CONST_TITLE]?></title>
 <link><? echo OPENSEARCH_SERVER_LINK . "/u?" .
    $record["collection"] . F"," . $record["pointer"]; ?></link>
 <!--<comments></comments>
 <pubDate></pubDate>-->
 <dc:creator><?=$record[CONST_CREATOR]?></dc:creator>
 <? $word_count = explode(" ", $record[CONST_DESCRIPT]); ?>
 <?php if ($word_count > 50) {?>
 <description><![CDATA[<?=extract_description($record
    [CONST_DESCRIPT], 50)?>]]></description>
 <?php if ($word_count > 255) {?>

 <content:encoded><![CDATA[<?=extract_description($record
    [CONST_DESCRIPT],255)?>]]></content:encoded>
 <?} else { ?>

 <content:encoded><![CDATA[<?=extract_description($record
    [CONST_DESCRIPT])?>]]></content:encoded>
 <? } ?>
 <? } else { echo "<description></description>"; } ?>
 </item>
 <?php $items_count++; ?>
 <?php } ?>
 <?php } ?>
 </channel>
 </rss>
```

Figure 7-6. Example of Plugin (continued)

This plugin implements basic OpenSearch functionality, which now allows the collection to be natively searched from within a Web browser (Figure 7-6) and A9. Given the rapid acceptance of this protocol by the Internet community at large, digital repository administrators would be well served to see how this protocol could expose their own collections to wider audiences. What will be more interesting to see is how the library community responds in the long term to the use and support of protocols like OpenSearch. While SRU/SRW offers a greater level of granularity in terms of search, protocols like OpenSearch offer the library community a way to interact with outside developers on the library community's own terms, allowing individuals and organizations a much straighter path to resource integration.

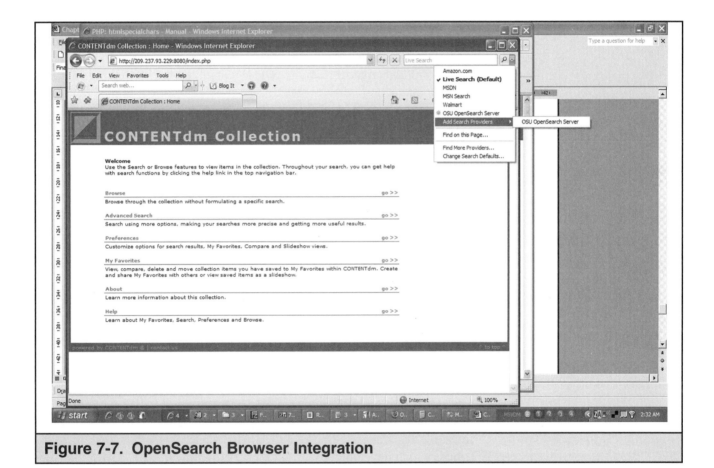

Figure 7-7. OpenSearch Browser Integration

LINKING PROTOCOLS

Linking protocols specify a standard method for generating uniform resource identifiers (URIs) to materials outside of one's repository. Nearly all of the current-generation digital repository platforms provide some method for generating a permanent URI to an item. For many platforms, this involves utilizing Persistent URLs (PURLs) or the handle system (CNRI, accessed: 2007).

In theory, these persistent URIs provide a permanent access point for a resource. However, what happens when a link is generated from a digital repository to an item outside of the resource? For example, a preprint of an article has been placed into a repository, but a link to the published article is desired. How would this type of linking take place? In general, two primary linking methods are emerging. The first method, OpenURL, utilizes a protocol that queries an outside service to determine if an organization has access to a specific resource from any of its vended content. The second, digital object identifiers (DOI), represents a type of fingerprint for digital documents. This is a widely used identifier in the publisher community that can be used to link directly to a resource. The use of either of these linking solutions requires interaction with an outside server or service, but digital repository administrators would be well served to evaluate both protocols if the linking to external items is required.

OPENURL

The original version of OpenURL (now called version 0.1) developed out of a research project at Ghent University in Belgium in early 2000. The concept was the product Herbert Van de Sompel and Patrick Hochstenbach's research project on ways to solve linking issues when dealing with digital articles (Van de Sompel and Beit-Arie, 2001). As more and more academic research moved into the online area, libraries and other information organizations were having increasing difficulty locating journals and articles within the various aggregate journal packages. Von de Sompel and Hochstenbach were exploring a linking system that could facilitate the discovery of access points for a digital item by evaluating all an organization's digital subscriptions or open-access resources. The process would generate a linking URI giving a user access to the resource as long as the organization had any valid access to the resource (Beit-Arie et al., 2001). In late 2001, Van de Sompel and Hochstenbach sold this concept to Ex Libris, which developed the first OpenURL resolver, SFX. Given the simplistic nature of the OpenURL protocol, the specification enjoyed a quick adoption rate, quickly becoming the de facto format supported by data vendors and leading a number of library vendors to produce OpenURL products.

The OpenURL protocol itself works as a resolution system. A request is sent from a user to an organization's OpenURL resolver, which stores information about that organization's digital assets holdings. The request is processed by the OpenURL resolver, generating a link to the resource if it exists.

Figure 7-8 illustrates very simply how an OpenURL request is handled by a generic OpenURL resolver. The resolver engine utilizes a holdings database to evaluate the incoming request. If the resource appears in the holdings database, a link can be generated to the item; if not, then a link is not generated and, per most OpenURL systems, a set of alternative access methods is provided to the requestor.

The OpenURL protocol itself is very much like OpenSearch in that it is executed over an HTTP GET connection. Requests are made using a specially crafted URL that includes citation-level bibliographic data that will be used by the resolver to identify the resource. For example, the URL in Figure 7-9 represents a simple OpenURL request to Oregon State

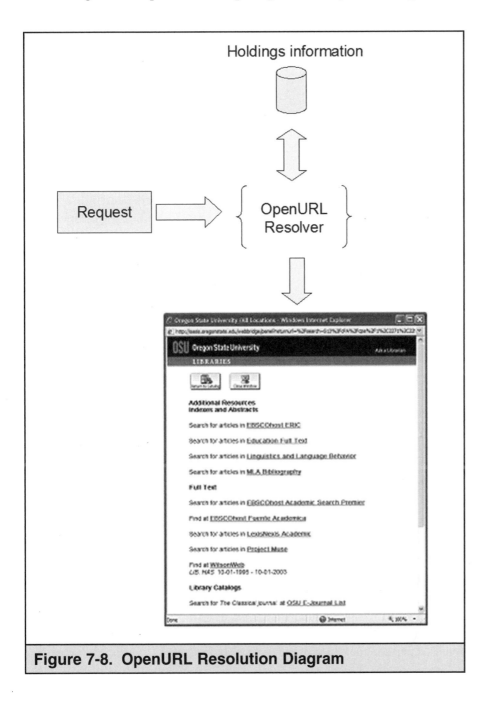

Figure 7-8. OpenURL Resolution Diagram

```
http://osulibrary.oregonstate.edu/digitalcollections/openurl/open.php?
url_ver=Z39.88-2004&amp;ctx_tim=2006-12-31T15%3A36%3A37-
0800&amp;ctx_ver=Z39.88-
2004&amp;ctx_enc=info%3Aofi%2Fenc%3AUTF-8&amp;ctx_id=&amp;rft.
isbn=&amp;rft.atitle=INFORMATION+PROFESSIONALS+Stay+FREE+in
+the+MARC+EDIT+METADATA+SUITE.&amp;rft.title=Computers+in+Libr
aries&amp;rft.spage=24&amp;rft.date=20040900&amp;rft.issn=1041-
7915&amp;rft.issue=8&amp;rft.volume=24&amp;rft.aulast=Reese&amp;rft
_val_fmt=info%3Aofi%2Ffmt%3Axml%3Axsd%3Ajournal
```

Figure 7-9. OpenURL Request for an Article

University's OpenURL server for an article titled "Information Professionals Stay Free in the MarcEdit Metadata Suite."

Currently, OpenURL exists in two flavors, the original OpenURL 0.1 specification and the more recent OpenURL Framework for Context-Sensitive Services (OpenURL 1.0), which was adopted as a NISO/ANSI standard (Z39.88-2004) in April 2005 (NISO, 2004). OpenURL 1.0 expands the OpenURL protocol beyond that of simple item linking, allowing the context of an item to be described as well as providing an XML specification for the protocol. This has made it possible to explore of new ways to utilize OpenURL to promote resource discovery, include auto resource discovery (Chudnov et al., 2005) and achieve integration with microformats through new protocols like Context Objects in Spans, ([COinS] Hellman n.d.) and unAPI (Chudnov et al., 2006). What's more, OpenURL is a very complementary standard in that it integrates well with other linking technologies. For example, handle IDs, PURLs, OAI identifiers, and DOIs can all be utilized in concert with the OpenURL protocol.

Fortunately for digital repository administrators looking to utilizing OpenURL as a linking system, OpenURL resolvers have become fairly ubiquitous and are likely to be available at one's organization. Administrators then will simply have to ensure that their software can generate the relevant OpenURL requests to the resolution server.

DOI (DIGITAL OBJECT IDENTIFIERS)

Digital object identifiers (DOIs) are a special implementation of the Handle System. The Handle System provides an architecture for digital objects so they can be managed in a networked environment (The Handle System, accessed: 2006). It provides a unique digital identifier that, once registered, is permanent to a particular item. In many ways, these identifiers are very much like an ISBN or a government document classification number in that a DOI is a string of characters making up a unique identifier for a resource.

Sample DOI: 10.0001/9876541

Like a government document number (SuDoc), a DOI is made up of two components, a prefix and a suffix (International DOI Foundation, accessed: 2006). In the above example, the prefix would be the information before the slash: 10.0001. The prefix itself is made up of two parts. The first part of the prefix is the first two digits, 10. This first part identifies this as a DOI. The second part of the prefix, 0001, is an assigned organization code. A DOI registration agency assigns this code to an organization. This value is unique to an organization, and all documents published by an individual organization will have the same prefix. The suffix of the DOI, 9876541, is a user-defined character string that uniquely identifies the resource. This string can contain any alphanumeric string so long as the data is unique to the organization. This could range from an ISBN to a local control number. For more information regarding the DOI numbering scheme, developers or potential DOI implementers should consult the *DOI Handbook* (www.doi.org/hb.html).

So how do DOIs and OpenURL fit together? Does one supersede the other? Actually, the two are complementary technologies. At this point, current generation browsers cannot natively resolve a DOI (i.e., it cannot convert it to a numerical IP address). DOIs must be sent to a DOI resolver like http://doi.org, where the identifier can be resolved directly to an article. However, direct resolution to an article re-raises the issue of organizational holdings and access to the item. Fortunately, DOIs can be used in conjunction with OpenURL. OpenURLs can wrap a DOI and use a service resolution service to resolve a DOI to an OpenURL for processing against the OpenURL resolver's holdings database. Currently, a number of such resolution services exist. The most widely used is probably CrossRef (www.crossref.org). CrossRef is a DOI linking service that is free for library and nonprofit organizations; it provides a Web services based interface that can be integrated into the OpenURL process.

Figure 7-10 updates the resolution diagram from Figure 7-8 by adding a resolution service like CrossRef to the infrastructure. In this diagram, the OpenURL resolver acts as the DOI resolution agent, transparently communicating with a DOI registry to resolve the submitted DOI to data that can be utilized within an OpenURL service. This data allows the OpenURL resolver to then query the resolver's holdings database to locate an accessible copy of the item or push data to an OpenURL-aware service like an interlibrary loan service.

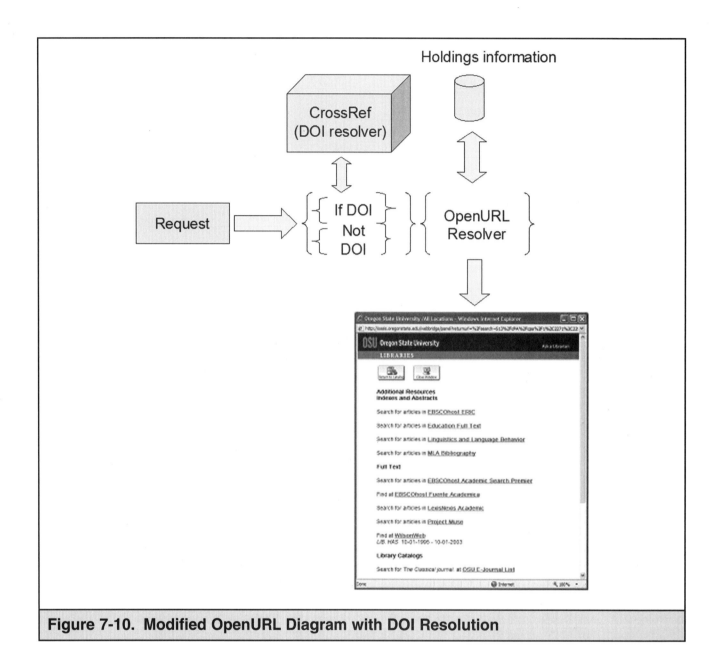

Figure 7-10. Modified OpenURL Diagram with DOI Resolution

SEARCH ENGINE SUPPORT

Within the past two years, commercial search engines like Google, MSN, and Yahoo! have started to offer more and more opportunities for digital repository administrators to find and link to materials stored in repository software. Through the support of harvesting standards like open search initiativ (OAI), discussed in Chapter 6, commercial search engines are making a concerted effort to harvest and index scholarly materials hosted by the library community. For repositories that don't support OAI, commercial search engines offer additional methods to facilitate harvesting and indexing. Initially started by Google, a concept known as Site Maps has been developed and has gained wide acceptance among the commercial search vendor community, allowing repository administrators to construct a special mapping file that allows their resource to be indexed. Site maps in general are simply XML files that provide linking information to the documents in a collection. The search engine uses these maps to "program" how a search engine's Web spiders crawl and index a site. This allows search engine crawlers the ability to index resources with dynamic URLs—items generally outside of a Web spider's field of vision.

In addition to site maps and metadata harvesting, commercial search engines are providing access to OpenURL linking and resolving of resources. Originally found in Google Scholar, these services allow organizations to embed OpenURL links to electronic resources held by the organization. These links could link to electronic articles, print books, or items in a digital repository. Unfortunately, unlike the Site Map concept, each commercial search engine supports this service in a different way, which requires organizations' OpenURL and electronic holdings information to be stored in different formats.

SERVICE REGISTRIES

Service registries are a fairly new concept within the library community and represent the next evolution in digital library development. Within today's digital library infrastructure, services are being created at a dizzying pace. Organizations are bringing OpenURL services online through digital repositories, image repositories, SRU/SRW services, Z39.50 services, and XML search gateways—and each of these services can require a different set of protocols and connection information. Since many of these digital services are designed to be used by individuals outside of the originating organization or can be mixed and co-mingled with other services, it would be useful to have a standard method or service that could be queried to retrieve service-related information. In essence, this is the problem that the service registry seeks to solve. A service registry is essentially the equivalent of a digital services "yellow pages." A service repository contains vital information about a service, its creator, and the necessary connection information needed to connect to and retrieve results from a specific set of resources. This allows automated services a single localized source from which connection information can be extracted, thereby making it possible for allowing digital library builders to more easily auto-discover new materials.

The sample network infrastructure in Figure 7-11 details the query service to poll the service repository for the connection and processing information needed to complete the users' search. This is different from a more traditional

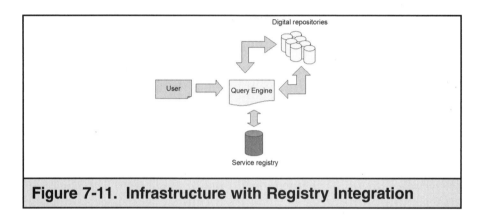

Figure 7-11. Infrastructure with Registry Integration

network infrastructure, where connection and protocol information would be stored within a locally created and maintained database or repository. As Figure 7-11 illustrates, this information is stored remotely and maintained by the individual service owners, thus reducing the total maintenance costs for all the service registry's participants. What's more, if a set of canonical service repositories did exist, digital library developers would have a fixed set of data nodes that could be queried to allow quicker tool development and reduce the need for redundant local systems filled with connection information.

In the past few years, a number of organizations have started working on service repository infrastructures. Within the digital library community, one such group is the Ockham Initiative. The Ockham Initiative is a multiyear study to create a functioning services infrastructure that could be used to connect various digital Web services together. It is a multi-institutional project that as of January 1, 2007, has released an initial server/client application to build a distributed service registry in addition to a handful of proof-of-concept services that use information stored within the service registry (The Ockham Initiative, accessed: 2006).

The Ockham Initiative has been envisioned as a global repository for library services. It would include information about an organization's digital repository, library catalog, and so forth. Currently, the Ockham registry uses a number of different interfaces to give individuals access to the repository.

Figure 7-12 shows the Web-based user interface (UI) to the Ockham Initiative. This gives an idea of the types of information that are being stored and made available through the service, and how each element might be utilized in other applications. Each service is broken down into three components: servant, agent, and collection.

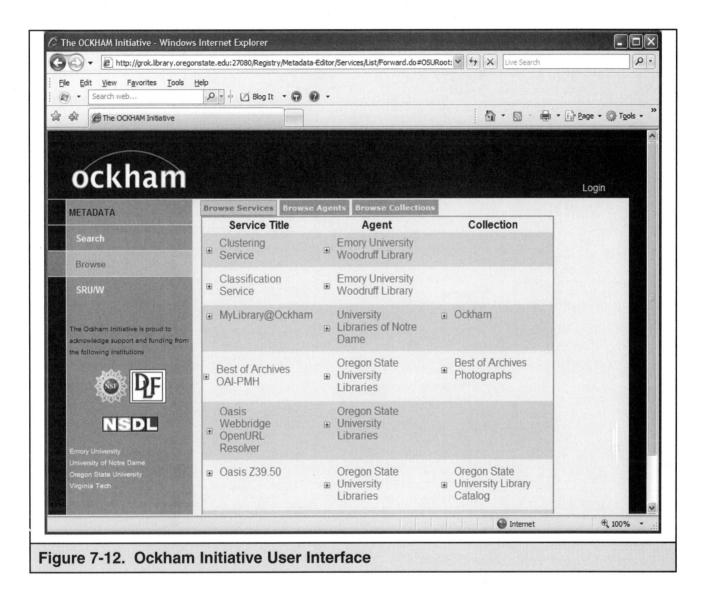

Figure 7-12. Ockham Initiative User Interface

SERVICE

The service represents the actual digital resource being described. This node includes connection and ownership information of the described service.

Figure 7-13 shows an example of a service node. Here one finds the connection information, access restrictions, and the protocol and standard being supported. In Figure 7-13, this is an OAI resource with the baseURL of the repository defined within the location URL. Moreover, access method and standards fields tell the user that this service supports Version 2 of OAI-PMH. Information within the services node is often the information most coveted by digital library developers. This information provides the necessary data needed to remotely connect to the specified server and gives a clue as to what methodology will need to be utilized in processing the returned data.

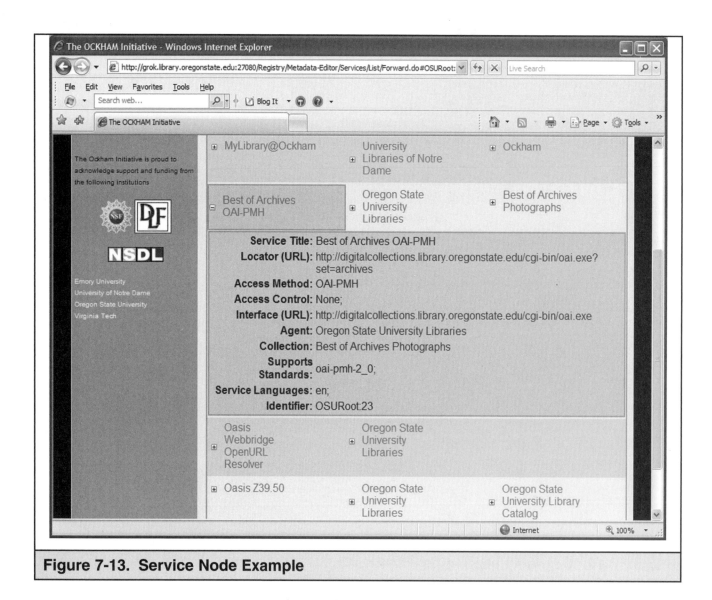

Figure 7-13. Service Node Example

AGENT

The agent is the institution or organization currently hosting a particular service. Within this node, users would expect to find information relating to an agent's contact information and title, as well as information relating to other services "owned" by the agent.

In Figure 7-14, the agent's primary contact information has been provided, along with information on the individual service and other services "owned" by the agent. Exposing the agent's information in a service registry allows an individual or process to search, display, or utilize all services related to a specific agent. For example, if organization A and organization B both store all their information in a service repository, but

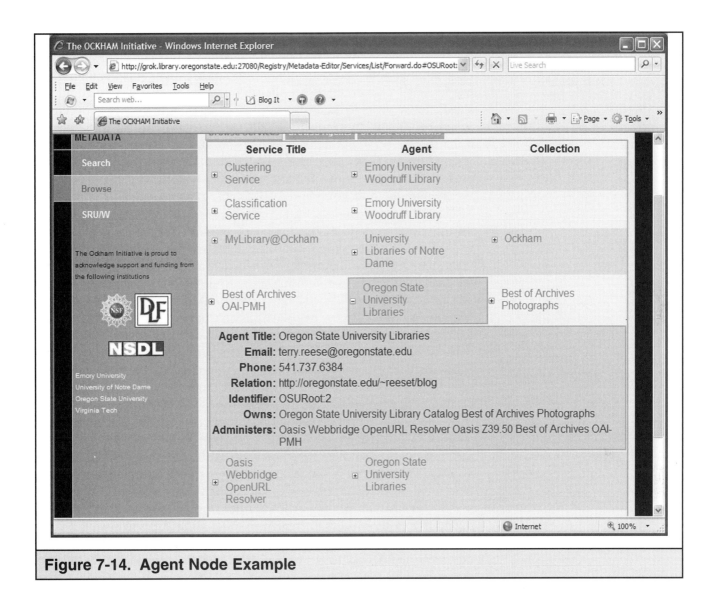

Figure 7-14. Agent Node Example

organization A builds a tool that can only utilize their own content, this ability to limit available services by agent allows organization A to utilize the service registry in this way.

COLLECTION

Collection provides a light set of descriptive metadata about the parent collection served by the service. How a service registry presents this information will vary, but it will generally include keyword, title, and creator information. The interesting aspect of this node is the inclusion of keyword information. This essentially provides an effective method for doing automated resource discovery. An individual or process could query a set of collections based on keyword and then utilize the attached Service node to pull up the necessary connection information. For example, a federated search tool could utilize the service repository to return additional suggested services to the uses for a search based on matches between the search terms and keywords in the collections. This could be manifested as a transparent service, that is, resources are discovered and automatically queried for the users, or a user-initiated service in which suggestions are presented to a user with a request for further action.

In addition to the Web-based UI, the Ockham service also provides an SRU interface to the repository. Here users can utilize a Web services request infrastructure to build automated query services against the repository to allow for easier integration with other tools or mashups. However, at this point, the Ockham Initiative is primarily a "proof of concept" service with the stated mission in the grant proposal to provide a registry network and services for National Science Digital Library (NSDL) projects (The Ockham Institute, accessed: 2006), this serves as an example of how a general service registry could function with a larger digital library environment. The main barrier to general adoption of the Ockham Initiative, and service registries in general, is the issue of provenance. For a digital registry infrastructure to be truly successful, a number of canonical registries will need to emerge to provide all developers with a trusted set of information.

In addition to general service registries like the Ockham Initiative, a number of specialized service registries have started to spring up in the past few years. The most noted of these is the OCLC OpenURL service registry. This registry is limited solely to providing information related to OpenURL services at various organizations. This allows developers to make their institution's OpenURL service portable for its users. It allows digital library developers to create tools that allow users to always resolve OpenURL requests through their organizations' OpenURL service, ensuring consistent access to resources. A number of services currently exist that utilize this type of functionality. Google Scholar, for example, allows users to specify an organization and will provide a link to the specified organization's OpenURL server, though Google currently utilizes its own service registry of information. The Yale Medical Library's Canary Database takes this one step further. Here, the resource actually utilizes the OCLC OpenURL service to provide OpenURL links based on the incoming IP address (Chudnov et al., 2005). For example, Figure 7-15 shows a query against the Canary Database on the Oregon State University campus. The page shows the Oregon State University OpenURL "Get this item" button linking to the OpenURL resolver.

The information needed to build this link all comes from the registry. In the OCLC registry, information relating to the organization's preferred linking text, images, and IP range are stored, allowing developers to create services and interfaces that mimic the individual user's functional expectations. If this query is repeated outside of the Oregon State University IP

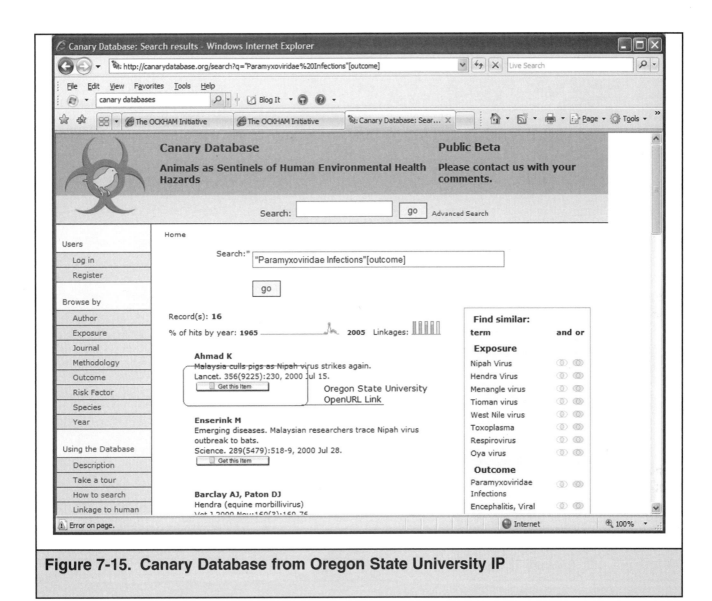

Figure 7-15. Canary Database from Oregon State University IP

range, one will see that a different set of OpenURL linking information is displayed. Again, the service will take the incoming IP address and resolve it against a known list of OpenURL resolvers and provide a link to the OpenURL if it exists.

If the IP address cannot be resolved, the service simply generates a link directly to the OCLC OpenURL registry for clarification. The Canary Database demonstrates one of the very powerful ways that a service registry could be utilized to enhance the user experience. In both Figures 7-15 and 7-16, the OpenURL links were built dynamically without user

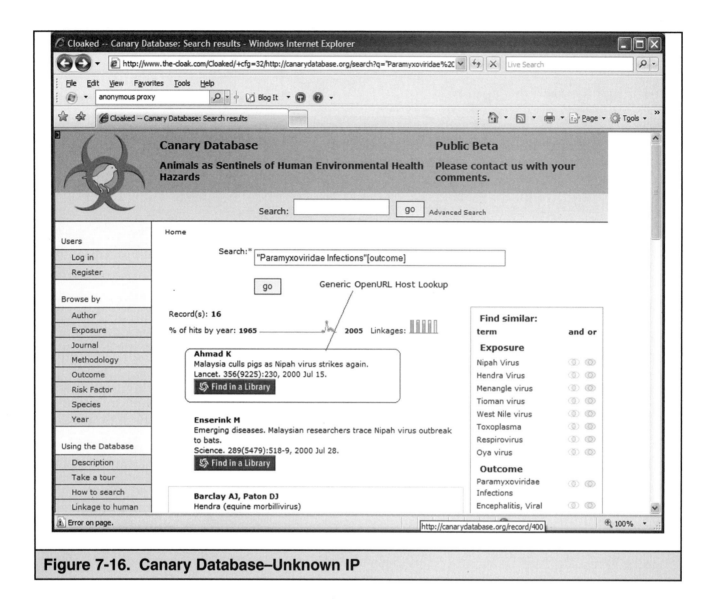

Figure 7-16. Canary Database–Unknown IP

interaction, allowing users to simply search for content while the system handles issues related to whether they have access to the content through their organizations.

To the digital repository administrator, the benefit of service registries should be keenly apparent. At present, if a digital repository administrator wishes to have materials indexed by various search engines or services, they must register the service themselves. In some cases, this could mean that digital repository owners may need to register their services many times before all available search vectors can be satisfied. However, with a digital registry, repository owners would only need to register their services once to give a host of tools and developers access to the collections' content.

EVALUATING NEEDS

Given the wide variety of protocols and metadata formats, how does one decide what to support? Since no current digital repository package supports every potential protocol or access point, evaluation of digital repository packages should include a discussion of what protocols and metadata have to be supported to meet the needs of one's organization and user community. But how to evaluate need? Ultimately, the evaluation process needs to involve members from throughout the organization to ensure that the widest range of necessary services is offered both to encourage organizational development and meet long-term user needs.

DEVELOPMENTAL NEEDS

A digital repository will likely be only one type of digital resource supported by an organization. The organization will need to consider how the digital repository fits into the larger information infrastructure of the organization and what protocols will need to be supported to allow for the development of services around the collection. Will the digital repository need to interact with a federated search tool? Should the tool be harvestable by commercial search engines? Will the metadata need to be repurposed outside of the digital repository system? These are but a few questions that digital repository administrators need to consider when selecting the digital repository package for their organizations. The digital repository administrator should work closely with the individual responsible for planning the corporate information infrastructure—as well as developers within the organization—to discover and plan for the necessary modes of access to support continued development.

Ideally, this evaluation is an ongoing process, as protocols and standards will change over the lifetime of the digital repository. A good digital repository administrator will need to keep the lines of communication open between him- or herself and the organization's development community to ensure that the repository platform continues to grow with the needs of the organization. Very likely, this might necessitate local customization of a digital repository platform through code customization or the purchase of subsequent software, but evaluation of the repository software must remain an ongoing task.

USER NEEDS

Unlike past generations, today's user presents a welcome problem for organizations. Many users today are very familiar with the concept of mashups, utilizing code API from various services to create their own custom services. These services may be very personal, serving a very specific need, or more general, open to a wider audience. But, users have become more active in looking for ways to search, store, and link to data in library collections. A digital repository will not be immune to this user tendency, and administrators will need to consider what level of user interaction the organization is willing to support. Should the repository support RSS or the Atom publishing protocol? Should the repository be searchable in commercial search engines or linkable from outside resources like blogs? Users' needs will vary widely between organizations, and it's up to the digital repository administrator to discern what tools and protocols users find necessary. For example, many users will require the presence of some type of citation service. Since different organizations will utilize different types of citation services, like EndNote or RefWorks, the way a digital repository provides citation support will vary with the needs of its user community.

Discerning those needs may not be a simple process. Functions like citation services, OpenURL linking, and cross-database linking are very general user services that most digital repositories are likely to support, but issues like a user API or support for syndication protocols are particular to an institution. Digital repository administrators will need to look to public services librarians and organizational usability studies to get a better idea of what is necessary to support their users' research and development.

SUMMARY

The widespread implementation of federated search tools is changing the way that the library community views digital services. In past years, Web services meant anything available over the Web. Web journals and databases provided access to users in ways that had not been previously available. Federated search tools offer this capacity; in addition organizations are now able to build services that can query multiple resources, saving the user the frustration of locating a single item in an ocean of digital assets. Even with its warts and shortcomings (slow, poor deduping and ranking, etc.), federated search offers users a set of tools that can be utilized to query all (or most) of an organization's resources.

The growth of service registries offers a glimpse into the future, as developers become more able to build services that are more responsive to their users needs. Registries offer opportunities for auto-discovery, service portability, and shared service maintenance in a way that is currently unattainable with today's federated search products. For digital repository administrators, understanding how these tools and services could affect long-term access and development will be important in the years to come.

REFERENCES

Baeza-Yates, R., and B. Ribeiro-Neto. 1999. *Modern Information Retrieval*. New York: ACM Press/Addison Wesley.

Beit-Arie, O., M. Blake, P. Caplan, D. Flecker, T. Ingoldsby, L. W. Lannom, W. H. Mischo, E. Pentz, S. Rogers, and H. Van de Sompel. 2001. "Linking to the Appropriate Copy." *D-Lib Magazine* 7, no. 9. Available: www.dlib.org/dlib/september01/caplan/09caplan.html

Chudnov, D., P. Binkley, J. Frumkin, M. Giarlo, M. Rylander, R. Singer, and E. Summers. 2006. "Introducing unAPI." *Ariadne* 48 (July). Available: www.ariadne.ac.uk/issue48/chudnov-et-al/

Chudnov, D., R. Cameron, J. Frumkin, R. Singer, and R. Yee. 2005. "Opening Up OpenURLs with Autodiscovery." *Ariadne* 43 (April). Available: www.ariadne.ac.uk/issue43/chudnov/

Corporation for National Research Initiatives (CNRI). "Handle System." Available: www.handle.net (accessed September 15, 2007).

CPAN. Available: http://search.cpan.org/~mirk/Net-Z3950-ZOOM/ (accessed November 12, 2006).

Emory State University. "MetaCombine Project." Available: www.meta-combine.org (accessed November 6, 2006).

ESRI. "Metadata and GIS: An ESRI White Paper." (Last updated October 2002). Available: www.esri.com/library/whitepapers/pdfs/metadata-and-gis.pdf

Google Site Maps. Available: www.google.com/webmasters/sitemaps/ (accessed March 3, 2007).

The Handle System. Available: www.handle.net/ (accessed November 13, 2006).

Hellman, E. "OpenURL COinS: A Convention to Embed Bibliographic Metadata in HTML." Available: http://ocoins.info/ (accessed November 13, 2006).

IndexData. "YAZ." Available: www.indexdata.dk/yaz/ (accessed November 9, 2006).

International DOI Foundation. "DOI Handbook." Available: www.doi.org/hb.html (accessed November 13, 2006).

Lynch, Clifford A. 1997. "The Z39.50 Information Retrieval Standard." *D-Lib Magazine* (April). Available: www.dlib.org/dlib/april97/ 04lynch.html

Lynch, Clifford A., and Cecilia M. Preston. 1990. "Internet Access to Information Resources." *Annual Review of Information Science and Technology (ARIST) Volume 25* (pp. 263-312). New York: Elsevier.

National Information Standards Organization (NISO). "NISO RP-2006-02, NISO Metasearch XML Gateway Implementers Guide." (Last updated August 2006). Available: www.niso.org/standards/resources/RP-2006-02.pdf

NISO. 2004. "Z39.88-2004, the OpenURL Framework for Context-Sensitive Services." Available: www.niso.org/standards/standard_detail.cfm? std_id=783 (accessed December 3, 2006).

The Ockham Initiative. Available: www.ockham.org/index.php (accessed December 13, 2006).

The Ockham Institute. "Ockham Grant Proposal." Available: http://wiki.osuosl.org/download/attachments/527/ockham.pdf (accessed December 3, 2006).

PHP. "YAZ Functions." Available: http://us2.php.net/manual/en/ref.yaz.php (accessed November 9, 2006).

Reese, Terry. 2006. "Building a Shared, Metadata-Driven Knowledge Base System." *Ariadne* 47. Available: www.ariadne.ac.uk/issue47/reese/

Ruby/ZOOM. Available: http://ruby-zoom.rubyforge.org/ (accessed November 9, 2006).

SourceForge.net. "Zoom.net." Available: http://sourceforge.net/projects/zoomdotnet/ (accessed November 9, 2006).

U.S. Library of Congress. "Context Sets." (Last updated February 13, 2004). Available: www.loc.gov/standards/sru/cql/index.html

Van de Sompel, H., and O. Beit-Arie. 2001. "Open Linking in the Scholarly Information Environment Using the OpenURL Framework." *D-Lib Magazine* 7, no. 3. Available: www.dlib.org/dlib/march01/vandesompel/03vandesompel.html

Webster, Janet, Seikyong Jung, and Jon Herlocker. 2004. "Collaborative Filtering: A New Approach to Searching Digital Libraries." *New Review of Information Networking* 10, no. 2: 177-190.

ZOOM Initative. (Last updated October 14, 2001). Available: http://zoom.z3950.org/

8 ACCESS MANAGEMENT

The preceding chapters have looked at the challenges and issues organizations need to consider as they work to bring their digital repository online. It's an exciting time for an organization when users start using and storing items within the digital repository, and a time for the organization to reflect on the many challenges they have overcome to realize this new service. However, the challenges don't stop when the repository comes online—they just change as the organization shifts from implementing the repository to moving content into the digital repository. As digital publishers, organizations must now take a more active role in the field of rights management, as they seek to manage the rights of the author against the mission of the organization.

Libraries traditionally have had to be concerned with issues related to access management of collections. Libraries toe the line between fair use and copyright clearance each day while dealing with interlibrary loan and electronic reserves requests. However, in both of these cases, libraries have been data consumers rather than data publishers. A digital repository requires organizations to take on both of these roles: that of the entity that secures rights for publication and the entity that enforces access rights for materials. It is with the latter that libraries traditionally have had very little experience. Within a digital repository, however, organizations need to balance data access between the author's expectations and the organization's mission. Researchers submitting documents on current research may require lengthy embargo periods before the work can be made available, or they may require access to be limited to a specific community. Likewise, some researchers may wish to supply their own copyright statements or use one of the many variations of the Creative Commons license. In the end, it's the job of the digital repository administrator to ensure that the license restrictions required by the contributor are honored, which means that organizations must take a much more active role in managing access to the digital materials placed within their care.

COPYRIGHT ISSUES

Any discussion of access management would be incomplete without addressing issues of digital copyright. However, it should be noted that this chapter will deal with this issue in very broad terms. The topic of digital copyright is at the same time precise and confusing.

Copyright is a set of legislative rights granted to the creator or author of a publication or work. (This book is going to ignore copyright law as it relates to organizations and consultants, since this falls outside this very basic discussion of copyright principles.) As legislative rights, copyright is often applied differently in different countries, particularly in regards to the types of works than can receive copyright. For example, within the United States, no materials created by local, state, or federal governments can be copyrighted, while in the United Kingdom, all government works are copyrighted as property of the Royal Crown. Likewise, differences regarding the duration of copyright and application of fair use will differ among nations, though nations have traditionally respected copyright law across boarders. Originally, copyright law was created as a way of spurring invention and innovation; the creator of an original work, publication, artistic piece, software, and so on would be granted exclusive protection to reproduce or profit from the work. However, the protections that copyright offers have always been a finite set of protections. After a prescribed period of time, a work falls out of copyright and into the public domain, allowing anyone the unrestricted right to reproduce or reuse it. At least, this is how copyright has traditionally worked prior to digital copyright laws.

In one sense, digital copyright law is still being written and legislated. Digital rights management (DRM) law is currently very organic, as digital consumers are quickly beginning to challenge the ethics and constitutionality of such practices. Within the United States, legislation like the Digital Millennium Copyright Act (DMCA) passed in 1998 has had a chilling affect on how large digital-content producers protect their materials. The DMCA specifically outlawed any practice that could be used to circumvent anti-piracy measures tied to specific software or media (Digital Millennium Copyright Act, 1998). This marked a change in current law, which allowed reverse engineering for the purposes of teaching and research. This law effectively allowed content producers to place their digitized content within virtual digital containers labeled in the name of anti-piracy measures to gain the extended protections of the DMCA governing the reverse-engineering of encrypted digital content. As a consequence, no standard form of DRM has been allowed to emerge because major content producers like Apple Inc., Microsoft, and others have explicitly built DRM systems that cannot easily interoperate with other platforms.

In cases such as these, the DRM mechanisms pose a major challenge for content holders seeking to archive content because of the extreme fragility of the material. DRM material tends to have two major points of failure: (1) the media reader and (2) the DRM format itself. Since many DRM materials are tied to specific hardware or software solutions, accessibility to the content itself is tied to a media reader's overall viability. Should the media reader cease to exist, so too would the ability to get at the stored content. Likewise, the DRM mechanism itself complicates long-term access to a collection given the rapid change of this platform and the necessity to make outdated DRM models obsolete. The current DRM model then actually works against content holders seeking to actively archive and protect their content. Likewise, content holders often find themselves locked into a specific set of technologies with their ability to innovate tied directly to the flexibility and limitations of the DRM under which the content falls.

Legislative actions like the DMCA have muddied the waters regarding how copyright law should be applied in the digital environment and have raised the hackles of digital consumers regarding the restrictive nature of most content under DRM. Consumer groups have consistently challenged DRM in its existing form, leading to uneven application of the laws between nations. For example, in January 2007, Norway moved to outlaw Apple, Inc.'s I-Tunes product specifically because of the restrictive nature imposed by I-Tune's proprietary DRM. The move was made in an attempt to force Apple and other media producers to work to create a shared DRM mechanism to allow for greater sharing of digital content.

Moreover, organizations like Google (with their Google Library Project) continue to challenge and stretch the definitions of fair use within the digital environment. Under current United States copyright law, fair use is a narrowly defined exception to the copyright law that allows individuals to make "fair" use of copyrighted material without seeking the copyright holder's explicit permission. Fair use has narrowly been defined as the reproduction of a work specifically for criticism, research, news, scholarship, teaching, and comment (U.S. Copyright Office, n.d.). In order for the use of a document to fall under the fair use guidelines, four factors need to be considered (U.S. Copyright Office, n.d.).

1. The type of use is the use of the work for commercial or educational purposes. Fair use only applies to non-profit, educational uses of copyrighted materials. Reproduction for commercial use would not traditionally fall under the guidelines of fair use.

2. The character of the copyrighted work.

3. The amount of the copyright work being reproduced. This is known as the substantiality test. Fair use traditionally has only been seen as an insubstantial reproduction of the whole.

4. The effect reproduction has on the value of the work–
or the ability of the copyright holder to profit from said
work. For reproduction of a work to be deemed fair use,
the reproduction itself cannot damage the value of the
copyrighted work or the ability of the copyright holder
to profit from the original work.

Given the subjective nature of many of these tests, determining the limits
of fair use has become a matter of much discussion within the digital
environment. Is fair use constituted when a digital object is used solely for
the purposes of research? Is fair use constituted when a commercial entity
makes publicly available snippets of whole reproductions to sell services?
Google's digitizing and indexing of copyrighted materials is one such test
to the fair use doctrine. While Google's use of the digital reproduction is
not made available to the general public, the reproduction of the copyrighted work allows Google to index and datamine these documents for
valuable information. Does this use constitute a breech in the fair use
doctrine? At this point, it's unclear, and the courts have been asked to
clarify this use case (The Author's Guild, 2005).

This chapter will focuses primarily on attributing copyright within a
digital repository environment and ensuring that the organization has the
legal right to store and provide access to submitted content. Each digital
repository platform performs this function differently, but all let the organization "filter" material submission through a specific copyright license
family or allow authors to attach their own licensing restrictions. How the
digital repository allows submitters to assign copyright will have a profound effect on how the repository must address issues of access management, as well as the legal exposure of the organization.

COPYRIGHT AS ORGANIZATIONAL POLICY

Access management within the context of a digital repository is really
about minimizing the risks of storing and providing access to digital content. Every digital repository exposes an organization to some level of
legal risk, in part because one of a repository's primary purposes is to
encourage the collection of an organization's digital artifacts. As a data
provider, a digital repository requires submitters to grant the repository
permission to store and digitally reproduce the document. However, this
assumes that the submitter is authorized to grant these types of rights to the
digital repository. This is true even of material contributed by a document's author. While likely more common within an academic environment, very often pre-publication or post-publication prints of a published
work cannot be self-archived into a digital repository. Often this is due to
the author's transferring reproduction rights to the publisher of a work. In
cases such as these, the author may have relinquished nearly all rights in

respect to the work to the publisher, and thus would have no legal right to archive the item in his or her organization's digital repository. This puts their organization in the awkward position of unknowingly infringing upon the actual copyright holder's reproduction and archival rights.

To help mediate the legal risks associated with having a digital repository, an organization should take a closer look at how copyright is granted and attributed in one's digital repository platform. Organizations traditionally will spend a great deal of time working out the details relating to the workflows and technical requirements for the digital repository. Even this book spends a great deal of effort discussing the planning and implementation steps of a digital repository platform. Likewise, organizations must create an equally thorough plan addressing copyright with the digital repository platform. And as a content provider, digital repository providers will need to be concerned with issues relating to how materials are assigned copyright, as well as the access management requirements for specific licenses. Repository planners will also need to create a plan to deal with the inevitable problems relating to the access of materials should someone raise questions about the reproducibility of a document. An organization can sharply reduce their legal exposure by setting guidelines for the types of licensed content that will be allowed in the digital repository and creating a policy for reviewing the archivability of a submitted work.

One of the most difficult aspects of hosting a digital repository is managing the license restrictions of a document imposed by the author of a work. Today, a number of license families exist that grant or restrict a broad range of rights regarding the reproduction and use of a work. As a content provider, it is the responsibility of the digital repository to provide access mechanisms that faithfully protect a document according to the license terms supplied by the document's author. A model that allows users to set their own distribution terms will potentially prove to be untenable, as access to documents could become uneven and difficult to manage.

Organizations hosting a digital repository need to take the proactive step of defining what license terms authors may distribute their works under within the digital repository. This means defining the types of materials the repository is willing to accept to meet its overall goals and mission. Defining terms gives the digital repository administrator the ability to administer documents more easily, as access management restrictions become narrowly defined by the acceptable distribution terms. The challenge for the institution comes in selecting a set of licenses that allows authors the freedom to share or restrict their work while still meeting the goals and mission of the repository.

Fortunately, a publication license family is available to digital repository developers, which provides an author with a broad range of license possibilities while, at the same time, simplifying the process of license management for the digital repository itself. This license family is known as the Creative Commons license. One of the rights that the digital repository itself needs to secure from the author is the right to redistribute the work in digital form. Since one of the primary functions of a digital repository is to provide access to an organization's documents, this right must be secured upfront. The Creative Commons license family provides a set of license options that grant the redistribution of a work or publication but allow the author to specify terms regarding the redistribution and use of a work. The Creative Commons' license family currently allows the following different types of licenses:

- **Creative Commons Non-commercial No Derivatives**
  This variant is the most restrictive license. It prohibits the creation of derivative works of a document and specifically restricts all commercial use of the document.

- **Creative Commons Non-commercial Share-Alike**
  This variant grants users the rights to build upon a work as long as this work is done outside of a commercial setting. Moreover, all work based upon the original document must be made available using a "Share-alike" licensing model.

- **Creative Commons Non-commercial**
  This variant restricts a document to non-commercial use.

- **Creative Commons No Derivative**
  This variant allows both commercial and non-commercial entities to reproduce and share a document, but it restricts the ability to create derivative works from the original.

- **Creative Commons Share-Alike**
  This variant allows both commercial and non-commercial entities to build upon a work, as long as all derivatives are made available using a "Share-alike" licensing model.

- **Creative Commons Attribution**
  This allows all users to distribute, share, and modify an existing work, as long as they acknowledge to the original.

- **Public Domain**
  This allows all users to distribute, share, and modify an existing work without restrictions.

The Creative Commons license is ideal for digital repositories because it makes the assumption that a work can be reproduced and shared. Since one of the primary purposes of a digital repository is to allow for the distribution of digital materials, requiring authors to acquire a Creative Commons license for inclusion within a digital repository allows the organization to solve a number of distribution-related challenges. Moreover, the Creative Commons organization itself provides a wizard at http://creativecommons.org/license/ to help authors select the specific type of Creative Commons license that best reflects how they want their materials used.

There are a number of reasons why Creative Commons is an excellent choice for digital repositories. First, Creative Commons is a widely used license format outside of the library community for dealing with electronic documents. A number of tools currently exist that allow the embedding of the Creative Commons license into an electronic document itself. For example, Microsoft and the Creative Commons organization worked together to create a plug-in specific to Microsoft Office that allows a user to automatically sign created documents with a particular Creative Commons license variant (Figure 8-1). Likewise, Open Office—an open-source productivity software—also provides a mechanism for automatically applying the Creative Commons license to created documents (Yergler and Linksvayer, 2004). Given the widespread use of the Creative Commons license family for specifying rights of born digital content, it makes sense that this model could easily work within a digital repository platform.

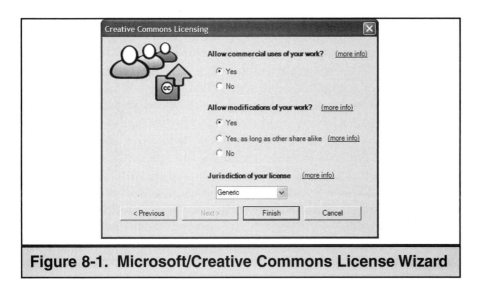

Figure 8-1. Microsoft/Creative Commons License Wizard

Second, some digital repository platforms, like DSpace, already support the use of the Creative Commons license as part of the document submission process. While DSpace and other digital repository platforms offer administrators a number of different methods of designating and assigning distribution rights to a specific document, the ability to provide native Creative Commons support gives contributing authors more choices from which to select the preferred license for their content. For example, in DSpace, two types of licensing are supported: a monolithic license structure that assigns a single license to all content, and the Creative Commons license model. Both models require the content submitter to grant distribution rights to the digital repository. However, only the Creative Commons model allows the author to set specific exclusions to how and under what circumstances the content can be shared, reproduced, and modified. Moreover, given the current popularity of DSpace within the academic community, it's very likely that a large number of repositories currently are, or will start, using the Creative Commons license to create a large pool of similar licensed materials.

CAN IT BE ARCHIVED? CAN IT BE DISTRIBUTED?

Setting an organizational copyright policy is done, in part, to provide the organization and content submitters with guidance regarding what type of content can be submitted and redistributed through the digital repository. In theory, the digital repository would be made up of content submitted directly by the primary content creator. However, as a digital repository evolves and becomes more widely used within an organization, questions regarding the inclusion of materials not specific to an organization or content creator are sure to come up. Can a Web site or group of Web documents be archived for long-term access into the digital repository? Can digitized slide collections be made available through the digital repository? The archiving and redistribution of materials for which the organization has no direct ownership or rights present a prickly problem for digital repository administrators, particularly if this content is submitted to the repository without being vetted.

For example, a common issue with digital repositories is the archiving and distribution of co-authored materials. Co-authored materials require all authors to authorize the archiving and redistribution of a work. How does the organization secure these rights or ensure that the content submitter has secured redistribution rights for the repository? An organizational policy on copyright and the submission of works into a digital repository would need to cover decisions regarding the type of documentation necessary for content submitters to place questionable materials into the digital repository. An organizational copyright policy helps protect the institution in cases where proper rights were not secured, but the item was still submitted to a repository. It gives the organization a way to evaluate questionable materials, and it simplifies the submission process by giving content providers a process they can follow. What's more, organizational policy can lay out how proper documentation will be retained and stored in the case of future disputes.

Challenges will arise as a digital repository becomes more successful. It's a good problem to have, but as users recognize the repository's ability to enhance access to the documents archived within it, the natural inclination will be to archive difficult-to-access materials in the digital repository. Traditionally difficult to locate materials, such as government gray literature, extension publications, or government publications, are generally good candidates for inclusion into one's repository, in part because government publications are free from the normal copyright entanglements. However, a plethora of other document types exist for which accessibility could readily benefit if they were included in one's digital repository. Historical newspapers, serial back runs, and theses collections offer ready-made collections with varying sets of challenges. For example, serial back runs that have fallen out of copyright protection can be freely digitalized and made available, but this will generally only apply to materials published before 1925. The same applies for historical newspapers and publications. However, if the publication is ongoing, weighing the potential fallout from the current publisher should be considered.

In many ways, digitizing a library's theses collection seems much more straightforward. Since the theses are a product of a university program, one could argue that the university itself has some right to the publication. But even here, unless a university has historically required graduates to transfer nonexclusive or exclusive redistribution rights to the university, permission will need to be sought from each author. While the thesis was created as part of a university's degree requirements, it doesn't fulfill the necessary conditions under which an organization could classify it as a "work for hire." With theses, the publication rights still remain with the document's author unless prior rights transfer agreements exist. What's more, prior agreements made by the author and other theses publication entities might further complicate this process, restricting the redistribution of the publication over digital media.

In the end, organizations need to have a clear understanding of how documents enter the digital repository and problems that may arise throughout the submittal process. Having a policy in place empowers the digital repository administrator and staff to make informed decisions regarding the types of items that can and cannot be submitted to the repository, while giving content providers a clear documented path for submitting content. It helps resolve disputes and protect both the content submitter and digital repository from potential legal challenges over the redistribution of an item.

LONG-TERM RIGHTS MANAGEMENT

Given the archival nature of a digital repository, consideration must also be given to any long-term rights management issues. In general, these issues will be limited to three categories of materials:

1. embargoed materials with temporary restrictions of a year or more
2. sensitive or confidential documents
3. DRM-protected content

The most problematic of these three categories is probably DRM-protected content. Embargoed and sensitive materials share many of the same challenges, with the length of the exclusionary period being the primary difference. Current-generation digital repository software has defined workflows for isolating sensitive content to a specific set of users, groups, or profiles. The long-term challenge is providing a method for documenting these decisions. In the case of embargoed materials, how is a restricted item made available? Current digital repository platforms have no built-in support for the embargoing of titles; they rely on human intervention and workflows that are developed outside the repository platform. These types of workflows are fragile by nature and could result in embargoed content being made available too soon, or worse, not at all. When dealing with confidential documents, the primary challenge over the long term will be maintaining their private status. As digital repository platforms are updated or replaced, mechanisms built around one system to suppress access may not be available in the future. However, should private documents even be stored in a general purpose digital repository? Probably not, given the assumptions built into the current generation of repository productions. This, again is something organizations must decide for themselves.

DRM-protected content, however, represents an entirely different challenge for repository administrators. DRM content, in its current incarnation, tends to be tied to specific hardware and system requirements. One of the dangers of allowing DRM-protected content into one's digital repository is the inability to move the content forward as hardware and software system change. Refreshing and migrating data from obsolete formats will always be problematic in a digital repository. Digital content is extremely ephemeral, as formats consistently are changed and updated. For non-DRM content, the problem of migrating content between formats is largely technical in nature. It may not be straightforward or simple, but a migration path exists for the content. For DRM-protected content, there is no such migration path. Once the hardware or software used to "read" the content expires, the content is essentially lost. Repository administrators would be well advised to simply avoid adding DRM-protected content to the repository given its limited lifespan.

ALLOWING/RESTRICTING ACCESS

While organizations will have a number of different reasons for building a digital repository, one of the primary functions of all repositories is the dissemination of information. Digital repository platforms are designed around the assumption that materials archived within the repository system will be made available to the repository's user community. This means that not all materials should be stored in an organization's digital repository system. Content that cannot or will not ever be made available to at least a part of the repository's user community is not a good candidate for inclusion. This is one of the reasons that organizations need to define a clear collection development and copyright policy when dealing with digital materials. Libraries have traditionally had well-developed collection development policies for their print collections, in part because of the physical space limitations presented by storing physical objects. Libraries routinely weed and shift print collections to make room for the materials that will have the greatest impact on its user community. As a result, they traditionally have very focused collections that emphasize the research strengths of the organization. Digital repositories need to adopt this same practice, with the expectation that materials collected will circulate to the larger user community.

Yet, even with the expectation that all materials submitted into one's digital repository will ultimately be made accessible to all members of the repository's user community, the reality is that this will not always be possible. Many of the reasons for this have already been stated. Publication agreements or the presence of sensitive information may require that a document be embargoed, or withheld, from the public for a set period of time. In an academic community, researchers are often required to suppress submitted documents and research to comply with contractual publication agreements. Likewise, graduate students submitting a thesis may request that the document be embargoed so they can present their ideas and research for outside publication or employment. In a corporate setting, some materials may be unsuitable for general access. In such cases, limited access might be provided just to the members of the organization. There are many scenarios in which access to submitted content may be delayed or indefinitely limited to a specific user group. However, the need to restrict access within a digital repository is a prickly issue—most digital repository platforms are created with the supposition that materials archived within the repository can be shared. While platforms have their authentication methodology, the ability to suppress or restrict access to a particular item within a collection is often time limited. Furthermore, digital repository systems like DSpace or CONTENTdm are, in general, self-contained systems; they have their own authentication methodologies, which may be difficult to integrate into an organization's existing infrastructure. A closer look at CONTENTdm and DSpace clarifies what some of these challenges may be.

CONTENTDM

The CONTENTdm repository software is representative of the number of lightweight digital repository platforms available to organizations looking for a low-dependency, easy-to-administer repository system. This simplicity of administration is one of the platform's main strengths, but it comes with tradeoffs. CONTENTdm has been designed to be a self-contained system that provides some limited ability to restrict access to materials on an item-by-item level by using the operating system's authentication architecture.

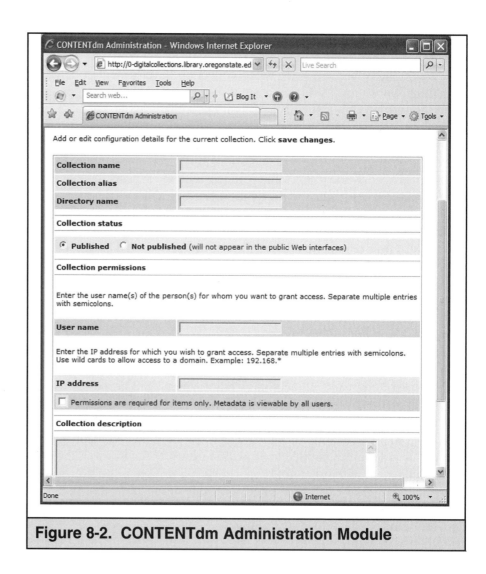

Figure 8-2. CONTENTdm Administration Module

Figure 8-2 shows CONTENTdm's collection administration module, Version 4.2. Here we can see the three levels of authentication provided by the platform. First, there is a collection status, which is used to mark an entire collection as public or private. With CONTENTdm, private collections are accessible only by registered users in the system, while public materials are made accessible to the public through the repository's Web front end. Secondly, CONTENTdm allows for the restriction of materials by username or IP. These restrictions can be set at a collection (from this screen) or item (through the metadata) level. Moreover, as one can see in Figure 8-2, these restrictions can be blanket restrictions, limiting access to the entire item, or they can simply be limited to the media object, allowing the metadata to be visible by all users.

Functionally, CONTENTdm provides collection administrators with a number of authentication options, providing item- and collection-level options. However, CONTENTdm is less flexible when it comes to how users are actually authenticated into the system. To a degree, CONTENTdm has two authentication mechanisms, one for collection editors and one for collection access. For collection editors, CONTENTdm provides the ability to create user categories with a number of different roles and privileges within the system. However, in general, CONTENTdm ignores the larger issue of authentication by shunting authentication of resources to the operating system level through the use of .htaccess files. So each user who needs to sign into the CONTENTdm system must also have a UNIX or Windows user account on the system. This makes single sign-on (SSO) systems nearly impossible in the current CONTENTdm environment given the reliance on the operating systems user/group model.

DSPACE

Like CONTENTdm, DSpace, right out of the box, is a very self-contained system. However, DSpace has a very different authentication model. Unlike CONTENTdm, DSpace utilizes more of a community-centric authentication model, which uses high-level collections that can have a number of child collections. Within this model, each collection can have its own administrators, users, and permitted actions by those users. So a collection administrator in one community may essentially be a "guest" in all others.

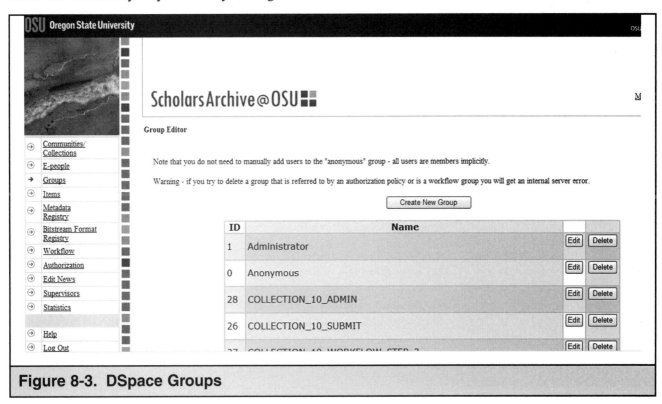

Figure 8-3. DSpace Groups

Within DSpace, permissions are granted at a group level. Individual users are associated with a particular group or given elevated group permissions within a specific collection. These are not system-prescribed groups; the digital repository administrator can create the groups. This gives the administrator a great deal of flexibility as to how permissions will be doled out between collection administrators, submitters, and staff working with the collection metadata. These decisions are made in the form of collection policies that define which user groups are allowed to perform actions on the collection. So, for example, submission, collection editing, even collection browsing is controlled by the collection policies. At the same time, DSpace was conceived as a publishing platform and does not by default support other common-access restriction mechanisms like IP authorization, at the item or collection level. This means that embargoed materials present a unique challenge with DSpace. DSpace offers little outside the normal workflow to accommodate embargoed materials, which leaves organizations to improvise their own solutions.

Like CONTENTdm, DSpace can be difficult to integrate with an SSO system. By default, DSpace's user/authentication system is a self-contained system with authorized users' needing to be registered on the DSpace system to inherit policy rights. However, as an open-source application, there are opportunities to enhance integration. At Oregon State University, for example, a Lightweight Directory Access Protocol (LDAP) authentication plug-in was developed to allow DSpace to interact with the campus' centralized LDAP authentication system. This tied DSpace authentication to the campuswide LDAP system for login. While this solved the login problem, DSpace still required users to be registered with a specific user group in order to interact with the system. For new users, the plug-in inserted the new user information into the DSpace user's table. This registered a new user with DSpace and allow the user to inherit the default group polices specific to the user type (e.g., student or faculty). This gave the new user a basic set of rights within the repository, which would later be augmented as necessary by the repository's administrator. So while this is a minor inconvenience for the DSpace administrator, it does help make the login process for this resource more transparent to the users.

CONTROL MECHANISMS

The decision regarding control mechanisms is generally not left to the digital repository administrator, but assigned by the organizational information technology (IT) services. The repository administrator's job is to find ways to make the repository fit into the organization's existing infrastructure or present incompatibilities to the authentication manager. Digital repositories support a wide range of authentication methods, ranging from IP recognition and individual system accounts to distributed authentication like LDAP and sign-on services. Organizations with little need for a distributed sign-on services will typically have an authentication system made up of individual user accounts and passwords, typically employed over the LDAP protocol. While primarily associated with e-mail, LDAP provides an ideal directory service that can be queried within a local network environment to sign authentic users onto a system, and a growing number of digital repository systems are moving to support LDAP authentication "out-of-the-box." Currently, most repository authentication is tied directly to the repository platform, taking it outside an organization's formal authentication infrastructure. And while direct support for distributed authentication schemes like LDAP can be added or emulated by modifying the source code, the difficulty integrating this support can become a major hurdle when trying to integrate one's repository authentication with that of the organization.

Given the varied authentication methods utilized over a networked environment, the use of a standard control access mechanism offers one viable possibility for creating an SSO environment. Products such as Shibboleth, Athens, or OpenID provide high-level protocols that make the authentication process transparent to the user. These high-level protocols act as a middle-tier, obscuring the authentication process from the user while defining how user-attribute information should be shared within a federated environment.

Determining what type of SSO to use depends largely on two factors:

1. network topology
2. the digital repository platform

In general, SSO options work best within a consortium network environment where information is shared among users at multiple institutions. Protocols like Shibboleth and OpenID thrive in this type of environment, providing a method for organizations to use their own internal-access infrastructure while still communicating with the larger network. And while these solutions could be implemented in a local network environment, it's likely that utilizing an LDAP authentication scheme would be more appropriate.

The digital repository platform also plays a role in determining what type of control mechanisms can be utilized. In part, this is because many digital repositories only support a specific type of authentication system. Systems like DSpace utilize a community policy system, while other tools may allow for IP recognition or direct support for a SSO solution. As a result, an organization may need to become more flexible regarding the types of authentication methods used on their networks, or the need to be willing to utilize and modify an open-source repository system like DSpace or Fedora to "fit" their infrastructure needs.

LDAP

LDAP, or Lightweight Directory Access Protocol, provides a distributed directory service commonly used by organizations for access control.

Technically a database optimized with a very specific access and search mechanism, LDAP provides an information model for querying information within a directory. While LDAP might be primarily thought of as a directory protocol used essentially for e-mail and address books, it may well currently be the most widely used authentication method. LDAP provides quick access to user data, allowing authentication services to make use of the protocol to access user attributes within the directory. LDAP makes an ideal authentication scheme for local authentication, as it can be accessed over a secure connection and provides a ready source of user information.

LDAP compliance within the digital repository environment is spotty at best. LDAP itself provides for reading, writing, and deleting entries within the LDAP database. For the purposes of authorization, an LDAP authentication service would need to be able to perform all these functions to allow a user or system to access and update information. Generally, however, LDAP compliance is limited to the ability to read data via LDAP. This means that information can be used for authentication but cannot be managed through the repository system. This sets up a model where user information needs to be managed on multiple systems, limiting some of the flexibility that LDAP provides.

The LDAP protocol translates binary data using a format known as LDIF (LDAP Interchange Format). LDIF provides a set of common user-attribute elements that can be utilized by an organization to identify a user. LDIF also has an objectclass element that an organization can use to define local attributes common within that organization. For example, an LDIF response could contain information like that in Figure 8-4.

postaladdress: My Library$My Institution$121 my street$my town

mail: nobody@example.com

givenname: Jane

cn: Doe, Jane

sn: Doe

telephonenumber: 1 404 111 1111

ou=people,o=example.com

Figure 8-4. LDIF Response Format

SHIBBOLETH

Shibboleth is a Web-based communications protocol that provides a standard method for sharing authentication data with both local and external organizations. Primarily an identity management system, Shibboleth provides secure protocol for sharing user data between systems. Originally designed for sharing authentication data between organizations in a consortia environment, Shibboleth federates authentication and distributes the management of user information across organizations. Implementing the OASIS SAML (Organization for the Advancement of Structured Information Standards Security Assertion Markup Language) specification, Shibboleth utilizes a federated authentication model, by which a target resource can receive information about a user from its parent organization (Shibboleth, n.d.). It's important to note that the Shibboleth middleware does not actually provide any authentication capabilities; it only defines a communication protocol to facilitate the sharing of user attributes between systems. There is no centralized authentication source within the Shibboleth infrastructure, but rather a federated set of origins that authentic and communicate user attributes to target resources.

OPENID

Like Shibboleth, OpenID is a federated identification management protocol. However, there are a number of keen differences. First, OpenID has been designed under the premise that user-identification management can function essentially like a URI (OpenID, n.d.). Within the OpenID model, a user signs in using a unique URI, which is resolved by a service run either by the user or authenticating organization. Like Shibboleth, the protocol defines how user information is securely transmitted between resources as well as what attributes are needed to authenticate users between targets. What makes OpenID different from many other authentication services is the notion of a secure URI that acts as a user's username and password. Within the OpenID model, the URI provides the authentication mechanism for the protocol, meaning that how one proves ownership of the URI directly relates to how authentication is verified within the system.

ATHENS

Athens is fundamentally different from Shibboleth and OpenID in that it is both a communications protocol and authentication scheme. Whereas Shibboleth is a distributed network, Athens provides a centralized authentication service. Within the Athens framework, there is a single authentication origin that authorizes all incoming requests from a target resource providing centralized user administration. In addition, it's important to note that Athens, unlike Shibboleth and OpenID, which are both open-source projects, is a commercial authentication venture. Moreover, the Athens authentication method can only be utilized by products that support it. Unlike Shibboleth and OpenID, which can be used on top of diverse systems, the Athens authentication scheme is limited by platform.

MONITORING REPOSITORY USE AND STATISTICS

How successful is the digital repository? How much will it cost to sustain the digital repository program? Organizations will ask many questions of its digital repository administrator once the resource is up and running. Given the number of resources needed to both implement and sustain a digital repository over the long term, finding a way to quantify the digital repository's use over time will become an important aspect of any digital repository administrator's duties. Where does one get the numbers? What do they mean? Obviously, some kind of method for measuring usage over time will remain important as the program competes with other services for finite people and budget resources. Regular assessment of the repository's use and usage patterns is equally worthwhile and can be used to inform decisions relating to collection development and usability to keep the information within the repository applicable to its user's needs. While statistics are important to generate, even here, one needs to understand how statistics, particularly when dealing with electronic materials, don't always tell the whole story.

INTELLECTUAL PROPERTY

One necessary role played by a digital repository administrator is that of an information gatekeeper. As a content publisher, the organization is responsible for providing reasonable assurance that the documents placed within its care will not be used inappropriately. It goes back to the discussion on licensing. Under what terms has the author licensed reproduction of the document, and how is the digital repository honoring that agreement? The repository has a responsibility to ensure that the author's terms are being honored and provide notification to the affected parties if problems arise.

SERVICE USABILITY

For years, the corporate world has understood that a successful service is defined not only by what it does, but also by how easily it does it. Google is a good example of this principle. In 1998, Google was a quirky project coming out of research at the Stanford University. Today, in 2007, it ranks as the world's most widely used Internet search tool. Whether Google has the smartest, fastest, or most relevant search engine is arguable, but the tool's ability to make the search process simple has been undeniably successful. By uncluttering the search page and presenting clear results, Google quickly was able to differentiate itself from a number of early and established competitors.

In the same way, organizations can work to make their digital platforms more successful by trying to understand both how users want to use the tool and where they are currently having difficulty. Log analysis provides a rich set of user data that can give a digital repository administrator a better idea of how users are searching for items. Understanding how users are querying a system can help in deciding how to best describe a submitted item or how to explore mechanisms that could be used to relate similar items for easier discovery. What's more, log analysis can be used to aid collection development by identifying common topics or areas of interest.

While some of this analysis can be done at the usage-log level to analyze how users are searching, a great deal of value can also be had by "seeing" how a tool's users find information. This can be done a number of ways, the most effective being formal usability studies in which researchers can observe a user attempting to complete an assigned task. However, there are less obtrusive methods for getting an overall picture of how users relate to a resource. Tools such as Crazy Egg can be used to generate click maps and heat maps to track user behavior by recording user clicks on a page.

Figure 8-5. Oregon State University CONTENTdm Archive Collection Click Map

Figure 8-5 shows a sample click map from an image collection at Oregon State University. Click maps and heat maps make it readily apparent which items on the page received the most attention from the sample users and which parts of the Web page received little or no attention. Repository administrators can utilize tools such as these to "watch" users and identify areas where content either is not being seen or is causing the user undue confusion. These types of tools can help identify when user patterns change, allowing the resource to react more quickly to the user communities' wants and needs.

STATISTICAL ANALYSIS

Statistical analysis of use patterns can also provide a rich set of data for a number of stake holders. While statistical analysis of a resource's usage log tends to be sketchy in terms of trying to draw very narrow conclusions about specific use patterns, it can provide a very broad overview of how and what collections are currently utilized. This type of information can prove to be invaluable when evaluating collections for digitization. Usage logs that point to a heavy concentration of user activity in a specific collection or over a specific type of resource can indicate a high level of interest from the user community and help inform digitization decisions.

Rightly or wrongly, success of the repository is likely to be tied to frequency of use. And while statistical reporting has never been particularly strong within any digital repository platform, each does provide a reporting tool that can be used to track searches, item views, and materials archived into the repository. Savvy digital repository administrators will recognize the need to understand and accept the importance of this type of statistical tracking and seek to gain a better understanding of what their repository platform tracks as well as how user actions are defined. For example, how is document usage tracked—by download or item record view.

In addition to the sometimes ambiguous nature presented by statistical tracking software, a number of outside influences can skew usage statistics to the point of making them useless for statistical analysis. One example of such an influence is Web spiders and harvesters.

WEB SPIDERS/HARVESTERS

A Web spider is a hungry little critter that crawls the Web, seeking documents and hyperlinks to index a document or Web page for retrieval with a search engine. Web spiders have the potential to skew usage statistics by the very frequency of their visits. Many popular sites can receive spider visits from multiple search engines frequently throughout the day. These spider "hits" add up, burying actual user searches and clicks. Fortunately, it is common practice for nearly all reporting software to filter out spider hits as part of the reporting process. However, metadata and data harvesting by large metadata repositories tends not to be filtered during statistics processing and can potentially introduce hundreds or thousands of "false" hits into the report log.

ITEM PREFETCHING

An interesting problem with current-generation browsers is the practice of prefetching documents. Web browsers like Firefox can actually be configured to prefetch documents from the links on a page. Furthermore, through the use of specially encoded <link> tags on an HTML page, a document itself can encourage the browser to prefetch page content. Search engines like Google are actively exploring and utilizing prefetching in its search results (Google Help Center, n.d.). While prefetching content allows the browser to load documents faster for the user, it also has the potential to record thousands of false "hits," complicating analysis. On the Web server, prefetch requests are generally recorded as a "hit," as if the user had visited the page him- or herself. The only difference is found in a custom message sent in the header of the browser request (Mozilla, 2006):

> **X-Moz: prefetch**
>
> The header is only visible when the document is fetched but not logged in the server logs. This means that unless the Web server is configured to **not** log a prefetch request, there is no measurable difference between a log entry for a prefetch "click" or a user "click."

Even given these problems, analysis of Web logs will play a vital role in securing funding and promoting success, in part, because numbers seem so objective. It's the role of the digital repository administrator to interpret the available statistical data so that they provide a representative snapshot of the repository's usage.

SUMMARY

As an institution works to bring a digital repository program online, it must not forget to prepare for the many new tasks and responsibilities that come with being a digital provider. Digital repository administrators would do well to familiarize themselves with their legal responsibility as content providers and work with the organization's legal department to craft a copyright policy that benefits both the contributing authors and the digital repository. This document should serve as a guide for the organization as it plans the digital repository's long-term management and assesses the types of materials for archiving.

A successful program is built on more than technical infrastructure and content. Within a digital repository, the process of assessment is always ongoing. Assessment of the collection, usability assessment, or use assessments—the digital repository administrator needs to be the project's advocate, representing the needs and success of the project to the larger user community.

REFERENCES

The Authors' Guild. "Authors' Guild Sues Google." (Last updated September 20, 2005). Available: www.authorsguild.org/?article=86

CrazyEgg Homepage. Available: www.crazyegg.com

Creative Commons. Available: http://creativecommons.org

Digital Millennium Copyright Act. Available: http://thomas.loc.gov/cgi-bin/query/z?c105:H.R.2281.ENR

Google Help Center. "Results Prefetching." Available: www.google.com/help/features.html#prefetch

Mozilla. "Link Prefetching FAQ." (Last updated 2006). Available: http://developer.mozilla.org/en/docs/Link_prefetching_FAQ#Do_prefetched_requests_contain_a_Referer:_header.3F

OpenID Homepage. Available: http://openid.net

Shibboleth Homepage. Available: http://shibboleth.internet2.edu

U.S. Copyright Office. "Fair-Use Fact Sheet." Available: www.copyright.gov/fls/fl102.html

Yergler, Nathan R., and Mike Linksvayer. "CreativeCommons OASIS Open Document Model." (Last updated March 2, 2004). Available: www.yergler.net/projects/cc-oasis/ccoasis.html

9 PLANNING FOR THE FUTURE

Cheap technology and network computing have fundamentally altered the way that information is created, distributed, organized, and used. For libraries, the most important of these effects has been the rapid decentralization of information and its storage in volatile formats. Since the function of libraries has traditionally been to preserve information resources and provide centralized access, recent technological developments have changed the primary function of the library from preserving physical information that it owns to providing access to electronic information that is often maintained by others.

The digital repository will play a very interesting role in the future. Although locally maintained by individual libraries, the repository's true value is derived from the role it plays as part of a network consisting of high-value resources. Consequently, even when libraries create substantial digital collections that they own and maintain, the library of the next generation will still need to achieve a high level of interoperability with digital repositories maintained by others as well as other information sources. Nonetheless, as time passes, digital repositories will play a progressively greater role in library services.

PROVIDING INFORMATION THAT PEOPLE NEED

Now that most information is created and used exclusively in electronic format, libraries must confront the challenges that digital repositories present if they are to maintain a prominent role in preserving and organizing information. Because most libraries have access to information that is unique to their organization or area, they also need to be familiar with methods that will allow them to share that information with others. In the process of learning to share information with other institutions, libraries will also become proficient with the methods necessary to integrate information from many remote sources. As the number of people who access libraries from remote computers increases, use of aggregate databases, electronic books, digital repositories, and Web sites will continue to grow. To serve these users well, libraries must develop tools so users can search all these resources without having to know which one contains the information that they need.

This is not to say that libraries will only provide access to digital information. For a variety of reasons, paper and other physical formats will continue to play an important role for the foreseeable future. Too much information that will never be digitized has accumulated over the years. Even if copyright were not an issue, there will never be enough money and labor to do the work because of the sheer amount of physical processing required. In some cases, paper is simply the most practical and efficient format to serve certain information needs. It is easier to quickly browse and read paper, and sometimes it is impractical to have an electronic device that requires special care and a continuous power supply. For these reasons, most libraries will continue to maintain and develop their paper collections despite the wealth of information available online and the access to excellent subscription databases.

Nonetheless, it is clear that people will expect and need mostly electronic information in the future. It is simply too convenient to use—especially in an environment characterized by wide geographic dispersal of information resources. Even information professionals often shun paper resources although they are aware that many high-value resources are only available in this format. One of the authors of this book has served for a number of years on the editorial board of a library science journal that does not specialize in technology. Over time, the number of references to paper resources has steadily decreased, and submissions often include only electronic citations. When paper resources are cited, they tend to be to "classics," material the author read as part of a degree program. The research process is very time consuming, and it takes far less time to discover, evaluate, and obtain an electronic resource than it does to acquire a paper book or journal, especially if it is not available locally.

Users' need to access a wide variety of electronic resources makes the creation of digital repositories inevitable. Libraries must embrace this new role or they will soon find themselves limited to maintaining paper collections that get progressively less use with time. People expect to have their needs satisfied quickly. Despite the fact that many large libraries still do not have their entire collections in their online catalog, and never will because the cost of converting the rest of the cards would be prohibitive, use of the card catalog has steadily declined. This is true even when it is the only access mechanism to significant parts of the collection. Even many librarians who are aware of this problem still use the online catalog exclusively themselves.

LIBRARIES' NEW ROLES

Given the extensive transformation of the information landscape in recent decades, the core services that libraries provide need to be reexamined. A growing trend over the past few decades has been to contract external entities to provide library services. Traditionally, library personnel have chosen which materials should be acquired. They also ordered, cataloged, physically processed, and shelved these resources. When patrons needed help, librarians provided assistance.

Today, it is common for libraries to use vendor-provided approval plans to select books and other materials for their collections. The vast majority of cataloging is performed by downloading records from OCLC. In many cases, libraries purchase books that arrive shelf ready from the vendor, complete with barcodes, labels, and embedded security tape. As collection budgets have failed to keep pace with inflation, libraries have increased their reliance on interlibrary loan. It is expected that other libraries will maintain many resources that users need. In other words, many tasks that used to be regarded as core functions have been outsourced.

In recent years, the trend has accelerated, and libraries have started relying on outside parties to maintain the collection and provide reference as well as access services. Electronic collections are rarely managed directly by libraries. Rather, access to them is licensed through vendors, and, in many cases, the library is not even responsible for providing proxy access or authentication. Vendors are becoming increasingly responsible for determining what belongs in the collection and for ensuring that the resources are adequately protected. If current trends continue, and libraries provide access to increasingly larger collections provided by a shrinking number of vendors, eventually a point will be reached where one could argue that the library is merely acting as a purchasing agent and that the vendor is performing the acquisitions, preservation, and access functions that have been traditionally associated with libraries.

Progressively fewer services require a librarian's mediation. Desktop access effectively outsources the reference interview and assistance finding items for the users and the people who design and configure systems. Virtual reference services such as L-net are to reference what OCLC is to cataloging. A patron might well have his or her reference question answered by someone thousands of miles away rather than by the local librarian. If a point is ever reached where librarians start relying exclusively on digital information to answer questions, there is no reason why libraries could not someday follow the example of many businesses and contract overseas call centers to provide phone and chat-style reference. Systems are being maintained outside the library as well as services. When campus or municipal IT departments do not absorb responsibility for system administration, libraries frequently opt to purchase hosted solutions. Libraries join progressively larger consortia, and, in recent years, the number of shared catalogs has rapidly expanded. Even when libraries maintain their own systems, they may choose to have the servers hosted by a service provider.

In short, almost all aspects of library work—selection, acquisitions, cataloging, interlibrary loan, reference, preservation, and systems—are increasingly being provided outside the library. As dependence on licensed content increases and libraries purchase fewer books and journals, it is clear that the library's role in archiving and preserving information is gradually diminishing. It is not clear what the future holds, but it is evident that the stereotypes of librarians shelving books or gently warning patrons to work more quietly will soon have little basis in fact. Clearly, the next generation of libraries will look very different than those of yesteryear.

Although many library administrators and staff have become very concerned by the transfer of responsibilities traditionally performed by the library to outside organizations and to the users themselves, these trends should be welcomed. Rather than characterizing a "dumbing down" of services and a reduction in quality, these trends represent a chance for libraries to provide a greater level and quality of service than was possible before. As an analogy, consider the travel industry. Just a few years ago, the only way consumers could purchase an airline ticket was through a travel agency or directly from the airline. Tickets could be obtained by mail or in person, but losing them often resulted in significant headaches and charges to replace them. On the day of travel, the customer had to stand in a long line because the gate agent had to enter information from the ticket into the system to issue a boarding pass.

Now, customers can compare fares on airlines quickly and even receive automated alerts when routes they are interested in can be bought at desirable prices. The customer enters all the relevant information into the system, chooses seats, prints out boarding passes, and can even check in without leaving the comfort of his or her own home. The new system is faster, easier, and more flexible for the customer despite the fact that he or she does most of the work and the airline can provide its service at significantly lower cost.

LEARNING FROM THE PAST

Like the people who used to process paper tickets for airlines, librarians must adapt their skills to match user needs and new realities. Most people type their own letters, dial phone numbers, and press the buttons when they enter an elevator despite the fact that several decades ago, secretaries typed letters, operators dialed phone calls, and elevator operators selected floors for people. Improved technologies and trends towards self-service have led to automation of many tasks and made it easy for people to serve themselves. As a result, computers now perform many jobs that used to be regarded as good careers.

Libraries serve as a cultural institution as well as an information resource, so it is essential to retain knowledge that has emerged over time. However, it is also necessary to embrace the future and recognize the difference between maintaining a connection with the past and clinging to practices that have lost their relevance. Every service that is now considered a part of "traditional" library service was at one time new and innovative, and it is important to realize that new traditions will continue to emerge. The long-term outlook for libraries that anticipate and respond to user needs is much better than it is for those who try to define user needs in terms of what services they provide now.

History teaches many lessons. For libraries, one of the most important of these is that change is inevitable, so the digital repository of today must be designed with this in mind. Digital resources have existed for only a few decades, and not enough time has passed for libraries to know what formats, methods, and systems are best suited to archiving and serving these materials. No system lasts forever, and it would be a mistake to presume that the best tools for running a digital repository have even been developed. Every generation believes it has attained the pinnacle of scientific knowledge and technological achievement. Great advancements have occurred throughout the ages, and there is every reason to expect that future generations will continue to improve current methods, tools, and knowledge.

The Great Library of Alexandria contained hundreds of thousands of items over two thousand years ago, but standardized call number schemes did not exist until very recently. Consistent authority files have only been in widespread use for a few decades at best—until network computing made producing collective authority files convenient, these were typically maintained separately at each library. As a result, headings varied from one environment to another. Classification systems that members of the public can use to find related books together have only been in general use for about a century. As of this writing, online catalogs have been in widespread use for barely two decades.

Digital repositories are still in their infancy. Although many libraries have embarked on repository projects, the impact of these initiatives is modest at this point in time. Some repositories look very polished on the surface, but contain very few resources. Those that contain many items frequently have collection development policies that add materials because they are free rather than because they are particularly useful. Libraries are still at a stage where repositories are frequently treated as proof of concept demonstration projects rather than as a true component of the library collection. For such repositories, one would expect relatively low usage. However, now that libraries are recognizing that digital repositories can succeed, the time has come to develop more ambitious projects that address larger scale and more sophisticated information needs.

Although digital repositories still play a relatively minor role in the information landscape, a growing number of significant electronic collections are becoming available. The Library of Congress' American Memory project is a well-funded endeavor to make unique and rare materials that document the American experience available online. Virginia Tech has required that students submit theses and dissertations electronically since 1997, and many other universities have followed suit (Virginia Polytechnic Institution and State University, accessed: 2006). Other institutions digitize unique photographs or make other special collections available online. Clearly, the role of digital archives maintained by libraries is growing.

Patterns are starting to emerge that suggest that digital repositories will be very different from their physical counterparts. Current examples of successful projects are all very limited in scope. The American Memory project does not simply digitize information relating to American history. Rather, it focuses on digitizing primary documents that are of particular historical or cultural significance. Successful university digital repositories typically make a special collection available online, or focus on very specific locally produced resources, such as theses and dissertations. Other digital archives focus on preserving access to specific titles or resources.

It is easy to dismiss these patterns as introductory growing pains and presume that libraries will collect all resources that their patrons use digitally just as they currently collect all resources that their patrons use in physical formats. However, there are a number of reasons why this apparent pattern of repositories that serve relatively specialized needs may be part of a growing and permanent trend. Identifying content that the library can reasonably expect to store and have the right to distribute is very difficult. Copyright regulations put severe limitations on the types of materials libraries can store in digital repositories. Rights management issues are complex; there is a strong incentive for libraries to focus on providing access to those items that they own the rights to distribute.

Even when copyright is not an issue, a number of technical and organizational challenges place significant constraints on what kind of resources can be archived. As Chapters 2 and 3 explained, certain types of resources lend themselves poorly towards the archival procedures normally used in digital repositories. It is important to keep a sense of perspective. Although there has been a great deal of hand-wringing about what is lost when digital information is archived, libraries have always limited their collections to what could be stored and managed properly. Few libraries accept materials they cannot preserve and provide access to, and it is difficult to argue that those that do are providing better service. Even when information is recorded on paper, most libraries provide minimal access at best to physical information that does not conform to a very rigid structure. On the rare occasions when significant efforts are made to store paper resources that do not have the properties of books or serials (e.g., correspondence, notes, etc.) in a special collection, access is often provided via sketchy information in a specialized finding aid or a collection-level catalog record, and finding the desired item requires searching through boxes of material. In short, libraries have traditionally addressed the problem of which resources they preserve by limiting their collections to items they can work with. It is perfectly reasonable to continue this same practice for digital resources.

ADAPTING TO CHANGE

Libraries will need to change if they are to remain relevant to serving peoples' information needs. The amount of information that people want access to is increasing, but the funding and number of library staff is not. As time passes, information will become progressively more decentralized and parties outside the library will maintain much of it. The role of digital information will continue to expand. Given that libraries have traditionally served as centralized repositories of information, the trend toward users' needing decentralized electronic information has major implications for delivery of library services.

Libraries already face significant competition even in their core business of providing patrons with books. Online booksellers deliver new and used books quickly and cheaply to patrons. Recognizing patrons' affinity for online bookstores as well as their brick and mortar counterparts complete with coffee shops, many libraries have started adopting methods developed by businesses known to be popular with users. Since the late 1990s, the library community has been discussing what can be done to make the online catalog more like Amazon.com and the interior of the library more like Borders. Libraries have started serving coffee, renting out popular books, and displaying colorful book jackets in their online catalogs.

While it is appropriate for libraries to incorporate certain ideas from the business world, libraries need to maintain their own niche. Simply emulating models adopted by for-profit entities with more efficient supply and distribution systems is not an effective long-term strategy for libraries. If the library provides a similar service to the business, but does so less effectively, the logical outcome would be for libraries to fade away, and users will gradually turn to other information providers to meet their needs. If libraries are to prosper, they need to do more than simply mimic services provided by others.

The key to libraries' continued success is to identify which services they are uniquely positioned to provide. There has been endless discussion in the library community about implementing features such as the ability for users to place comments in online catalogs, recommend other books, display book jackets, and similar features. However, it is highly unlikely that libraries will be able to perform these tasks as well as large businesses. Making accurate recommendations requires a great deal of statistical data about individual as well as group preferences and behavior. For many reasons, including privacy and freedom to explore without surveillance, libraries do not track user behavior at this level. Even if they did, they would need to compile the data centrally for it to be useful. Millions of people use Amazon.com, but much smaller groups use individual libraries. Libraries use a large number of separate and often incompatible systems, so it would not be technically feasible for them to combine their data so that it could be used for local purposes, even if they wanted to.

Statistically based methods require large sample sizes. Even aspects of the vendor systems that do not rely on statistics might be difficult to implement in local catalogs. For example, it is unlikely that enough patrons would attach thoughtful comments in a local catalog to affect more than a tiny minority of books. The online booksellers have millions of users, yet the number of comments is relatively small and they appear mostly on popular books that sell many copies. Allowing patrons to view book jackets or browse a few pages requires time-consuming digitization. If libraries focus on copying business practices such as these, they will find that the product they deliver will be inferior and at higher cost. Consequently, it makes more sense to purchase these services.

As a practical matter, libraries cannot expect to rely on any method that requires sophisticated and large-scale technological integration. All examples of technologies that have proven successful for purposes of integrating library collections are very simple. Even moderately complex technologies such as Z39.50 are barely utilized despite widespread vendor support, lack of a viable alternative for many years, and strong advocacy on the part of the library community. Because technology skills vary so widely from one library to the next and many library staff have demands placed on them that do not allow them to spend significant amounts of time developing technical skills and debugging software, all technological integration must use robust protocols and standards that are simple enough that they can be understood and implemented very quickly by people without highly specialized technical knowledge.

For libraries to thrive, they need to concentrate on those services that they are structured to provide faster and more efficiently than anyone else. Many services can be automated, but many cannot. Libraries excel at services that require large-scale cooperative efforts or human evaluation of information resources. One inherent advantage libraries have over any other information provider is that they have cataloged and organized materials that have been created over a period of centuries. In addition, libraries have established practices that allow them to quickly identify what materials other libraries have as well as where a particular resource can be found. Consequently, even if a library does not have what a user needs, chances are that it can be quickly obtained through interlibrary loan (ILL).

Although digital information will continue to increase in importance, an enormous amount of critical information from the past will be available only in paper, and the only way to find it will be through a library. Library catalogs have their faults, but the methods they use to organize materials have proven effective for organizing hundreds of millions of unique items. People may rave about Amazon.com, but it is far easier to find all books written by an author in a library catalog, particularly if he or she has a common name with multiple spelling variations. Most major research libraries can provide access to far more books than Amazon.com. Now that dozens of major libraries can be searched at once in large consortia catalogs, it is clear that libraries still have much to offer.

In addition to the well-organized materials they have collected over the years and the cooperative arrangements they have made to maximize use of resources, libraries are positioned to provide certain services better than businesses. If a user does not know what he or she needs, a reference librarian is still much more helpful than a search engine or a vendor database. A reference librarian will know which content providers are most likely to have resources that could help the user, and will not fail to recommend materials to a user because a competitor owns them or because they are not listed near the top of a keyword relevancy search. By leveraging these and other strengths, libraries will provide critical information services well into the future.

CONSOLIDATION AND SPECIALIZATION

Just as it has transformed other institutions and businesses, the global Internet economy is also changing how libraries operate. Patrons expect libraries to deliver a greater variety of materials than ever before, and they want these faster, cheaper, and better. Libraries must pool resources and enter cooperative agreements to take advantage of economies of scale, consolidated purchasing power, and other efficiencies. Fortunately, libraries have been doing exactly that for many years. Thousands of libraries use the OCLC cooperative to share cataloging and holdings information. This helps make efficient copy cataloging, large-scale authority control, and ILL possible. Large consortia such as OhioLINK and the Orbis Cascade Alliance provide a shared catalog and distribution system to make it possible to share materials almost seamlessly. Consortia and cooperative organizations can also take advantage of combined purchasing power to negotiate better terms for databases and other products.

Digital repositories reflect the dual library trends towards consolidation and specialization. The Networked Library of Theses and Dissertations represents an effort to lower the costs for providing access to electronic theses and dissertations (ETDs) and to share graduate-level research produced at major research universities around the world (Networked Digital Library of Theses and Dissertations, accessed: 2006). By making information about ETDs widely available through normal cataloging channels, OAI-PMH, and other means, universities and other information providers can share a unique and valuable resource very efficiently. Enthusiastic support within the library community for Dublin Core, OAI-PMH, and other generic standards discussed in Chapter 5 helps libraries conveniently share unique resources. That is precisely why major repository software such as DSpace and CONTENTdm support these standards.

A good digital repository does much more than simply store and provide access to a collection of electronic documents. Rather, it represents a permanent and unique archive of useful materials that serve the library community as well as local users. Just as libraries have banded together to provide collective cataloging and even reference, the next logical path for libraries is to collectively capture information so that it can be made accessible. In many ways, this task is an extension of ILL services into the electronic realm.

The Internet has enormous value because it allows millions of computers to communicate with each other. Individually, even the powerful computers have limited value. Collectively, they comprise an incredibly powerful resource that allows a user at an inexpensive workstation to do things that would be impossible even with a non-networked supercomputer. Digital repositories are also more valuable when they are part of a greater network. Just as a coin, stamp, card, or a book has more worth as part of a collection than by itself, an electronic document is more useful as part of a greater collection. As the collection becomes richer and more extensive, the value of the component parts continues to increase. For this reason, a digital repository is far more valuable as part of a great network of information resources that can be searched conveniently than it is as a silo of information on the Internet.

Consolidating services, employing technologies to share metadata and information, and collaborating with other organizations enables libraries to take advantage of work and resources at other institutions so that they can serve their patrons better, cheaper, and faster. By specializing in services and materials that a library is positioned especially well to provide and turning to partners and vendors for addressing other needs, libraries can maintain and even expand their niche well into the future.

FEDERATED COLLECTION MANAGEMENT

If libraries want digital repositories to represent more than a fringe of special collections, a model based on the premise that libraries physically manage the resources patrons will use is not adequate for the future; that will only put them at the same status as many other content providers. Users need all kinds of information, and an individual library can only own the rights to a small fraction of the resources a community of users is likely to want. Thus, for digital repositories to play an important role in the future, it must be possible to discover materials in them using federated searching techniques (discussed in Chapter 7). It is unreasonable to expect users to search thousands of digital repositories located around the globe for materials of interest. Just as most users find what they want on the Web by consulting one of a small number of search engines, they will most likely want to find all library materials in a single search.

Digital repositories that lack the capability of sharing information with systems that users want to use have the effect of hiding important resources from all users except those who are especially persistent or lucky enough to stumble upon what they need. Good digital repositories must allow users to search for what they want across multiple information sources at the same time, preferably without the user having to know which information sources need to be searched.

Efforts have been made to incorporate library materials in Web search engines, but it is unlikely that this approach will provide effective access to entire categories of content that are essential for many library users. Web search engines cannot construct OpenURLs that allow immediate access to resources in subscription databases, nor can they automatically place interlibrary loan requests for materials that must be obtained from other libraries. Web search engines cannot display local holdings or availability information, or allow for searches when the search target is an item that has a common title (e.g., reports, bulletins, proceedings, etc.) or all items by a specific author.

It is clear that as time passes, other libraries and organizations will maintain a growing proportion of the resources that individual libraries have owned and maintained. Thus, management of library collections will ultimately be based on access to rather than ownership of materials.

A well-managed digital repository that contains unique and useful information is a critical component of the next-generation library. Just as the Internet decentralized computing, it is also decentralizing library services. Figure 9-1 illustrates how libraries have traditionally managed and provided information to users. According to this model, the library owns all materials and provides what is requested. When the user needs something, he or she searches the appropriate collection directly to find resources.

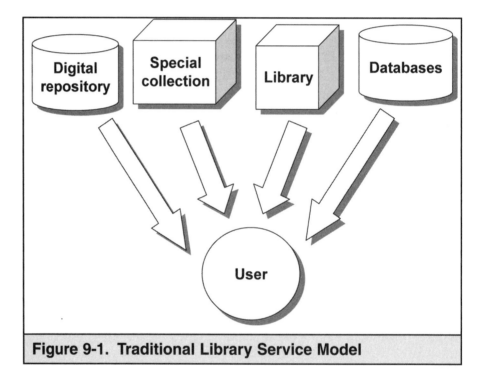

Figure 9-1. Traditional Library Service Model

Figure 9-2 depicts how the next-generation library will serve patrons. There are two important differences between this diagram and the traditional model. The first is that users do not need to search individual resources; in fact, they do not need to know which resources are being searched. The library simply finds and combines metadata from various content providers (including the library itself) that are likely to be useful. The second difference is that, in many cases, the user does not obtain the resource from the library. The library may act as an intermediary in some cases, such as interlibrary loan or proxy access to subscription materials, but its primary function would be to provide access by integrating metadata from a variety of sources and making it searchable in a way that helps the user.

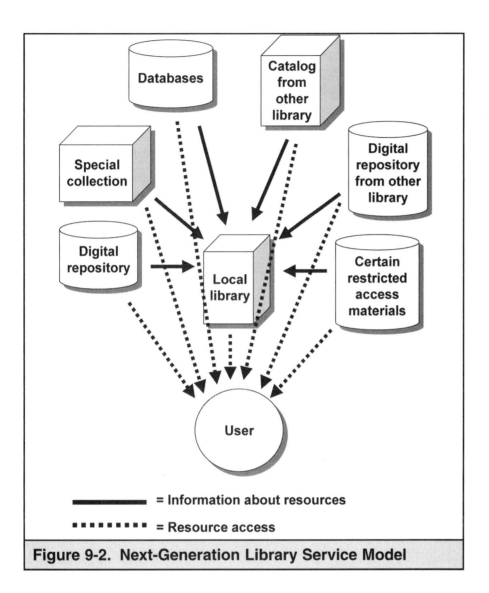

Figure 9-2. Next-Generation Library Service Model

Figure 9-2 is displayed from the user's perspective and has been simplified for clarity. In this diagram, the user's home library harvests information about resources (i.e., metadata) from other information providers. In practice, the very entities that the library harvests metadata from would also be harvesting metadata themselves to serve their own users. Viewed from a universal perspective, there is no "main" library except from the perspective of an individual user. Rather they all work together in a seamless information fabric. Notice that this model allows access to certain resources maintained by other libraries that have access restricted. This is possible because of distributed access-control mechanisms such as those discussed in Chapter 8.

Proponents of a vision where all libraries both collect and distribute metadata must answer must ask why all metadata is not simply included in a single repository. The answer is simple: for information to be useful, it needs to be provided within context. By allowing individual libraries to choose which metadata is harvested and how it is presented, users may browse and search different virtual collections. Just as many shoppers would be better served by a small store that specializes in a particular type of product than by a shopping mall containing thousands of stores of all sizes that sell goods expected to appeal to the vast majority of consumers, many people will need specialized information spaces that are optimized towards their needs. While it would be technically feasible for all information providers to keep all metadata in a single physical location, the organizational and technical challenges are considerable enough that the disadvantages outweigh the benefits of doing so. By sharing metadata according to standard protocols, libraries can use the operating environments and software that best serve local needs to provide access to all materials.

In this next-generation model, the number of information providers has greatly expanded, and a service point can be provided anywhere a user has network access. This means that many users will never see the inside of a library, and librarians will not see their most loyal customers. Just as the Internet has made it possible for people to maintain close relationships with people they have never met in person, it also allows libraries to make resources scattered all over the globe seem as if they were part of a single collection and provide highly personalized services to users who will never enter the building.

To move towards the next-generation library, where information is stored in distributed repositories around the world, library systems must invest in common protocols and standards that allow information to be discovered, transmitted, and used. Fortunately, many of these protocols, such as SRU/SRW, OAI-PMH, OpenURL, and Dublin Core, are supported by most repository software. It is important to be aware that the most successful protocols and standards may not originate from the library community. For example, OpenSearch may eventually emerge as the *de facto* generic search protocol. OpenSearch is easier to implement than SRU/SRW, has enormous support outside the library community, and has a simple but elegant design that can be easily extended. (OpenSearch is discussed and compared with SRU/SRW in Chapter 7). As the number of resources that require mediated access for rights-management reasons increases, it may well prove impractical for libraries to configure all proxy connections. If this is the case, Shibboleth, Athens, or some other distributed access-control mechanism discussed in Chapter 8 in combination with a DOI or OpenURL resolver may well prove to be the solution, even though these tools were not specifically created for library use.

In many ways, the most important aspect of the digital repository of the future is not that the information is being stored in electronic format. Rather, it is that otherwise relatively insignificant repositories will be able to play a role in a large peer-to-peer network containing a rich collection that can be used to serve diverse needs. Once the technical and organizational challenges of creating digital repositories are overcome, the next critical hurdle will be make sure these systems can share information seamlessly with each other.

Libraries will distinguish themselves by providing federated content management. The complexity of this task is significant, but the basic tools and methods necessary to achieve this already exist, and libraries know how to use them. For example, librarians have long taken relatively sophisticated authority control mechanisms for granted. Although it is common for naive technologists to claim that authority control is not necessary when sophisticated keyword searching is available, people usually quickly discover through experience that it is indeed necessary.

To illustrate this point, Wikipedia uses a process called "disambiguation" that is not only functionally equivalent to authority control, but which also uses the same methods (Wikipedia, accessed: 2006a). Among other things, disambiguation specifies rules for qualifying common terms, expressing relationships between different entries, and it even prescribes how headings for certain types of resources such as ships are constructed (Wikipedia, accessed: 2006b). A disambiguation page has a structure very similar to that of an authority record.

FEDERATED VOCABULARIES

Effective searching is difficult to achieve without vocabularies that allow users to specify what they need. Algorithms based on resource popularity may work well for general Web searching, but when highly specialized resources are needed that do not have equally unique vocabularies, these materials become difficult, or even impossible, to find. For this reason, vocabularies that allow users to search for items within a knowledge domain are necessary for searching across multiple repositories.

The maintenance of vocabularies implies authority control. However, just as resources become more decentralized, vocabulary maintenance will also become decentralized. While it would be impractical for librarians to maintain vocabularies using committees, as is currently done with Library of Congress Subject Headings, it would be perfectly feasible for them to identify vocabularies maintained by appropriate bodies that could be used to manage access across multiple repositories. As digital repositories and library services mature, it seems a natural extension for librarians to manage vocabularies belonging to different domains.

The skeleton of such a structure has already been in place on the Internet for years. XML namespaces are based on this same concept of managing vocabularies belonging to different domains. Although the cascading style sheets used to display Web pages do not reflect vocabularies in the normal sense of the word, their structure is based on the idea that contradictory display information may be provided from a variety of sources, and a simple way to prioritize that information must exist. Likewise, rules can be established for resolving conflicts between overlapping vocabularies, depending on what the user needs.

Although federated vocabularies that comprise the semantic Web (discussed in Chapter 7) have been criticized for being impractical, there is still ample reason to believe that the library community can make them succeed even when they have not been particularly successful in the Web environment in general. In a well-known essay, Cory Doctorow explained the futility of metadata on the Web, claiming that there are a number of inherent and insurmountable problems in the metadata creation process that make it impractical to use on a large scale. Specifically, he found that differences of interests in metadata creators, lack of time or inclination to be accurate, sloppiness, the fact that each schema represents a different conceptual universe, differences in how people describe things, and the impossibility of devising a ranking algorithm that suits all needs equally severely limit the utility of human-created metadata (Doctorow, 2001).

Many respected technologists agree with Doctorow's premise that human-created metadata has little value, especially when used with Web search engines. That major search engines have increasingly ignored human-created metadata over time would seem to support his conclusions. However, the next-generation library model that is already emerging addresses virtually all of Doctorow's concerns.

Unlike individual authors and information providers who may be interested only in promoting their own materials or even impeding access to works created by others, libraries have a vested interest in presenting information resources within the context of a larger collection. This dynamic explains why most libraries obtain the vast majority of their catalog records from OCLC WorldCat rather than creating new ones themselves. Library staff are trained professionals, so although there are certainly discrepancies in how they describe things, the level of consistently is very high. If there is one thing that the library community recognizes, it is the importance of consistency in organizing a collection. As has been described in the chapters of this book, the standards that make participation of digital repositories in federated collections possible also allow searching that mitigates conflicts in the schemas that describe information. Consequently, the prospects of success are very good.

SUMMARY

Libraries have traditionally served as centralized repositories of information, so the rapid decentralization of information brought about by the Internet and cheap technology presents significant challenges to libraries.

To maintain a prominent role in provision of information services, libraries must develop digital repositories and other services that are designed to provide access to distributed resources so that user needs can be met.

Among other things, such a shift will require librarians to focus more on providing access to materials maintained by others and less on physically maintaining control over resources. It will also require librarians to identify and expand services that libraries are uniquely positioned to deliver. By leveraging the enormous amount of data libraries have already collected for cataloging and ILL purposes and the enormous amount of experience librarians have performing information identification and organizing functions requiring human evaluation of information, libraries will continue to be a critical components of the infrastructure people need to find what they want. While librarians can learn from popular features of the online booksellers and search engines, they should not simply attempt to emulate successful commercial entities that have developed business models based on relative strengths and weaknesses that are different from those of libraries.

Digital repositories maintained by libraries will perform an important function in this new, decentralized environment since they will contain a wide variety of specialized and unique collections. To be useful to local users as well as to the greater library community, these repositories must support common protocols for sharing metadata so that libraries can effectively manage federated collections. To support robust federated search, libraries will also have to identify and develop vocabularies that describe their local collections but that also translate well into generic standards such as Dublin Core. Just as libraries have shared cataloging for many years to provide better service at lower cost, they will need to share collections stored in digital repositories on a large scale.

Physical libraries have traditionally limited acquisitions to materials they can effectively preserve and process. Likewise, digital repositories will need to define their collections in terms of what they have rights to provide access to and what can be preserved. As a practical matter, this implies that most successful digital repositories will serve specialized needs because the best tools and methods for acquiring, storing, and accessing digital resources depends on the type of resource.

REFERENCES

Doctorow, Cory. "Metacrap: Putting the Torch to Seven Straw-men of the Meta-utopia." (Last updated August 26, 2001). Available: www.well.com/~doctorow/metacrap.htm (accessed January 7, 2007).

Networked Digital Library of Theses and Dissertations. "Networked Digital Library of Theses and Dissertations." Available: www.ndltd.org (accessed December 17, 2006).

Virginia Polytechnic Institute and State University. "VT ETDs from the Digital Library and Archives." Available: http://scholar.lib.vt.edu/theses/ (accessed December 17, 2006).

Wikipedia. "Wikipedia: Disambiguation." Available: http://en.wikipedia.org/wiki/Wikipedia:Disambiguation (accessed December 26, 2006a).

Wikipedia. "Wikipedia: WikiProject Ships." Available: http://en.wikipedia.org/wiki/Wikipedia:WikiProject_Ships (accessed December 26, 2006b).

10 CONCLUSIONS

Designing and building a digital repository is exciting work, providing an opportunity for electronic-resources people to work with each other and technology in new ways. As of this writing, digital repositories are still new enough that many of the challenges they present remain unresolved. Therefore, libraries choosing to embark on repository projects should do so with the expectation that they will help advance understanding of how repositories work and how they can be improved. A great deal of excellent work has been done by organizations of all sizes, but methods and technologies have not yet matured to the point that libraries can simply adopt solutions developed elsewhere, except when very limited projects are concerned.

Establishing a repository is like adding a special collection. It is a major responsibility that involves a permanent commitment of significant financial and staff resources. For this reason, a library should launch a digital repository project only after considering how the repository can be operated using available resources in a way that supports the library's mission. To remain usable, a digital repository must be actively maintained. Electronic files can only be used with the aid of technology. If the files themselves or any platform required to use them are allowed to become obsolete, they eventually become inaccessible.

A digital repository is a virtual space where electronic resources are processed and housed. Just as simple design choices during a library renovation project can have enormous lasting effects on the usability of a physical library and the ability of staff to perform their responsibilities, early technical and policy decisions on a repository project can have a major impact on the functionality, usability, workflow, and even long-term viability of the resource. It is therefore essential to be aware of the major implications of key alternatives with regards to platform, formats, metadata, workflow, and standards supported before making final decisions.

Success demands a sense of enthusiasm for the project, a willingness to learn, and a desire to contribute to the field. Administrative and staff buy-in as well as long-term organizational commitment are also indispensable. Maintaining a digital repository requires specialized knowledge and skills. Staff must have a broad understanding of repository processes, including those relating to acquiring, reformatting, describing, classifying, and processing materials. Any locally hosted solution requires systems administration and some programming skills. For these reasons, maintaining a digital repository should be assigned to staff who have the time and skills to adequately support the project.

During the planning stages, it is critical for designers to articulate the goals of the repository clearly. Planners need to identify what types of materials will be stored, who the repository will serve, how resources will be protected against modification and disaster, how intellectual property rights will be managed, what systems it must interact with, and what resources will be available for maintenance. Digital repositories are still in a stage of rapid development, and more likely than not, in a few decades they will look very different from the way they do right now. Repositories must be flexible enough to accommodate types of information that do not yet exist, as well as any workflows, procedures, or special capabilities those new resources may require. Just as libraries have added microfilm, tapes, CDs, and DVDs to their collections as resources and user needs evolved, it will undoubtedly be necessary to someday add resources that have not even been imagined yet to digital repositories.

To date, successful digital repositories have well-defined scopes that focus on acquisitions of very particular types of materials. There are numerous reasons for this, but one of them is that different purposes are best addressed by different philosophical, organizational, and technical approaches. Highly centralized repositories require different tools from those designed to grow organically with content providers submitting their own materials. Systems that are optimized to search and display graphic materials or maps might not be as effective at organizing textual documents into conceptual hierarchies and vice versa. The quantity, sophistication, syntax, and granularity of metadata have an enormous impact on how resources can be used in the local collection or as part of a federated collection. Virtually all decisions affect the cost and staff requirements for maintaining the repository. Especially at the beginning, it is impossible to know which of the decisions that will prove best for a particular library. Therefore, it is best to start with a simple but extendable plan, and expand functionality as staff and systems become better equipped to address increasingly complex challenges.

When developing a digital repository plan, it is sometimes more important to understand problems than it is to solve them. For example, any Web-based digital repository will be accessible from areas governed by different and contradictory laws. The laws that govern electronic resources are still not entirely clear, but it is imperative not to let this fact prevent a digital repository from being launched. While there are many serious copyright issues surrounding digital resources, the focus must be on identifying and managing risks rather than on anticipating and solving any problem that may arise. If one waits until all unknowns are solved before taking action, it is unlikely that work will ever begin.

A good repository plan includes many separate components, including a realistic collection development policy and well-conceived workflows. It also requires a clear idea of who will be responsible for identifying, acquiring, and reformatting materials, as well as who will assign metadata or perform other key functions. As the plan is developed, more details must be provided—people will not do what is needed until they know what is expected of them and have received adequate training.

Just as no responsible administrator of a physical library would be satisfied with a collection development policy that relies exclusively on authors to submit their works or staff members to encounter them by chance, he or she should not accept such a policy simply because the resources are downloaded over a network and stored on hard disks. While information flow on a computer network is different from the one in the analog world, and there may be a substantial role for more direct involvement with content providers, it is naïve to presume that unknown individuals can be relied on to determine which digital resources a library should collect. Therefore, a systematic means for identifying appropriate content must be developed using available staff and tools. This is a difficult task because the number of potential content providers is large, and many tools that are normally used to aid in the selection process (such as approval plans, catalogs, and marketing literature) are not available.

A digital repository is distinguished from other information resources on the Internet by which information resources it includes, how these resources are organized, and how they are preserved. On the Web, any type of information resource can be found. However, not all of these belong in a repository because they cannot all be preserved. Some resources are inseparable from very specific technologies that will soon be obsolete. Just as physical libraries do not accept items that do not fit collection goals, low-value resources, materials requiring special viewing equipment the library does not have, or materials that simply cannot be preserved, digital repositories should only include materials that the library can maintain properly.

As a practical matter, all resources in a repository must be in one of a limited number of formats that the library can support. Just as a book or serial is unlikely to be re-cataloged once it is added to the collection, a library that ignores the challenges an electronic resource presents at the time it is acquired will be unlikely to find time to determine what special treatment that resource needs and to take appropriate measures later.

Working with digital resources is an inherently complex endeavor. For example, an XML document may point to images, sound files, or other binary formats that may be located on disparate systems. There are multiple versions of the PDF format, and while all are intended to be stable, none has yet had a chance to pass the test of time. Although XML is presented as a format that can be used on any platform, XML resources cannot be used without an appropriate program. There is an enormous difference between a program that can read XML and one that knows what to do with the tags and attributes that it has read. Clearly, the challenges that repositories present cannot be solved by simply implementing a few well-regarded technologies. Digital repository planners must use their knowledge of how people create and use resources to choose appropriate technologies and develop workflows that allow the library to maintain the repository and the resources it contains over the long term.

Resources in digital repositories are acquired, processed, and accessed using computers. Nonetheless, an enormous amount of manual work and human judgment is necessary to maintain a high-quality collection, even if many processes can be partially or totally automated. Therefore, the procedures used to identify, acquire, process, and store electronic resources must be developed carefully. Different types of electronic resources present different challenges, so different workflows, tools, and procedures will be needed, just as they are to address various challenges presented by different kinds of physical resources.

Acquiring, processing, and maintaining electronic resources is time consuming. Except when self-contained resources (e.g., word-processed documents) are involved, many have significant external dependencies containing formatting information, graphics, or other external files intended to be used with the resource. Establishing procedures that allow staff to efficiently determine which files to download, convert them to an appropriate archival format, and establish necessary linkages between related files is inherently problematic.

Adding metadata is an essential step that takes a considerable amount of labor. The utility of a digital repository depends on how it is organized. Metadata is essential for categorizing resources, dividing them into subcollections, and making it easy to discover materials in local or federated environments. Consistency and the level of granularity of metadata are important, and access points must be created in a way that is compatible with existing metadata in other collections (e.g., information from the online catalog) for them to be searched at the same time.

Although ranking algorithms are very useful, metadata are still necessary because relevancy-based search results rank some materials too low to be found. Keyword searching is especially problematic for critical but low-use resources that do not contain unique terminology. The search mechanism for a digital repository should allow a researcher to find anything in the repository; there is no reason for a library to expend staff labor processing acquiring resources that cannot be used. Besides, many resources (e.g., images, sound files, video, etc.) cannot be used with keyword searching alone. Metadata can associate related publications by title, author, and subject. It allows people to identify things by date or collection. Keywords may be useful, but when searching for a known resource, two of the most helpful access points are the name of the resource and those responsible for creating it.

A repository's platform is inseparable from the repository itself because it determines how information is added, processed, searched, and used. Different hardware and software architectures are optimized for different needs, so a platform that works very well for one library may prove to be a poor choice in another environment. Platforms are based on different assumptions of how a repository should work. Some presume that the library will manage resources centrally, while others are based on a more organic approach relying on content providers to add resources. Others may work best with certain types of resources. For example, some might be specifically designed in a way that facilitates browsing images, while others presume that materials have a document-like structure. A great deal of manual labor is necessary to acquire and process digital resources, so a platform should be chosen that will facilitate identifying, acquiring, processing, organizing, and presenting the type of resources that are expected to be kept in the library. It should also provide administrative functionality that makes it easy to perform tasks such as adding users, ensuring the integrity of files, or providing rights management.

Because digital repositories are so technology dependent, planners must develop a basic level of understanding of core technologies and standards before committing to any particular solution. Most librarians are familiar with XML. However, XML is not really a language; rather, it is a grammar that defines how languages can be created. Specially written programs are necessary for reading documents that are written in XML. Other technologies, such as SOAP, are very useful for providing services in a Web-based environment. It is not necessary to learn the technical details of the myriad of technologies that libraries depend on. However, it is essential to understand the purpose, advantages, and major limitations of technologies to get the most benefit from them.

XML is particularly important because it is the foundation of many key standards used in digital repositories. Of these, Dublin Core is the most widely known, but it is meant as a "lowest common denominator" metadata standard that is designed to support basic resource discovery. Other XML-based standards that are very useful include OAI-PMH, which allows libraries to discover and share new metadata; SRU/SRW, which is useful for information discovery; and a variety of standards that contain information about resources, such as MARCXML, MODS, and EAD. There are many XML standards that can be used in repositories, and it is important to understand the function, strengths, and weaknesses of any standard a repository will use before deciding which ones will be utilized. However, keep in mind that no system lasts forever, and all formats must be expected to eventually become obsolete. Even materials stored in XML or PDF should be assumed to need conversion at some point.

Although metadata can be converted from one format to another, meaning is often lost during conversion since analogous fields are not always available in the target format, because there are different standards to support different purposes. For example, EAD has a very flexible structure that can be used to store both collection- and item-level metadata. If an EAD document is converted to Dublin Core, most of the information will simply be lost, because there is no place in the Dublin Core record to store it. In fact, converting from almost any format used in libraries to

Dublin Core will normally result in data loss for the simple reason that Dublin Core is a simple, general-purpose scheme for describing resources. Consequently, it lacks the expressive power of more specialized metadata formats, such as TEI, MARCXML, or MODS.

The number of online resources that libraries provide access to is constantly expanding, and it is unreasonable to expect users to wade through dozens, or even hundreds, of Web pages and search interfaces to find what they need. From the perspective of a user in an academic setting, a digital repository is just one of hundreds of databases that a library provides access to. Sometimes, there is no substitute for the power that can be achieved using a repository's native search interface. However, a repository must also be searchable as part of existing collections as well as others that do not yet exist. This means that it must be able not only to share information with other systems, but to deliver responses to live searches that can easily be interpreted so that it can be searched alongside other resources using federated search tools.

For a repository to be used as part of a federated collection, it must support protocols that allow it to communicate with other systems. Although there are many protocols, a small number of searching and linking protocols are particularly useful for providing digital repository services. Searching protocols allow users to search for known as well as unknown items. For example, Z39.50 and SRU/SRW can be used to search for resources by keyword, author, title, or a number of other fields. OpenSearch, a standard developed outside the library community with widespread support on the Internet, can also be used for this purpose. Linking protocols help the user connect to a resource that has been identified. If a user locates an item that is in a subscription database, he or she needs to be redirected through a proxy server or other form of authentication. This can be accomplished with technologies such as DOIs and OpenURL. DOIs uniquely identify a resource much as an ISBN identifies a book. OpenURL allows for the transmission of limited bibliographic data (such as DOI) to connect a user directly to a resource via proxy server, or however it is appropriate given the circumstances.

Unless a repository is only expected to provide access to information that is in the public domain, some form of access control will be required. Access restrictions may be necessary even when access does not need to be limited to particular classes of individuals and only locally produced information is kept. Embargo periods are common. Authors of theses or dissertations may signed away some or all rights so that the manuscript can be published in a peer-reviewed journal, some units may rely on sales of a print publication to finance production of the free online version, and there are other cases in which information may need to be restricted because it is legally, commercially, or politically sensitive.

Any access control mechanism needs to integrate with those already available. It is useful for repository software to contain its own authentication mechanism, but it is impractical to expect staff to manually maintain logons detailing who can access what. It is also undesirable to require users to obtain a new logon just so they can read materials in the repository. Most organizations already have an LDAP server, so a repository's authentication needs to work with whatever that organization already uses. If it is necessary to authenticate users from other organizations, a mechanism that supports federated authentication, such as Shibboleth or Athens, needs to be present.

The success of a repository is measured by how well it accommodates changing needs and technologies. It could easily be argued that the Internet has been the most significant development for libraries since the printing press, and it is possibly had an even greater effect on library services. The very idea of a library implies a repository of information that is stored in a centralized location and administered by a single organization. The Internet is based on a diametrically opposed principle—namely that information is distributed around the globe and maintained by different entities. Despite the fact that it is still very new, it is clear that the Internet is a valuable resource that will play a key role in the provision of library services for the foreseeable future.

Libraries' long-term success depends on their ability to adapt to the challenges presented by an information landscape characterized by decentralized and unstable electronic resources. Librarians have been gradually recognizing that meeting user needs in a networked environment requires institutions to focus on the principle of fulfilling information needs by obtaining access to resources rather than owning them outright. However, most library practices are still based on a model that presumes that libraries must physically control all materials that their users need.

Historically, the library catalog has functioned largely as an information silo that must be searched by itself. In recent years, however, a growing number of libraries and users have started to turn to consortium-level catalogs, WorldCat, or metasearch tools to find what is needed. These practices reflect a clear trend towards consolidation of resources and federated searching of materials.

Despite the fact that digital repositories allow libraries to maintain individual collections of electronic resources, they represent a shift towards the model of the next-generation library. In a world where there are so many sources of information, most users will not encounter repositories that function solely as stand-alone resources, except by chance. To be successful, digital repositories must serve as part of a greater network of electronic services. This means that repositories must be able to share metadata with other systems and process searches using standard protocols.

This book has explained how to plan, design, and construct digital repositories. It has explored the problems repositories have been developed to solve and described the qualities repositories need to be successful. It has discussed methods that can be used to address the organizational and processing challenges electronic resources present. It has explained the technologies and standards needed to maintain a repository, and it has detailed how repositories can be incorporated into a broad array of online services, including other repositories scattered around the globe.

We are entering a fundamentally new age of library services in which digital repositories will play an important role. When Sir Isaac Newton first invented calculus and described his theory of universal gravitation, he started a revolution that sparked some of the greatest advances in the history of science. Progress moves in fits and starts. It was not until over 200 years after Newton did his pioneering work that Einstein succeeded in describing how gravity actually worked and discovering its connection with space and time.

Just as Newton's work revolutionalized science, the Internet has transformed the way people interact with each other and information almost overnight. Enormous progress has already been made with regards to identifying, accessing, and preserving access to distributed electronic resources. However, there is still much to be learned. Those that embark upon digital repository projects will help find solutions to the complex challenges electronic resources present while improving access to resources that users need.

INDEX

ABOUT THE AUTHORS

Terry Reese is the Digital Production Unit Head for Oregon State University Libraries. In that capacity, he oversees the digitization efforts at OSU. Additionally, Terry serves as a member of the OSU research and development team working on projects like LibraryFind, an open-source metasearch/OpenURL application being developed by the library.

Kyle Banerjee is the Digital Services Program Manager for the Orbis Cascade Alliance in Eugene, Oregon. He has written numerous articles about digital library issues and co-authored a book entitled *Digital Libraries: Integrating Content and Systems*. He is one of the key architects of the state of Oregon's electronic documents repository. Kyle enjoys riding his bicycles and experimental human-powered vehicles any time of year in any kind of weather. He particularly likes to ride in the mountains.